1 CUP ACQUA FREDDA,
1 pezzetto CIRCA 1 CM. cannella
2 chiodi DI GAROFANO
SI FA BOLLIRE PER 4 MINUTI
SI COPRE SI FA RIPOSARE P
30 M... FILTRARE. SI
AGGIU...
LIM...
ML...
DI C...

Check No.

...KC100   Guest

...co...le

...olio

e di acqua
...ito

MAR 1064

COOKING WITH

NONNA

COOKING WITH

CELEBRATE FOOD & FAMILY WITH OVER 100 CLASSIC RECIPES FROM ITALIAN GRANDMOTHERS

ROSSELLA RAGO

Race Point
PUBLISHING

For all the Nonne.
Your love makes the world go round.

Brimming with creative inspiration, how-to projects, and useful information to enrich your everyday life, Quarto Knows is a favorite destination for those pursuing their interests and passions. Visit our site and dig deeper with our books into your area of interest: Quarto Creates, Quarto Cooks, Quarto Homes, Quarto Lives, Quarto Drives, Quarto Explores, Quarto Gifts, or Quarto Kids.

First published in 2017 by Race Point Publishing,
an imprint of The Quarto Group
142 West 36th Street, 4th Floor
New York, NY 10018 USA
www.QuartoKnows.com

ISBN 978-1-63106-294-0

Editorial Director: Jeannine Dillon
Project Editor: Erin Canning
Art Director: Merideth Harte
Photographer: Evi Abeler, Big Leo Productions
Hair Stylist: Enza Cristino
Makeup: Gabriella Trantino

10 9 8 7 6 5 4 3 2

Printed in China

CONTENTS

Domenica per le
ricetta di Rosa
500 g. di farina
500 l. di mando
250 g. di zucche
uova

circa

le uova

INTRODUCTION

Ricordati una cosa a' Nonna. Un giorno la Nonna non ci sarà più. E voglio che tu devi saper fare tutte le cose che fa la Nonna!

("Remember one thing, my darling. One day nonna won't be here anymore. And I want you to be able to do all the things that nonna does!")

The very first thing I attempted to make in the kitchen was a disastrous fruitcake. My Nonna Romana loves to tell this story. I was six years old, and I was on a mission to make the best fruitcake I could. I had mixed together the eggs, milk, flour, and fruit until I had made a complete mess of myself and the kitchen. When I finished mixing, I asked nonna to bake it for me. She agreed, with a knowing smile. But when my cake came out of the oven, it hadn't risen at all. I was crushed.

"What happened?" I asked her.

"You didn't put in any baking powder, my darling. But that's okay, next time you know. *Sbagliando s'impara* ('Making mistakes, you learn')!"

I have always joked that I attended Nonna's Brooklyn Basement Culinary Academy. You see, if you're in a traditional Italian household, Sundays are for eating. There is always food to prepare because the house is filled with family. And in our house, nonna always needed my help if we were going to feed everyone. She usually had already made the *focaccia* that served as my aromatic alarm clock on Sunday mornings, but there was also a feast of *pasta al forno, zucchine alla poverella, braciole,* and *ciambella* that I helped to prepare every week. The small dining table in my nonna's apartment would be set for at least ten people. After the meal, even more people would drop in for coffee and desserts—usually almond paste cookies that nonna and her sister Zia Rosa had made—with everyone talking over Italian TV shows blaring in the background.

With very few exceptions, this is every Sunday I have ever known. These are not days to spend worrying about what to do with your life; however, it was on a Sunday that the course of my life would change forever. I was straddling two careers at the time. I was in college studying to be a high school Italian teacher, and though I loved my native tongue, I wasn't sure I could handle teaching it to a bunch of teenagers simply looking to fulfill a foreign-language requirement. I have also always loved the entertainment business and have moonlighted my whole life as an actress, but I did not want to commit to living in perpetual worry about being a size two. No thank you!

So, on this particular Sunday, as everyone left the table one by one, there remained only nonna, my father, Vito, and me. I was moving the bottles of *Amaro* to take the sauce-stained tablecloth into the laundry room, when my father asked me, "So what is it that you really want to do with your life?" He knew I had been floundering with my career choices, and in that moment, I honestly had no idea what to tell him. Suddenly, something popped into my head and it seemed so silly that when the words came out of my mouth, I was laughing as I said them: "I should host a cooking show. That's the greatest job in the world!"

Now my father is usually a stern man with a dry sense of humor. I didn't expect him to be enthusiastic, or even amused, but his eyes lit up immediately and he said, "Yeah! It should be a show about nonna! There aren't any shows about Italian grandmas and their recipes!" By now we were both laughing, and my nonna probably thought we had lost our minds. That's when it hit me. "Let's call it *Cooking with Nonna*!" I said.

That night, I began a chapter in my life that I had unknowingly been preparing for since that very first fruitcake. Looking back, it's very clear to me that the years I had spent living with my nonna had served as my unwitting culinary education. When we decided to start the *Cooking with Nonna* show for real, I began to see the extraordinary importance of nonna's tattered recipes, which could be found anywhere and everywhere: from hanging from a broken magnet on the refrigerator door to an old Post-it note to an entire address book detailing the perfect amount of yeast for bread. These things would become my bible. *Once she isn't here, who would make them?* I realized that it was up to me to carry the torch.

These old papers were my family's history: they told a story of what my family ate, why they ate it, what food was even available at the time, what a special meal looked like, what everyday nutrition was like, and what my family's palate was like. I had found exactly what I was searching for, but there was one problem: trying to replicate any of these recipes without my nonna was going to be a disaster. I had no magical knack for eyeballing measurements with coffee cups the way nonna did. If I was going to recreate any of her recipes, I was going to have to adapt them.

After spending some time working on my own nonna's recipes, it occurred to me that there might be other children and grandchildren in my position, desperately wanting to preserve their traditions through the food of their mothers and grandmothers, but finding it way too complicated. I felt a calling to make sure that these recipes did not die in the back of a drawer somewhere. This book is a testament that a meal is more than just food on dishes. It can be a piece of your family's legacy.

When I decided to sit down and write this cookbook, I knew immediately that I wanted to tell the stories of the women who have contributed recipes to the *Cooking with Nonna* show over the years. I wanted to tell each woman's story because life events have flavored each nonna's unique cooking style. The truth is, I've met countless extraordinary women on my journey, all with one thing in common: *they have no idea they're extraordinary*. Their excellence in the kitchen was always expected of them. In one of her Italian cookbooks, Carol Field writes, "According to tradition in Piedmont, bread is so important that a girl wasn't considered ready for marriage until she could make the dough for the family and bring it to the communal oven for baking."

To me, a nonna's modesty is what usually sets her apart from traditional master chefs. As a society, we can sometimes forget or downplay the role of these secret culinary heroines of the food world. Most Michelin-starred chefs will tell you a story about being inspired by their grandmothers. To me, a nonna's food, skills, and contributions are timeless. The women behind the food that I make have made me see the culinary arts from a whole new perspective, and have inspired my conviction that unlike the ingredients we cook with, women have no expiration date.

The recipes and stories in this book serve as a foundation to explore and create. Finalizing a list of only 110 recipes was next to impossible, and if I had been left to my own devices, this book would have been published in several volumes as I tried to include something for everyone (and every nonna)! I want people to flip through the pages and look at the photos while getting a rush of nostalgia for Sunday dinner. I truly hope everyone finds something in this book that his or her nonna once made.

One of the most important things I have discovered through *Cooking with Nonna* is that traditions of the past are not commandments written in stone, never to be changed. They are fundamental building blocks for the present and the future. My nonna's recipes— or any traditional recipes—are meant to evolve. They are merely the foundation for your own personal culinary evolution, just as the recipes handed down to nonna were for her. Don't be afraid to be adventurous, make a mess, or make a mistake, because it can lead to something wonderful. If an ingredient doesn't excite you, simply change it. If you think something needs ten more minutes in the oven, let it cook. So many of a nonna's recipes came into existence because of a seasonal, improvisational mentality. You can create something wonderful all on your own.

And finally, I just want to say that my journey has been just that: a journey. I did not come into this world wearing an apron and endowed with the masterful knowledge of handcrafting fresh pasta. I was incredibly blessed to be born into a family that appreciated and celebrated food, perhaps more than most, but I began like many people—I was curious, tenacious, and, above all, hungry!

Now get cooking!

GETTING STARTED

TOOLS

If you want to cook like a nonna, you should be well equipped. When it comes to kitchen tools, my own Nonna Romana has a basic rule that she lives by: *basta che funziona* (whatever works!). In other words, no fancy crap! Don't worry about finding the latest tools and gadgets at expensive stores. Be creative, look around, and utilize everyday objects that can double as useful tools. One of my nonna's most prized possessions was a rolling pin that her mother, my great-grandmother Regina, had fashioned out of the leg of an old chair. Seriously! The slender length of wood was perfect for rolling out pastas and doughs and quickly became the most comfortable rolling pin to work with. I'm sure the warm memories of cooking with her own mother made every time she used it an unforgettable experience for my nonna.

Of course, we are in the twenty-first century, and having modern appliances like stand mixers and food processors is a tremendous help, but I think there is something special about learning things the old-school way. Here are a few tools every nonna has in her kitchen.

The Nonna Knife: Every time I open the kitchen drawer of a nonna I find these plastic-handled knives, often in a rainbow of colors. Usually it's because she has a family member in Italy who bought them for her for a few dollars a dozen and sent them to America. Today, they're available at many Italian specialty stores, including my website! These inexpensive serrated knives are made out of pressed steel, which means they aren't necessarily of the fanciest quality, but their small size and sharpness makes them the handiest paring knives I've ever used. They're ideal for peeling and cutting vegetables and making small cuts of pasta like orecchiette and cavatelli. Let's be real: everyone has those fancy knives that came with their china pattern and look pretty but don't cut anything! My parents have had a set of these knives since they got married in 1980 and they're still sharp!

Rolling pin: What's in a name, anyway? When it comes to rolling pins, don't think that they can only be found in the rolling pin section of a store. Many nonne have utilized some crazy things to make a rolling pin that works for them. A slim leg of an old table or chair has worked for generations in my family (I also personally prefer a slimmer rolling pin), but even a wine bottle can be used. Just make sure you drink all the wine first!

Wooden board: If you're going to be making fresh pasta—or any kind of dough, for that matter—

nonna's favorite surface for rolling is a good sturdy wooden board. Ideally, you should find one with a raised edge so mixing dough is a snap and you don't have to worry about any runoff.

A good wooden spoon: If your house is anything like mine, you have more than one wooden spoon, but every nonna I've ever known has had her favorite spoon that may even look like it's been through some battles. Usually it has turned from a pale wooden color to a deep amber tone from years of stirring sauces. Curing a good wooden spoon may take some time, so be patient.

Ravioli cutter: A good ravioli cutter is essential to making decorative edges and sealing certain pastries or pasta doughs. The best ones are made of metal instead of plastic and will last much longer.

Pasta roller: A pasta roller is something every pasta lover should own! I have so many memories of my nonna and me working together on her old-school pasta roller that attached to the table. She would hold the dough as my hands would turn the handle as fast as I could. She would say that my hands were ideal for this job because they were so little! Pasta rollers can be either manual or electric, and will usually come with different attachments to make flat sheets for lasagna as well as thin spaghetti or fettuccine. If you have a stand mixer, you can purchase additional attachments that can create a variety of pasta shapes.

Chitarra (guitar): A pasta chitarra is a wooden box fitted with strings of different widths on each side and resembles the belly of a real guitar. Sheets of pasta can be placed on either side and rolled with a rolling pin to cut out long pasta like spaghetti and fettuccine.

Mortar and pestle: A mortar and pestle is a heavy bowl and club-shaped grinder that is used to grind ingredients into a paste. It can be made from different materials, ranging from wood to marble. Using a mortar and pestle can be a labor of love, as some can be very heavy to work with, but it tends to open up the flavors and aromas of many ingredients.

Measuring cups: Now if there were ever a relative term when it came to Italian grandmothers in the kitchen, it's measuring cups! Every single nonna I have ever known has developed her own personal measuring system that could stump the FBI. Nonna Romana measures exclusively in espresso cups and American coffee mugs that she refers to as "brown coffee" cups. I won't discount this measuring method because it speaks to the incredibly personal relationship each special lady has with food. Wouldn't it be wonderful to get to a place where we know exactly how much to add of any ingredient without measuring anything? As long as you understand your measuring system, then, as Nonna Romana says, "No worry about nothing!"

Kitchen scale: Measuring by weight is so much more accurate than measuring in cups. Remember, a pound of flour is always a pound of flour. Nowadays, you can find scales that are digital and measure in both metric and imperial.

Microplane: This is the one semi-modern tool every nonna seems to have. A microplane is really a long, thin grater with a handle. Nonna loves it for grating hard cheeses and garlic when you want it super fine!

Storage containers: Plastic containers with lids are considered nonna gold! For as long as I can remember, my nonna had an entire cabinet filled with washed containers that served as her own special Tupperware. Ricotta containers are especially good for storing soups and home-cooked legumes. Smaller containers are reserved for sending leftovers home with people. No one leaves nonna's house empty-handed!

IN NONNA'S KITCHEN
Nella Cucina di Nonna

IN THE CANTINA

Extra-virgin olive oil: For raw use on a salad or for light sautéing.

Olive oil (not extra virgin): For frying. Back in the day, nonne had only olive oil to fry in, and it worked for them!

Spices: Dried oregano, crushed red pepper flakes, bay leaves, black pepper, and maybe dried rosemary are the only dried spices you will find in a nonna's kitchen. Garlic, parsley, onions, and basil should all be fresh whenever possible!

Salt: Use kosher salt or sea salt, or *sale grosso*, as nonna calls it.

Canned tomatoes: Everyone has his or her personal favorites. Some nonne only use whole peeled tomatoes and they will crush and process them themselves.

Others only use crushed tomatoes or passata, which is made from boiled tomatoes that have been put through a strainer. They're all good to have on hand.

Dried beans: There's something comforting about a big pot of beans cooking low and slow on the stove, just the way nonna does it. She makes a large batch every week so she can add them to anything. You can also stock canned beans if you want to have them on hand.

Dried pasta: Get various cuts like spaghetti, rotini, pastina, etc.

Rice: Arborio, carnaroli, brown, and white.

Bouillon cubes: These are fantastic to have on hand to make a quick soup in no time. Beef, chicken, porcini, and vegetable.

IN THE BAKING CUPBOARD
Active dry yeast
Baking powder
Baking soda
Cinnamon
Confectioners' sugar
Cornstarch
Espresso powder
Flour, all-purpose and 00
Granulated sugar
Pure vanilla extract
Vanilla beans

IN THE REFRIGERATOR
Basil
Butter, salted and unsalted
Eggs
Garlic
Heavy cream
Lard or vegetable shortening
Lemons
Mascarpone cheese
Onions
Parmigiano-Reggiano and Pecorino Romano
    (preferably in whole hunks for grating)
Ricotta impastata or whole milk ricotta, drained
    (see Nonna Says on page 104)

IN THE FREEZER
Assorted blanched vegetables
Fresh pasta
Peas
Ice cream

tortelli (filled pasta)

pappardelle

tagliatelle

fettuccine

spaghetti
(alla chitarra)

BASIC PASTA DOUGHS

My relationship with pasta dough is a tumultuous one. From my very first memories of my nonna and her three sisters making orecchiette together at my aunt's villa in Italy to when I first visited a small street in the historic district of the city of Bari where women sit outside and make pastas all day, I was fascinated. Making pasta always seemed like magic to me, and no matter how many times I tried and failed I was determined to be successful at it. Making pasta dough may take a bit of practice. Often it looks like a mess before it looks like anything remotely edible. When those moments arise, I wish you could hear the voice of a nonna cheering you on and saying, "You do very good!" The most important thing to remember about making fresh pasta is that you literally can't mess it up! If it comes out too dry, you can almost always fix it with a little water. Too wet and you can always dry it out with semolina or flour!

Should you ever get discouraged, just remember that every nonna has decades of experience making pasta behind her and once upon a time she stood behind a floured board and felt just like you!

SEMOLINA PASTA DOUGH

PREP TIME: 1 HOUR • YIELD: ABOUT 16 OUNCES, OR 454 G, FRESH PASTA (ENOUGH FOR 4 TO 6 SERVINGS)

This is the pasta dough my family has been making for generations. It is more common in Southern Italy and can be used for many cuts but is most commonly used for shorter cuts of pasta. Using a refined semolina (technically a bread semolina flour) is the secret to achieving a smoother dough with a little less effort. Semolina pasta dough has a bit more bite than a dough made of regular flour.

   This dough is best suited for short cuts of pasta like orecchiette, cavatelli, maccheroni, and capunti. If using a pasta extruder attachment to make rigatoni, rotini, and others, use the semolina dough.

2¼ cups (375 g) refined semolina flour (semolina rimacinata*)

⅔ cup (160 ml) tepid water

* Semolina rimacinata is available at most supermarkets and Italian specialty stores, but if you have a hard time finding it, try going to an Italian bakery and they will usually sell you some of what they refer to as "bread semolina flour."

Method A

1. Pour the semolina onto a clean work surface and make a well in the center. Add the water little by little, a few tablespoons at a time. Begin to mix with your fingers, catching any water that tries to escape from the sides. Keep adding the water while trying to form a uniform ball of dough. The dough will be crumbly at first but will begin to come together after 5 to 7 minutes of kneading.

2. Once you have obtained a uniform ball of dough and the dough no longer sticks to your hands, keep kneading with the heels of your hands for an additional 7 to 10 minutes, until the dough is smooth and soft but firm enough to hold an indentation. The end result should feel somewhat like playdough—damp to the touch but not sticky. If the dough feels too wet, dust it and your work surface with extra semolina. If the dough feels too dry, add a teaspoon of water at a time and knead it through.

3. Follow steps 3 through 4 for Method B on page 20.

Method B

1. Add the semolina to the bowl of a stand mixer fitted with the dough hook attachment. With the mixer on low speed, add the water a little at a time until fully absorbed. Continue mixing on low speed for 5 to 6 minutes. The dough will be crumbly.

continued

cavatelli

orecchiette

capunti

maccheroni

2. Turn out the dough onto a clean work surface and knead by hand until the dough is soft and smooth, 5 to 7 minutes. Be sure to collect any small crumbs of dough.

3. Wrap the ball of dough in plastic wrap and let it rest at room temperature for about 30 minutes. After the dough has rested, roll it out to desired thickness. Keep any dough that is not in use under a damp kitchen towel to prevent drying while you roll out the rest of the dough.

4. To roll out the dough by hand, cut the dough into 10 pieces and roll one piece at a time into a ½-inch (13 mm) thick rope. While rolling keep your fingers together and spread them apart to lengthen the rope.

Cavatelli: Cut off ¼-inch (6 mm) pieces from the rope. With a serrated knife like the Nonna Knife (see page 12), press down on the piece of dough with your left index finger on the tip. Drag the piece of dough toward you while applying moderate pressure.

Capunti: Cut off 1½-inch (4 cm) pieces from the rope. Drag the piece of dough toward you while applying moderate pressure with your three middle fingers, creating the look of an empty pea pod.

Orecchiette: Cut off ¼-inch (6 mm) pieces from the rope. With a serrated knife like the Nonna Knife (see page 12), press down on the piece of dough with your left index finger on the tip. Drag the piece of dough toward you while applying moderate pressure. Keep the dough on the knife and turn the piece of dough inside out over your left thumb so that the rough side is exposed.

Maccheroni: Cut off ½-inch (13 mm) pieces from the rope and place a bamboo skewer in the center of each piece lengthwise. Using the palm of your hand, roll each piece of dough around the skewer so that it is wrapped around. Pull the maccheroni off the skewer.

---

5. The pasta will keep for about 2 days in the refrigerator wrapped in plastic wrap.

To dry the pasta before cooking: For short cuts of pasta, lay the shapes on a cotton tablecloth or a screen and dry overnight at room temperature, making sure none of the pieces are touching. For long pasta like spaghetti, hang the noodles over the back of a chair covered with a floured dish towel or use a drying rack. Once the pasta is completely dry, store it in an airtight container at room temperature for several months.

To freeze pasta: Layer the pasta in a tray as soon as you're finished rolling it out, separating layers with sheets of parchment paper and sprinkling with plenty of flour or semolina. Frozen pasta does not need to be thawed before it's cooked. Just toss it frozen into the boiling water.

To cook fresh pasta: Cook the pasta in salted boiling water for 1 to 6 minutes, depending on thickness, or until al dente. Never add oil to the water!

NONNA ROSETTA RAUSEO'S

EGG PASTA DOUGH

**PREP TIME: 1 HOUR • YIELD: ABOUT 16 OUNCES, OR 454 G, FRESH PASTA
(ENOUGH FOR 4 TO 6 SERVINGS)**

Egg pasta dough, which is more prevalent in Northern Italian cooking, is perhaps the better-known pasta dough in the United States. It's very easily made by combining eggs and flour, which everyone has in the kitchen already. The soft flour produces a tender pasta with a delicate flavor that everyone will love.

This dough is best suited for longer cuts of pasta like pappardelle, tagliatelle, spaghetti, and filled pastas.

2½ cups (300 g) 00 or all-purpose flour

3 large eggs plus 1 egg yolk, at room temperature, well beaten

2 tablespoons (30 ml) tepid water

¼ teaspoon salt

Method A

1. Pour the flour onto a clean work surface and make a wide well in the center with your hands. Pour the beaten eggs into the well and add the water and salt.

2. Begin whisking the flour and eggs in the center of the well vigorously with a fork, gradually mixing in the flour on the sides of the well. When the sides of the well collapse, begin mixing with your hands until a dough forms. Knead the dough for 8 to 10 minutes, or until it is smooth and supple and damp to the touch but not sticky.

3. Follow steps 3 through 5 for Method B below and on page 23.

Method B:

1. Place all the ingredients in the bowl of a stand mixer fitted with the dough hook attachment. Mix on low speed for 5 to 6 minutes, until all the ingredients are incorporated and a dough begins to form.

2. Turn the contents of the bowl out onto a clean work surface and begin kneading with your hands and trying to pick up any particles of dough. Knead by hand for 8 to 10 minutes, or until the dough is smooth and supple.

3. Wrap the ball of dough in plastic wrap and let it rest at room temperature for about 30 minutes. After the dough has rested, roll it out to desired thickness. Keep any dough that is not in use under a wet kitchen towel to prevent drying while you roll out the rest of the dough.

continued

4. To roll out the pasta by hand, cut the dough into 3 equal portions and place it on a clean work surface sprinkled with flour. Roll the dough out with a rolling pin into a rectangle shape, starting from the center and rolling out toward the edge. Flip the dough over every so often until your dough is as thin as possible (about ⅛-inch, or 3 mm). Once the dough is thin enough, trim it into a clean rectangle. Add the scraps to the remaining dough. Roll the dough up horizontally. To roll out the pasta by machine, use a pasta roller and pass the dough through until it is a thin as possible, and then select your desired width to cut the pasta. Use different attachments to cut different shapes of pasta.

Pappardelle: With a sharp knife, cut the dough into 1-inch (2.5 cm) wide ribbons. Toss the pasta with extra flour to prevent sticking.

Tagliatelle: With a sharp knife, cut the dough into ½-inch (13 mm) ribbons. Toss the pasta with extra flour to prevent sticking.

Fettuccine: With a sharp knife, cut the dough into ¼-inch (6 mm) ribbons. Toss the pasta with extra flour to prevent sticking.

Lasagna: With a sharp knife, cut 10 × 2-inch (25 × 5 cm) sheets of pasta.

Filled pasta: With a sharp knife, cut 3 × 3-inch (7.5 × 7.5 cm) squares of pasta.

5. The pasta will keep for about 2 days in the refrigerator wrapped in plastic wrap with generous amounts of flour or semolina.

To dry the pasta before cooking: For short cuts of pasta, lay the shapes out on a cotton tablecloth or a screen and dry overnight at room temperature, making sure none of the pieces are touching. For long pasta like spaghetti, hang the noodles over the back of a chair covered with a floured dish towel or use a drying rack. Once the pasta is completely dry, you may store it in an airtight container at room temperature for several months.

To freeze pasta: Layer the pasta in a tray as soon as you're finished rolling it out, separating layers with sheets of parchment paper and sprinkling with plenty of flour or semolina. Frozen pasta does not need to be thawed before it's cooked. Just toss it frozen into the boiling water.

To cook fresh pasta: Cook the pasta in salted boiling water for 1 to 6 minutes, depending on thickness, or until al dente. Never add oil to the water!

NONNA ROMANA SCIDDURLO

"It was in that moment that I decided to be strong for my family. There was no other choice but to survive."

Over the years, my Nonna Romana has often captured the hearts of people she meets with two simple words, "*Allo*, everybody!"

I like to say that she has become a nonna to the world.

Sitting at our family dining room table, nonna Romana takes her espresso with no sugar, but grabs a cookie to dip for its sweetness. "I put no sugar in the coffee," she says, hoping the cookie will go unnoticed, but I shoot her a look of disapproval. Sugar isn't the best thing for her, and as far as I'm concerned, my nonna must live forever. As we sit together, she begins to tell me a story that I know all too well, but one that I never grow tired of hearing.

"I am the first born of seven children. Three boys and four girls. Four girls like the four seasons. All of us are different," Nonna Romana says. Born in 1933 to Leonardo and Regina Valentini, in Mola di Bari, Italy, Romana was named after her paternal grandmother, as was customary at the time. When she was born, my great-grandfather exclaimed, *Donna sei e donna hai fatto!* ("A woman you are, and a woman you have made!")

"They were happy when I was born, but back then you wanted boys more than girls because boys could work harder. But me and my sisters worked harder than any boys I knew," my Nonna Romana says, smiling. A half-dozen siblings would soon join her. My great-aunt Rosa, born in 1935, would become my great-grandmother's right hand in the household. Twin boys Vincenzo and Vito came next, and Mussolini rewarded my great-grandparents with a prize for making future soldiers for the Italian army. "They sent us 600 lire, which was a lot of money at the time," Nonna tells me. Caterina and Chiara arrived in 1942 and 1944, and the two formed an unbreakable lifelong bond. One final boy, Antonio, would arrive in 1947, making the Valentini family complete.

"By the time my last brother was born, my father had become sick with chronic bronchitis, and couldn't cultivate our land anymore. In 1944, he requested a license to open a small grocery store in town, and that was the salvation of our family," my nonna says. When her father passed away in 1948, he left her mother, Regina, alone with seven mouths to feed. "My father's death was the first time I realized life was not fair. I was the oldest at fifteen, and little Antonio was barely a year old. I could understand more than the other children, and all of our hearts were broken, but it was in that moment that I decided to be strong for my family. There was no other choice but to survive. After that, we all took on different roles. I would cook for everyone. It wasn't always easy. Sometimes everyone would be in a picky mood and want to eat something different. My baby brother, Antonio, would only eat rice and potatoes, so I had to make that for him or he wouldn't eat."

My great-aunt Rosa was in charge of the children at home and worked at her mother's side whenever the store was busy, which was often. Although the economy in postwar Southern Italy was struggling, business thankfully was plentiful at the grocery store, because my great-grandmother Regina had a reputation for honesty and quality. "The war was very bad for Mola di Bari. Many artisans could not work, and people couldn't buy food. My mother felt bad for these people, and they would come to our store and sign for credit. I remember many of the people who couldn't read would sign by making an X in this book she had. My mother knew in most cases she wouldn't be paid, but she wanted people to eat."

At the age of twenty, my nonna met the love of her life, a dark, handsome man named Vitantonio Sciddurlo. "He was a very *simpatico* man. We even had the same birthday!" At that time, many men left Southern Italy for South America because of the failing economy, and Vitantonio was one of these men. "A month after I was married, I was pregnant with my son Geppino. My husband went back to Venezuela three months after that, and I didn't see him again until Geppino was nearly four years old. He would ask me to send him a photograph every month so he could see him grow up." Soon after he returned, she gave birth to my mother, Angela. When Angela was just eighteen months old, my nonna and her two small children boarded a boat bound for Caracas to be close to my grandfather. By now he was in poor health, and like a true Italian, he attributed it to not having regular home cooking. "I remember my husband asked me to make fresh *orecchiette* for all his friends there. They were all away from their families, and hadn't had a good home-cooked meal in a long time, so I cooked for all of them." She smiles briefly, but we both know she

is reaching a painful part of her past. "His health got worse, and we decided to go back to Italy to be with my family again. Two years later he passed away just two months after my twenty-ninth birthday. Geppino was eight, and your mother Angela was four." My nonna never remarried.

The next few years were filled with tremendous change. Romana left Italy to join the rest of her siblings in America. They lived on 2nd Place in Carroll Gardens, Brooklyn, which was then home to many immigrants from Mola di Bari. "I stayed with my sisters, but there was only room for me and one of my children. Geppino was older, and he could work," she says sadly. It was decided that my mother, Angela, would stay back in Italy with my nonna's younger sister Caterina, and once again my nonna found herself far away from someone she loved very much. "It was a difficult thing for me. Every time I saw a little girl I would feel sad, but I found happiness in making beautiful things for her. I would buy fabric and sew her clothes when I had extra time at work. It was a way for me to be with her to know she would wear the clothes that I made and look beautiful."

What amazes me about my nonna is not how she suffered, or how she survived, but that she did it with such grace. She possesses the extraordinary talent of accepting each moment for what it is, and her love and warmth are even more abundant than her pasta bowls.

My brother, Leonardo, and my cousins, Cristina and Anthony, and I know that our nonna is the perfect nonna, and our love for her grows with every tray of baked ziti. "I live for my grandkids. I want to see them happy and settled, because that makes me feel like life will go on forever, and that's very important. I was never a rich person in my life, but I look at my friends who have no grandkids, and I say to myself that I am more rich than them because I have all of you."

BASIC SAUCES

NONNA ROMANA SCIDDURLO'S

MARINARA SAUCE

Sugo alla Marinara

PREP TIME: 10 MINUTES • COOK TIME: 15 MINUTES • YIELD: 3½ CUPS (895 G)
(ENOUGH FOR 16 OUNCES, OR 454 G, OF PASTA; 4 TO 6 SERVINGS)

To Italians, a *marinara* sauce is as personal as a fingerprint. All cooks have their own combinations of spices and flavors that are important to them. This marinara is as simple as it gets—oil, garlic, onion, tomatoes, and very little else. Nonna Romana doesn't spend hours and hours cooking this sauce either, since she uses canned tomatoes that are already technically "cooked." These tomatoes are picked at the height of freshness and are low in acidity. The point is to taste the star of the show: the *pomodoro*!

1 can (28 ounces, or 794 g) whole
    peeled tomatoes

3 tablespoons (45 ml) extra-virgin
    olive oil

3 cloves garlic, finely minced

1 small onion, finely minced

1 teaspoon salt

Red pepper flakes (optional)

3 fresh basil leaves, roughly chopped

1. Pour the tomatoes into a medium mixing bowl and crush by hand, trying to get them as smooth as possible.

2. Heat the oil in a medium saucepan over medium heat and add the garlic and onion. Cook and stir until they just begin to color, about 5 minutes.

3. Add the tomatoes, salt, and red pepper flakes, if using, and cook until the sauce comes to a light boil, 4 to 5 minutes.

4. Reduce the heat to low and add the basil. Cook for another 5 minutes.

Nonna Romana Says

This sauce is great to have on hand at any time. I save it in the refrigerator for about a week in my favorite plastic containers, or when I have a lot left over I keep it in the freezer for about a month.

BOLOGNESE SAUCE

Sugo alla Bolognese

PREP TIME: 15 MINUTES • COOK TIME: 45 MINUTES • YIELD: 3½ CUPS (910 G)
(ENOUGH FOR 16 OUNCES, OR 454 G, OF PASTA; 4 TO 6 SERVINGS)

Few can resist a big bowl of pasta with a hearty meat sauce like *Bolognese*. Just the thought of it brings me right back to Sunday dinner! Named after the city of Bologna, the capital of Emilia Romagna, this sauce has become synonymous with classic Italian cuisine. A good Bolognese uses less tomato than you would imagine and showcases a mix of meats that are simmered to bring out their flavors. This sauce pairs ideally with thick egg pasta like pappardelle or tagliatelle and should be served with a generous sprinkle of Parmigiano-Reggiano cheese.

3 tablespoons (45 ml) extra-virgin olive oil

1 medium onion, cut into ¼-inch (6 mm) dice

1 large carrot, cut into ¼-inch (6 mm) dice

1 stalk celery, cut into ¼-inch (6 mm) dice

2 bay leaves

Dash of nutmeg

Red pepper flakes, to taste

1½ pounds (680 g) ground meatloaf mix (equal parts beef, pork, and veal)

1 teaspoon salt, plus more to taste

½ cup (120 ml) dry red wine

6 ounces (170 g) canned crushed tomatoes (about ⅔ cup)

3 ounces (85 g) tomato paste (about 5½ tablespoons)

3 tablespoons (45 g) unsalted butter

1. Heat the oil in a Dutch oven over medium heat for 1 minute. Add the onion and cook and stir for 2 to 3 minutes.

2. Add the carrot, celery, bay leaves, nutmeg, and red pepper flakes, and cook and stir until the vegetables are softened, 3 to 4 minutes.

3. Add the meat and 1 teaspoon salt, breaking up the meat with a wooden spoon. Cook until the meat is browned and mostly cooked through, about 5 minutes.

4. Add the wine and raise the heat to high. Cook for about 3 minutes, or until you can no longer smell the alcohol.

5. Reduce the heat to as low as possible and add the tomatoes, tomato paste, butter, and salt to taste. Cover and simmer for 30 minutes, checking and stirring occasionally. If the sauce appears dry, you may loosen it with ¼ cup (60 ml) of water at a time (preferably pasta cooking water).

6. Remove and discard the bay leaves before serving.

Nonna Rina Says

This sauce is great to make the night before, as all the flavors have a chance to meld together. To reheat and serve with pasta, add a little starchy pasta cooking water to loosen it up and toss with al dente pasta.

WHITE SAUCE

Besciamella

PREP TIME: 5 MINUTES • COOK TIME: 12 MINUTES • YIELD: 1¾ CUPS (438 G)
(USE 1 CUP, OR 250 G, FOR 16 OUNCES, OR 454 G, OF PASTA)

Besciamella is a staple sauce in Northern Italian cooking and is used as a base for many dishes. It works best in baked pastas like lasagna and pasta al forno because of its creamy, velvety texture. The richness of besciamella also complements many vegetarian dishes.

3 tablespoons (45 g) unsalted butter
¼ cup (30 g) 00 or all-purpose flour
1¾ cups (420 ml) whole milk
Dash of nutmeg
1½ teaspoons salt

Nonna Rina Says

If you're not going to use the sauce right away, place plastic wrap directly against the sauce to prevent a skin from forming. If the sauce thickens too much when cooled, whisk in 1 tablespoon (15 ml) of milk at a time to return it to the desired consistency.

1. Melt the butter in a medium saucepan over medium heat.

2. Add the flour and stir with a wooden spoon until the mixture begins to brown, 4 to 5 minutes.

3. Add the milk and whisk vigorously until the sauce is very smooth and begins to thicken, 5 to 6 minutes.

4. Once thickened, remove from the heat and add the nutmeg and salt. Whisk for another 30 seconds.

BASIL PESTO

Pesto di Basilico

PREP TIME: 5 MINUTES • YIELD: 2½ CUPS (650 G)
(USE 1 CUP, OR 260 G, FOR 16 OUNCES, OR 454 G, OF PASTA)

This basil pesto is just like Nonna Vivian: classic and full of flavor! Pesto is so easy to prepare and goes well with pasta or simply on some bread when company shows up out of the blue. If you want to keep it old school, use a mortar and pestle to grind the pesto and give it some elbow grease. Nonna will be proud of you!

5 ounces (142 g) fresh basil
(about 5 packed cups)
½ cup (60 g) grated Parmigiano-
Reggiano cheese
1 cup (120 g) grated Pecorino Sardo
cheese
4 cloves garlic, or to taste
½ cup (68 g) pinoli (pine nuts)
½ cup (120 ml) extra-virgin olive oil

1. Add the basil, both cheeses, the garlic, and the pinoli to a food processor, and process for 30 seconds.

2. Add the oil in a stream with the processor running and process for an additional 30 seconds, or until smooth. Use immediately or transfer to a jar for storage.

Nonna Vivian Says

To store the pesto, transfer it to a glass jar and cover the top with oil. It will keep nicely for a few weeks in the refrigerator as long as there is a layer of oil on top.

APPETIZERS

Antipasti

BATTERED ZUCCHINI BLOSSOMS

Fiori di Zucca in Pastella

PREP TIME: 15 MINUTES • COOK TIME: 15 MINUTES • YIELD: 12 BLOSSOMS, 4 TO 6 SERVINGS

Fried zucchini blossoms are a mouthwatering, seasonal treat. They're a great way to utilize the bounty of flowers that grow in your own zucchini yields every summer. If you don't have your own plant, make friends with someone who does; otherwise, you can find these beauties at many farmers' markets and Italian specialty stores. In Puglia, the blossoms are stuffed with mozzarella and capers and dipped into a flavorful batter called *pastella* before they are fried to a gorgeous golden brown color. Nonna Rina has to guard them carefully before serving them because these blossoms have a tendency to disappear.

BLOSSOMS

12 zucchini blossoms, stems trimmed, washed, and dried (some remove the stems and pistils completely, but they are totally edible and not harmful. Nonna Rina never removes them, as nonne don't waste anything!)

1 ounce (30 g) fresh mozzarella, cut into twelve 1-inch (2.5 cm) chunks

1 tablespoon (9 g) capers

BATTER

½ cup (60 g) 00 or all-purpose flour

¼ cup (30 g) grated Parmigiano-Reggiano cheese

3 cloves garlic, finely minced

2 tablespoons (12 g) finely minced fresh mint

1 egg

¾ cup (180 ml) water

Olive oil, for frying (or any frying oil you like)

1. **To make the blossoms:** With your fingers, gently open the petals of the blossoms and insert a mozzarella chunk and 1 to 3 capers, depending on the size of the blossom. Set the flowers aside.

2. **To make the batter:** In a medium mixing bowl, add the flour, cheese, garlic, and mint. Whisk to combine.

3. Add the egg and water to the mixture and whisk to combine. Set aside.

4. Heat 1½ inches (4 cm) of oil in a large (2.8 L) heavy-bottomed saucepan over high heat.

5. Dip each of the filled blossoms into the batter and coat evenly. Shake off any excess and drop them into the oil 2 or 3 at a time. Fry the blossoms, turning them occasionally with tongs, until they are golden brown, 1 to 3 minutes per batch.

6. Transfer to a paper towel–lined dish to drain. Serve immediately.

Nonna Rina Says
If you are picking your blossoms fresh, try to pick them in the morning, while they are open, to make sure they're clean.

PEPPERS AND EGGS

Uova e Peperoni

PREP TIME: 10 MINUTES • COOK TIME: 25 MINUTES • YIELD: 4 SERVINGS

Peppers and eggs is a humble Italian-American classic. This is one of Nonna Theresa's go-to dishes for a quick meal that packs in the flavor. Although traditionally made with cubanelles, it works beautifully with the addition of red peppers for color and texture. Serve it on crusty bread as a hero or by itself.

4 eggs

1 tablespoon (15 ml) water

¼ cup (30 g) grated Pecorino Romano cheese

Salt and black pepper, to taste

¼ cup (60 ml) olive oil, for frying

2 green bell peppers, seeded, and sliced into 2-inch (5 cm) chunks

2 red bell peppers, seeded and sliced into 2-inch (5 cm) chunks

1. In a small mixing bowl, beat the eggs with the water, cheese, and salt and black pepper. Set aside.

2. Heat the oil in a medium skillet over medium heat. Add the peppers and a dash of salt and black pepper. Cook until the peppers are soft, 20 to 25 minutes.

3. Add the beaten eggs and swirl with a wooden spoon until the eggs are fully cooked, 2 to 3 minutes.

Nonna Theresa Says
Make sure you cook everything low and slow to prevent burning. Cooking the peppers takes some patience, so hang in there!

NONNA GRAZIELLA RANDAZZO'S

SICILIAN CHICKPEA FRITTERS

Panelle

PREP TIME: 5 MINUTES • COOK TIME: 1 HOUR 30 MINUTES
YIELD: ABOUT 36 PANELLE, 4 TO 6 SERVINGS

Panelle are a famous street food in Palermo. Typically, they are eaten with a bit of lemon juice between two halves of crusty bread as a sandwich called *pane e panelle*, but they work wonderfully as "fries" as well. Nonna Graziella carefully stirs a simple mix of chickpea flour and water over low heat until it resembles a thick porridge like polenta. Once the mixture is formed and cooled, it can be cut into various shapes and fried to perfection.

1 cup (92 g) chickpea flour
2 cups (475 ml) water
1 tablespoon (4 g) chopped
   fresh parsley
½ teaspoon salt
Olive oil, for frying
Crusty bread, for serving
Lemon wedges, for serving

> **Nonna Graziella Says**
> *Make sure the panelle are cooled completely before cutting and frying them, or they will break apart in the oil.*

1. Put a medium saucepan over low heat and add the flour and water, stirring with a wooden spoon. When the mixture begins to thicken, after 3 or 4 minutes, add the parsley and the salt. Continue stirring for an additional 3 to 4 minutes. The mixture is ready when a spoon can make a line across the pan.

2. Pour the batter into three 8-ounce (230 g) ramekins just until the fill line. Let cool for 10 to 12 minutes. Once cooled, turn out onto a cutting board or a flat surface and cool completely, about 1 hour.

3. Heat about 1½ inches (4 cm) of oil in a medium heavy-bottomed saucepan over high heat. Cut the panelle into ¼-inch (6 mm) slices and fry 3 or 4 at a time until golden brown, 3 to 5 minutes per batch.

4. Transfer to a paper towel–lined plate to drain.

5. Serve with crusty bread and fresh lemon juice.

BAKED MUSSELS

Cozze con Battuto

PREP TIME: 20 MINUTES • COOK TIME: 23 MINUTES • YIELD: 4 TO 6 SERVINGS

Baked mussels is a classic dish that Nonna Romana has carried with her from her days in Mola di Bari, Puglia. Even when times were hard, mussels were always plentiful in the fishing village, so plentiful that you could practically go down to the beach and scoop up your own! Baking them with a savory, garlicky mixture of cheese and bread crumbs is a quick, easy, and inexpensive way to make an impressive appetizer. You might want to make a few extra because these are addictive!

½ cup (30 g) grated Pecorino Romano cheese

¼ cup (27 g) plain bread crumbs

2 eggs, beaten

4 cloves garlic, shaved

1 tablespoon (4 g) finely chopped fresh parsley

2 tablespoons (30 ml) extra-virgin olive oil

1 tablespoon (15 ml) milk

¼ teaspoon black pepper

1 pound (454 g) mussels, rinsed, scrubbed, and beards removed

1. Preheat the oven to 400°F (200°C).

2. Open all of the mussels and leave the fruit on the half shell, discarding the other shell halves. Reserve the juice of the mussels in a glass. Set aside.

3. In a medium mixing bowl, add the cheese, bread crumbs, eggs, garlic, parsley, olive oil, milk, and black pepper, and mix with a wooden spoon until smooth. The mixture should be quite soft.

4. Arrange the mussels in a 13 × 9-inch (33 × 23 cm) baking pan. Add any juices from the mussels to the pan.

5. Using two small spoons, drop about 1 teaspoon of stuffing over each mussel and spread to completely cover.

6. Bake the mussels for 20 minutes, and then place under the broiler for 2 to 3 minutes, or until golden brown on top.

Nonna Romana Says

Make sure you broil these after baking so they get some good color. The best part is the golden brown crust on the outside!

NONNA ANTOINETTE CAPODICCI'S

POTATO CROQUETTES

Crocchette di Patate

PREP TIME: 30 MINUTES • COOK TIME: 48 MINUTES • YIELD: 12 CROQUETTES

Nonna Antoinette's versatile potato croquettes make an appearance at almost all of her family meals. Feel free to change up the meat in the filling depending on what you have on hand. These can also be made in smaller sizes for a bite-sized appetizer or more substantial for a side dish or—let's face it—a whole meal!

CROQUETTES

4 russet potatoes, unpeeled

¼ cup (30 g) grated Parmigiano-
  Reggiano cheese

¼ cup (30 g) grated Pecorino Romano
  cheese

1 tablespoon (4 g) minced fresh
  parsley

½ teaspoon garlic powder

Salt and black pepper, to taste

1 large egg

3 ounces (85 g) sliced mortadella,
  cut into ½-inch (13 mm) dice

BREADING

All-purpose flour, for dredging

1 egg, beaten

1 cup (108 g) plain bread crumbs

Olive oil, for frying (or use any frying oil
  you like)

Nonna Antoinette Says

These can be made the night before. Prepare them up to step 4, making the mix and shaping them, and refrigerate them, covered in plastic wrap.

1. **To make the croquettes:** Bring a large pot of water to a boil. Drop in the potatoes and cook for 30 to 40 minutes, or until easily pierced with a fork. Drain the potatoes and scrape the skins off with a knife once they are cool enough to handle.

2. Transfer to a large mixing bowl. Using a potato ricer, mash the potatoes and let them cool, uncovered, for 15 to 20 minutes.

3. Once cooled, add the cheeses, parsley, garlic powder, and salt and black pepper. Mix well to combine. Add in the egg and mortadella, and mix until just combined. If the mixture seems too wet, add 1 or 2 tablespoons (15 or 30 g) of flour.

4. Shape the potato mixture into 12 equal rolls about 3 inches (7.5 cm) long.

5. **To make the breading:** Place the flour, beaten egg, and bread crumbs in 3 separate dishes.

6. Coat each roll in the flour, then the egg, and finally the bread crumbs.

7. Heat ½ inch (13 mm) of oil in a medium heavy-bottomed skillet over medium-high heat. Add the croquettes in 2 batches and fry until golden brown on all sides, 3 to 4 minutes per batch. Transfer to a paper towel–lined plate to drain. Serve immediately.

"Cooking is very personal, and you have to bring a little of yourself into everything you make."

Nonna Antoinette Capodicci is far from what you'd expect when you hear the word *nonna*. Barely in her sixties, she is a stunning woman with killer cheekbones, long eyelashes, and an impeccable posture.

We walk into her kitchen where she has prepared fresh cookies and a chilled, spiked Neapolitan coffee drink called Caffe Sport. I take a sip, and I'm in sweet caffeinated ecstasy.

Antoinette's interest in the kitchen was nurtured by her family when she was growing up in both Venezuela and Italy. "My love for cooking started from being around my grandmothers. I was eight years old and had a play stove. I was blessed with two wonderful grandmothers. One cooked more rustic in style and the other would cater weddings, so her cooking was a bit more chic. They both taught me so much, and I was very eager to help," she explains.

Antoinette's enthusiasm in the kitchen was a blessing for her family, too. During Antoinette's birth, her mother suffered a stroke that left her paralyzed on her left side. Even though her mother's condition meant more responsibility for Antoinette, her mother made her feel as if anything were possible. "My mother was paralyzed, and I swear I never realized she was handicapped. She never let anything stop her. To peel a potato, she would position it tightly in her left hand and peel it with the right. I suppose it's where I get my determination. I was always surrounded by strong women," she says. "It has never been good enough for me to just do something well. I had to be exceptional."

Antoinette has passed that philosophy on to her three children. "My children are all successful, and cooking for them is the greatest bonus I can pass on," she says. Her two small grandchildren also appreciate her efforts. "They want to help and I want them to learn. Italians love through cooking. When I watch them savoring something I made, I feel truly fulfilled."

Her desire to be exceptional means that she is, without a doubt, a passionate perfectionist. "Cooking started as a hobby, but it's a love. If I'm stressed out, I actually start cooking a five-course meal, and it makes me feel better," she says. In her spare time, Antoinette creates recipes and enters them in contests for fun (she has won many). "When I cook, I only use recipes as a suggestion. Cooking is very personal, and you have to bring a little of yourself into everything you make."

I find her confidence inspiring. The more you believe in your abilities, the more successful you become. "Some things, especially good things, don't always come easy," she says. "I spent my sixteenth birthday in a sweatshop because my father didn't believe I needed to go to school. I got married and became a mother very young. But I never let anything stop me. At forty, I got my GED, went to college, and became the valedictorian of my graduating class. It might take time, but it's never too late."

ZUCCHINI PIE

Torta di Zucchine

PREP TIME: 20 MINUTES • COOK TIME: 45 MINUTES • YIELD: 4 TO 6 SERVINGS

One bite of this moist and flavorful zucchini pie and it's no wonder everyone begs Nonna Gilda to bring it over. This pie is a breeze to prepare, and it's a great way to use those extra zucchini that grow abundantly in the summertime. It's perfect to serve as an appetizer or to have on hand as a savory snack!

1 pound (454 g) zucchini, grated (about 2 small zucchini)

1 small onion, cut into ¼-inch (6 mm) dice

3 eggs, beaten

2 tablespoons (15 g) grated Pecorino Romano cheese

⅓ cup (80 ml) extra-virgin olive oil

1 tablespoon (15 g) unsalted butter, melted and cooled

1 tablespoon (4 g) chopped fresh parsley

¼ teaspoon black pepper

1 cup (120 g) all-purpose flour

1½ teaspoons baking powder

1 teaspoon salt

1. Preheat the oven to 375°F (190°C). Grease an 11 × 7-inch (28 × 18 cm) baking pan.

2. In a large mixing bowl, combine the zucchini and onion.

3. Add the eggs, cheese, oil, butter, parsley, and black pepper, and mix well.

4. In a smaller mixing bowl, whisk together the flour, baking powder, and salt.

5. Mix the dry ingredients into the wet until just combined.

6. Pour the batter into the prepared pan and bake for 45 minutes, or until the top is golden brown.

7. Let cool before cutting.

Nonna Gilda Says

You can switch up the cheeses and even add shallots instead of onions. This pie works beautifully with yellow squash as well!

ARTICHOKE PIE

Carciofi con Battuto

PREP TIME: 5 MINUTES • COOK TIME: 1 HOUR 15 MINUTES • YIELD: 6 TO 8 SERVINGS

Carciofi con battuto is a wonderful example of Italian peasant food, *cucina povera* at its finest. Nonna Anna remembers a time when this dish would be served as a main course because of Puglia's seasonal abundance of artichokes—meat was a luxury in that era. Today, the rich flavors of the cheese and hearty texture of the artichoke make for a flavorful, delicious treat that can be cut into squares for an appetizer or served as a beautiful side dish.

ARTICHOKES

24 ounces (680 g) frozen
 artichoke hearts

3 cloves garlic, minced

4 sprigs fresh parsley

2 tablespoons (30 ml) extra-virgin
 olive oil

1 teaspoon salt

TOPPING

1 cup (108 g) plain bread crumbs

1½ cups (180 g) grated Parmigiano-
 Reggiano cheese

5 eggs

1 cup (235 ml) water

1 teaspoon extra-virgin olive oil

1. **To make the artichokes:** Place the frozen artichokes in a large saucepan with enough water to cover them, 3 to 4 cups (705 to 940 ml). Add the garlic, parsley, and olive oil. Cover and bring to a boil, 12 to 14 minutes.

2. Uncover and add the salt. Boil, uncovered, for an additional 10 minutes. Remove from the heat.

3. Using a slotted spoon, transfer the artichokes to a 13 × 9-inch (33 × 23 cm) baking pan and spread them into a single layer. Cool for about 15 minutes.

4. Preheat the oven to 400°F (200°C).

5. **To make the topping:** In a large mixing bowl, combine the bread crumbs, cheese, eggs, water, and olive oil, and mix well with a spoon. Spread the mixture evenly over the artichokes.

6. Bake for 5 minutes at 400°F (200°C), then lower the temperature to 375°F (190°C) and bake for 30 to 35 minutes longer, or until the topping is golden brown.

7. Cool before cutting. Serve at room temperature.

STUFFED MUSHROOMS

Funghi Ripieni

PREP TIME: 10 MINUTES • COOK TIME: 45 MINUTES • YIELD: 10 MEDIUM MUSHROOMS

These stove-top stuffed mushrooms are a hit at every family gathering for Nonna Carmela. They can be made with smaller mushrooms as an elegant appetizer or with larger mushrooms for a delicious side dish. Either way, the mixture of sauce and cheese will have you cleaning your plate.

SAUCE

2 tablespoons (30 ml) extra-virgin olive oil

3 cloves garlic, minced

2 teaspoons finely chopped fresh mint

1 can (28 ounces, or 794 g) crushed tomatoes

½ cup (120 ml) water

STUFFING

10 medium white or cremini mushrooms (about 1 pound, or 454 g)

3 tablespoons (45 ml) extra-virgin olive oil

¼ cup (40 g) ¼-inch (6 mm) diced onion

½ teaspoon salt, plus a dash

¼ cup (30 g) grated Pecorino Romano cheese

¼ cup (27 g) plain bread crumbs

1 tablespoon (4 g) chopped fresh parsley

¼ teaspoon black pepper

¼ cup (30 g) shredded provolone cheese

Nonna Carmela Says

Watch your cooking time when the pan is covered. Smaller mushrooms will be ready faster than larger mushrooms, so keep your eyes open!

1. **To make the sauce:** Heat the oil in a small saucepan over medium heat and add the garlic and mint. Cook and stir for 2 to 3 minutes, until the garlic just begins to color. Add the tomatoes and water, and cook, stirring occasionally, until the sauce comes to a boil. Reduce the heat to a simmer and cook for 8 to 10 minutes.

2. Remove from the heat and set aside.

3. **To make the stuffing:** Remove the stems from the mushrooms and chop the stems into a ¼-inch (6 mm) dice.

4. Heat the olive oil in a large skillet over medium heat, add the onion, and cook and stir until translucent, 4 to 6 minutes. Add the mushroom stems and a dash of salt, and sauté for another 2 to 3 minutes. Set aside and let cool.

5. In a medium mixing bowl, combine the Pecorino Romano, bread crumbs, parsley, ½ teaspoon of salt, and black pepper, and mix well.

6. Once cooled, add the mushroom stems and onions to the mixing bowl and stir to combine.

7. In the same skillet used for cooking the mushroom stems and onions, add a layer of sauce, about 1½ cups (380 g).

8. Fill each mushroom with about 2 tablespoons (30 g) of filling and place in the skillet.

9. Spoon 1 to 2 teaspoons of sauce over each mushroom and add 1 teaspoon of provolone over the sauce.

10. Cover the skillet and place it back on the stove over medium heat until the sauce begins to bubble, 1 to 2 minutes. Reduce the heat to a simmer and cook for 10 to 12 minutes, or until the mushrooms are tender and easily pierced with a fork.

SEVEN FISHES SEAFOOD SALAD

Insalata di Mare

PREP TIME: 3 HOURS* • COOK TIME: 1 HOUR 50 MINUTES • YIELD: 8 TO 10 SERVINGS
*REQUIRES AT LEAST 1 TO 3 DAYS OF SOAKING

Okay, so this recipe can be a labor of love, but every single bite will be absolutely worth it (if you manage to get some on your plate)! No matter how much seafood salad Nonna Giuseppa makes, there never seems to be enough to go around. Traditionally, she makes it every Christmas Eve as part of her legendary Feast of the Seven Fishes, but it's so light and refreshing that it works beautifully as a summer antipasto as well.

SEAFOOD

1 pound (454 g) baccalà (salt cod)

½ cup (120 ml) dry white wine

3 pounds (1.3 kg) mussels, rinsed, scrubbed, and beards removed

1 pound (454 g) calamari, cleaned, bodies cut into ½-inch (1.3 cm) rings, tentacles left whole

1 pound (454 g) small scallops, washed

1 pound (454 g) shrimp, washed, peeled, and deveined

1 pound (454 g) scungilli (whelk)

1 pound (454 g) tenderized octopus

Nonna Giuseppa Says

Feel free to change up the seafood depending on your taste. Lobster is a special and delicious addition. When I'm making this for Christmas, I always make the salad a day or two before so the flavors intensify.

1. **To make the seafood:** Put the baccalà in a large bowl and cover it with cold water. Place the bowl in the refrigerator and change the water 3 times a day. Soak for 1 to 3 days, depending on saltiness. Some varieties are saltier than others. Drain.

2. Put a large heavy-bottomed saucepan over medium heat. Add the wine and mussels, and cover. Cook the mussels until they have all opened and the meat is detached from the shell, about 10 minutes. Discard any mussels that haven't opened.

3. Remove the meat from the shells of the mussels and set aside. Discard the shells.

4. Filter the broth of the mussels through a cheesecloth into a medium bowl and set aside.

5. **To make the broth and cook the seafood:** Fill a 6-quart (5.7 L) double boiler halfway with water. If you don't have a double boiler, a regular stockpot can be used with a large strainer or colander to scoop out the fish. Add all the broth ingredients to the pot and bring the water to a boil.

6. Add the baccalà and cook it for 6 to 7 minutes, then remove it from the water and set aside. Bring the water back to a boil.

7. Add the calamari to the pot and cook them for 4 to 5 minutes, then remove from the water and set aside. Bring the water back to a boil.

BROTH

3 cloves garlic, left whole

3 bay leaves

12 black peppercorns

1 teaspoon fennel seeds

1 tablespoon (4 g) minced
   fresh parsley

Peel of ½ lemon

½ cup (120 ml) dry white wine

1 tablespoon (15 ml) salt

VEGETABLES

2 stalks celery, cut into ½-inch
   (13 cm) dice

½ cup (30 g) chopped fresh parsley

2 medium carrots, grated

1 cup (192 g) green olives
   with pimento

SALAD DRESSING

1 cup (235 ml) fresh squeezed
   lemon juice

¾ cup (180 ml) extra-virgin olive oil

12 cloves garlic, minced

1 tablespoon (15 ml) white wine vinegar

Dash dried oregano

Salt

Red pepper flakes (optional)

8. Add the scallops to the pot and cook them for 4 to 5 minutes, then remove from the water and set aside. Bring the water back to a boil.

9. Add the shrimp to the pot and cook them until pink and tender, 6 to 7 minutes (depending on the size), then remove from the water and set aside. Bring the water back to a boil.

10. Add the scungilli to the pot and cook them until firm but tender, about 50 minutes. Remove from the pot and set aside. Bring the water back to a boil.

11. Finally, add the octopus to the pot, dip the colander in and out 2 times, and then let the octopus cook for about 20 minutes, or until the octopus is tender and the tentacles have curled. Remove from the pot and set aside.

12. In a large mixing bowl, combine the mussels, calamari, scallops, and shrimp.

13. Slice the scungilli into ½-inch (13 mm) pieces and add to the bowl. Cut the octopus into ½-inch (13 mm) pieces and add to the bowl as well. Finally, shred the baccalà by hand into bite-size pieces and add to the bowl.

14. **To make the vegetables:** Add the celery, parsley, carrots, and olives to the bowl, and toss well.

15. **To make the dressing:** Add all the dressing ingredients to a medium bowl, mix well, and then drizzle the mixture over the seafood. Toss well.

16. Cover the bowl and let it marinate in the fridge for at least 3 hours or overnight. The salad can be chilled for up to 2 days.

SICILIAN RICE BALLS

Arancini

PREP TIME: 1 HOUR • COOK TIME: 30 MINUTES • YIELD: 15 ARANCINI

Arancini, which is Italian for "little oranges," have a golden crust and an irresistible risotto filling. The classic center is usually a slow-cooked meat sauce with peas, but a center of mozzarella and Italian ham cuts down the prep time and packs in the flavor. The secret to Nonna Graziella's crispy crust is her unique "glue" of flour and water to coat the outside instead of egg wash; it seals off the rice from the hot frying oil, resulting in a perfectly crispy on the outside, creamy on the inside ball of deliciousness!

RICE

3 cups (700 ml) water

1 chicken bouillon cube

3 or 4 strands saffron

1 cup (185 g) Arborio rice

¼ cup (½ stick/60 g) unsalted butter

¼ cup (30 g) grated Parmigiano-
  Reggiano cheese

3 ounces (85 g) fresh mozzarella,
  cut into ½-inch (13 mm) chunks

2 ounces (56 g) Parmacotto or any
  Italian ham, cut into ¼-inch
  (6 mm) dice

COATING

5 tablespoons (38 g) all-purpose flour

½ cup (120 ml) water

2 to 3 cups (216 to 324 g) plain
  bread crumbs

Olive oil, for frying (or use any frying
  oil you like)

Nonna Graziella Says
*The rice for the arancini can
be made the night before and
refrigerated. Take the rice out
30 to 45 minutes before shaping,
filling, and frying.*

1. **To make the rice:** In a large saucepan over medium-high heat, add the water, bouillon cube, and saffron to the pot, and bring to a boil.

2. Stir in the rice and reduce the heat to a simmer. Cook the rice until tender and most of the water has been absorbed, about 20 minutes. Remove from the heat.

3. Let stand for 15 minutes, and then stir in the butter and Parmigiano-Reggiano. Cool completely.

4. Shape the rice into 2-inch (5 cm) balls. Press your finger into the center of each ball and insert 1 or 2 chunks of mozzarella and a few pieces of ham.

5. Pinch the rice around the filling to enclose. If necessary, enclose the filling with a bit more rice.

6. **To make the coating:** Whisk the flour and water together in a small bowl and put the bread crumbs into a separate shallow bowl. Set aside.

7. Line a baking sheet with parchment paper and set aside.

8. Roll each ball in the flour mixture and then roll in the bread crumbs. Place on the prepared baking sheet.

9. Heat 2 inches (5 cm) of oil in a large heavy-bottomed saucepan over medium-high heat. Add the balls in small batches, 2 or 3 at a time, and fry until golden brown, 1 to 2 minutes each. Transfer to a paper towel–lined plate to drain. Serve hot or at room temperature.

EGGPLANT PURSES

Melanzane alla Tabacchiera

PREP TIME: 30 MINUTES • COOK TIME: 1 HOUR 15 MINUTES • YIELD: ABOUT 10 PURSES,
8 TO 10 SERVINGS

This dish gets its name from the tiny tobacco cases Nonna Graziella remembers everyone carrying back in Carini, Sicily. These stuffed eggplant pockets pack in so much flavor with such simple ingredients that you may even be able to make an entire meal out of them. The medley of textures and flavors from the Sicilian *mollica* (bread-crumb mixture) and melted mozzarella that wraps around the crisp ham and meaty, roasted eggplant, makes for an earthy and rich combination everyone will love.

1 medium eggplant (about 1½ pounds, or 680 g)

¼ cup (27 g) plain bread crumbs

½ cup (60 g) grated Parmigiano-Reggiano cheese

3 tablespoons (45 ml) extra-virgin olive oil, plus more for brushing

2 cloves garlic, finely minced

1 tablespoon (4 g) finely minced fresh parsley

½ teaspoon dried oregano

¼ teaspoon black pepper

2 or 3 slices Parmacotto ham or any Italian smoked ham, shredded by hand into bite-size pieces

1 cup (115 g) shredded fresh mozzarella

1. Preheat the oven to 400°F (200°C). Line a baking sheet with parchment paper and set aside.

2. Trim the ends of the eggplant and slice it into ¾-inch (2 cm) round slices. Slice each round in half three-quarters of the way through lengthwise, making a pocket.

3. In a small mixing bowl, combine the bread crumbs, Parmigiano-Reggiano, olive oil, garlic, parsley, oregano, and black pepper, and mix well. Set aside.

4. Spoon 1 to 2 tablespoons (15 to 30 g) of the bread crumb filling into each eggplant pocket depending on size. Add 1 tablespoon (9 g) of ham and 1 tablespoon (7 g) of mozzarella to the pockets as well.

5. Arrange all of the pockets on the prepared baking sheet and brush each side with oil. Bake for 20 to 25 minutes, turning over halfway through. Turn on the broiler to high and broil for 1 to 2 minutes, or until slightly browned on top. Serve hot.

"Destiny gives us the best and worst things, and we have to be happy no matter what happens."

"*La vita è gioia, mia Cara!*" (Life is funny, my darling!) Nonna Graziella says as she sits across from me at her "downstairs kitchen" table in Brooklyn, the place where most of the family gathers for meals. Italian television blares in the background while she worries aloud that she isn't confident she can give a good interview. I beg to differ.

Looking at her, it's so hard to believe she's a nonna to five grandchildren. I still see the young woman who begged her father to let her leave the small town of Carini and continue her education in Palermo. "I wanted to study, but my father, a lemon farmer, would see the modern girls who went to the city to school, and he said 'no!' "

In a time and a place with limited professional options for women, Nonna Graziella decided to teach. "I began to tutor children. That was what I could do with my eighth-grade diploma so that's what I did. When I had to leave them to come to America, they were all so sad."

The decision to leave Carini came with a desire for upward mobility for Graziella and her family. "We arrived in Flushing, Queens, and we stayed with people in an apartment. It was already furnished. We had no idea who the bed or the chairs or the coffee table belonged to."

Graziella soon found work in a clothing factory in America, but the town of Carini and fate seemed to follow her. "I didn't know my husband in Carini, even though our families lived very close by. I'm sure I even kissed them goodbye before we left. He had already been living in Brooklyn, so his aunt gave me a package for him. Once he came to the house to pick it up, he decided he wanted me as well. He was much older but we fell in love."

Like many Italian girls, Nonna Graziella's experiences with cooking were limited before she got married. "My mother cooked most of the time, but if she had to go out she would ask me to make sauce for her, and I used to panic. Luckily I had a photographic memory from watching her, and I remembered everything she did when I had to."

Today, Graziella still cooks with the same flavors of her home in Sicily, and she has passed her knowledge on to her sons, who own Graziella's a restaurant in Williamsburg, which serves up many of its namesake's famous dishes, especially her unique *arancini* (Sicilian Rice Balls; see page 46 for the recipe).

In the end, Graziella says she owes her life to destiny. "I do believe in destiny. I don't believe we go out and make our own, because if it were up to me I wouldn't have created the hard things in my life. Destiny gives us the best and worst things, and we have to be happy no matter what happens."

FRIED CALAMARI

Calamari Fritti

PREP TIME: 15 MINUTES • COOK TIME: 20 MINUTES • YIELD: 4 TO 6 SERVINGS

Fried calamari hits everyone's Italian comfort-food spot. The plate never makes it more than once around the dinner table! Nonna Romana's calamari are coated in refined semolina flour, which gives them a little more texture and a gorgeous golden color. In Italy, fried calamari aren't quite as crunchy as they are here in the States. The outside coating is light and delicate and doesn't overpower the seafood. These can be served Italian-American style with Nonna Romana's marinara sauce (page 26), but my favorite is just with a squeeze of fresh lemon.

2 cups (334 g) refined semolina flour

2 tablespoons (30 ml) salt, plus more for sprinkling

Olive oil, for frying (or use any frying oil you like)

2 pounds (907 g) cleaned calamari, bodies cut into ½-inch (13 mm) rings, tentacles left whole

Nonna Romana Says
Calamari need room!
Don't overcrowd the pan
when you're frying, or the
calamari won't brown.

1. In a large mixing bowl, whisk the semolina and salt together, breaking up any lumps.

2. Heat about 2 inches (5 cm) of oil in a large heavy-bottomed skillet over high heat.

3. With a paper towel, pat the calamari dry. Try and get them as dry as possible or else they will be soggy.

4. Dredge the calamari in the semolina mixture and transfer to a fine-mesh strainer to shake off any excess. Make sure all the pieces have an even coating.

5. Place the calamari in the oil and fry in 5 or 6 batches for 3 to 4 minutes at a time, or until lightly golden brown.

6. Transfer to a paper towel–lined plate to drain.

7. Sprinkle with extra salt. Serve immediately.

SOUPS AND SALADS

Zuppe ed Insalate

ESCAROLE SOUP WITH TINY MEATBALLS

Zuppa di Scarola con Polpettine

PREP TIME: 35 MINUTES • COOK TIME: 57 MINUTES • YIELD: 6 TO 8 SERVINGS

After many years, I came to the accidental realization that this is Nonna Romana's version of an Italian-American wedding soup. It's totally appropriate, because no soup could ever get you in the mood to cuddle up with someone like this one. The basic flavors of the greens and vegetables melt together beautifully in the savory chicken broth, and there's something about those tiny meatballs that is just so darn cute! If you're not already married, this could be renamed "husband-catching soup"!

SOUP

2 tablespoons (30 ml) extra-virgin olive oil

2 medium carrots, cut into ½-inch (13 mm) dice

1 medium yellow onion, cut into ¼-inch (6 mm) dice

2 stalks celery, cut into ½-inch (13 mm) dice

Salt and black pepper, to taste

3 quarts (96 ounces, or 2.8 L) chicken broth (about 12 cups)

2 or 3 bay leaves

1 head escarole, trimmed, washed, and cut into 1-inch (2.5 cm) strips

MEATBALLS

1 pound (454 g) meatloaf mix (equal parts beef, pork, and veal)

3 cloves garlic, finely minced

2 tablespoons (8 g) finely minced parsley

2 eggs

½ cup (54 g) plain bread crumbs

½ cup (60 g) grated Parmigiano-Reggiano cheese, plus more for serving

½ cup (60 g) grated Pecorino Romano cheese

1. **To make the soup:** Heat the oil in a 6-quart (5.7 L) stockpot over medium-high heat. Add the carrot, onion, and celery, and salt and black pepper. Cook and stir until the onion becomes translucent and the vegetables become soft, about 7 minutes.

2. Add the broth and bay leaves and bring to a boil. Drop in the escarole and reduce the heat to a simmer. Cook for 20 to 30 minutes, stirring occasionally.

3. **To make the meatballs:** In a large mixing bowl, combine all the meatball ingredients and shape the mixture into small meatballs, about 1 teaspoon of mixture per meatball.

4. When the escarole is wilted and tender, drop the meatballs into the soup and stir gently until cooked through, 15 to 20 minutes. Remove and discard the bay leaves, season with salt and black pepper, and serve with lots of grated Parmigiano-Reggiano.

Nonna Romana Says
You can also cook some pasta separately and add it to the soup. Delizioso!!

PASTA E FAGIOLI SOUP

PREP TIME: 6 HOURS • COOK TIME: 2 HOURS 30 MINUTES • YIELD: 6 TO 8 SERVINGS

The years I lived with Nonna Romana, I often remember waking up to the smell of cannellini beans simmering on the stove for her amazingly simple *pasta e fagioli*. She would sometimes wake up very early in the morning just to turn on the heat and go back to bed. Today, there still isn't a dish I find more comforting than a humble plate of pasta and beans. Sometimes the memories are enough to fill up my heart and stomach. Serve with hunks of crusty bread.

16 ounces (454 g) dried cannellini beans

½ tablespoon (8 ml) salt

4 bay leaves

4 cloves garlic, minced

3 plum tomatoes, cut into ½-inch (13 mm) dice

2 stalks celery, cut into ½-inch (13 mm) dice

¼ cup (60 ml) extra-virgin olive oil, plus more for serving

8 ounces (227 g) dried ditalini

Red pepper flakes (optional)

Nonna Romana Says

I like to make the beans in large batches in the beginning of the week and add them to pasta when needed. Having a refrigerator full of beans makes me so happy because I know I can make some pasta e fagioli *whenever I want!*

1. In a 6-quart (5.7 L) stockpot, add the beans, salt, bay leaves, and enough water to cover them by 2 inches (5 cm), about 10 cups (2.4 L). Soak the beans for at least 6 hours or overnight.

2. The beans will have absorbed some of the water while soaking overnight. Before you start cooking, add more water so you once again have 2 inches (5 cm) of water above the beans. Then add the garlic, tomatoes, celery, and olive oil to the water. Cook over low heat until the beans are tender, 2 to 2½ hours. (Some beans may take more time to cook than others. The idea is to cook them low and slow, so they cook without absorbing too much water and evaporating your broth. If you taste the beans and they seem tender and done, then they are. You got this!) Remove and discard the bay leaves.

3. Bring a medium pot of salted water to a boil, add the pasta, and cook until al dente. Drain the pasta and portion into bowls. Add the broth and beans to the pasta and top with some olive oil and red pepper flakes, if using.

"My kitchen is always open. Even now, I keep going because I can't bear to take the joy away from my family."

As I approach the large gold door that guards Nonna Nina's Park Avenue apartment, I'll admit that I'm slightly intimidated. It's been years since I last saw her, when she appeared on my freshman season of *Cooking with Nonna*.

When Nonna Nina answers the door, I can't believe how thin she is, a fraction of her former shapely figure. When I ask about her dramatic weight loss she snaps back, "Yeah, because now I eat alone! You know something? I was happier when I was fat!" she says.

In a few short minutes I feel at home with Nonna Nina. "I was born in Brooklyn, and I've been here on the Upper East Side for forty-eight years now, and I'm at home. Growing up, my mother had help [cooking and cleaning] for $40 a week. Once I moved to the city when I was married, I wanted to start cooking what my husband wanted," she says.

While she may have a different address than the usual Brooklyn-born nonna, Nina's Italian hospitality always shines through. "I don't have the biggest kitchen, but I've had up to thirty people here to eat. When you cook for someone, it's love!" It's a sentiment she has continued to honor, even after the passing of her beloved husband, Vinny. "My kitchen is always open. Even now, I kept going because I can't bear to take the joy away from my family."

Nonna Nina lives somewhat far away from my nonna (an hour subway ride to be exact) but she takes just as much pride in being a nonna, even if she's not always what people expect. "As I travel, people are shocked when I use the word nonna. They ask me why I'm not in a housedress stirring sauce, but I tell them a nonna of today is educated and well-traveled, and can dress well too. We have it all!" She prides herself on embracing modern tools with classic influences. "I have no problem using a Cuisinart, but I'm still old school from Brooklyn and I married an old school Italian guy."

Nina has always maintained a traditional Italian household. Her two children were always congregating in the main dining area of the house. "I could see my kids from the kitchen while they did their homework on our dining room table, and we would clear it to have dinner, and I always made a big dinner." Her eyes light up as she recalls these happy times with her children.

"The truth is, Rossella, I'm content. I'm never happy the way I was when my husband was alive. And part of it is there's no one to cook and show off for. I am content in myself, but I'm not happy."

I'm so moved by the bond Nina and her husband shared over food. As an Italian woman, I know firsthand the joy and satisfaction that lie in preparing a meal for someone you love. "I know one day I'll get to heaven and see Vinny again, and the first thing he's going to ask me is why I couldn't lose this weight when he was alive!" We both erupted in laughter. "He loved and accepted me exactly the way I was. I was never perfect. I couldn't make pasta the way some people can. I never got filet mignon right, but I believe that passion and perseverance count more than talent and that's always the way I've lived my life."

ARUGULA AND FENNEL SALAD

Insalata di Rucola e Finocchio

PREP TIME: 10 MINUTES • COOK TIME: 5 MINUTES • YIELD: 6 SERVINGS

This beautiful salad is as elegant as Nonna Nina. "Everything in it is Tuscan, like me," she says of the big mix that she can prepare on a whim if anyone important decides to drop by. This salad is full of assertive flavors that will please everyone's palate. The light and crisp fennel and the slightly bitter arugula create a beautiful contrast with the crunch of the almonds.

½ cup (46 g) sliced unblanched almonds

5 ounces (142 g) baby arugula (about 7 cups)

1 can (15 ounces, or 425 g) cannellini beans, drained and rinsed

1 fennel bulb trimmed, cored, and very thinly sliced

½ cup (96 g) pitted Gaeta olives

1 cup (150 g) halved cherry tomatoes

1 small red onion, thinly sliced

½ cup (120 ml) extra-virgin olive oil

¼ cup (60 ml) balsamic vinegar, preferably from Modena

Salt and black pepper, to taste

2 ounces (56 g) prosciutto di Parma, sliced and broken apart into small pieces by hand

¼ cup (30 g) shaved Parmigiano-Reggiano

1. Preheat the oven to 350°F (175°C).

2. Spread the almonds on an ungreased baking sheet in a single layer. Toast the almonds for 4 to 5 minutes, until golden and fragrant, keeping an eye on their color so they don't burn. Transfer to a plate and let cool.

3. Add the arugula, beans, fennel, olives, tomatoes, onion, olive oil, and vinegar to a large bowl, and mix well. Season with salt and black pepper. Top with the almonds, prosciutto, and shaved cheese, and serve.

Nonna Nina Says

Sometimes I make a big bowl of this salad and keep it in the fridge undressed. If someone drops by around lunchtime, I finish it with the olive oil and vinegar and it's always very elegant.

STELLINE PASTINA WITH PARMIGIANO

Stelline Pastina con Parmigiano-Reggiano

PREP TIME: 10 MINUTES • COOK TIME: 1 HOUR 10 MINUTES • YIELD: 6 TO 8 SERVINGS

Many who grew up on this soup would agree that *pastina* has healing powers. I like to think of it as Italian penicillin. It warms the heart and stomach, and brings back so many fond childhood memories of my nonna cooking for me. Her pastina recipe is very simple—almost too simple—but I've never had the heart to change a thing about it. The recipe calls for pastina, water, and bouillon cubes that my nonna calls *dadini*—that's it. I love the cubes because you can adjust the salt by cutting them in half or sneaking in an extra one like I always did to make it a little more *saporito!*

10 cups (2.4 L) water
1 or 2 chicken bouillon cubes
¾ cup (105 g) dried stelline pastina
¾ to 1½ cups (90 to 180 g) grated
    Parmigiano-Reggiano cheese,
    for serving

1. Put a large heavy-bottomed saucepan over high heat. Add the water and bouillon cubes, bring to a boil, and stir in the pastina.

2. Cook for 4 to 5 minutes, until the pastina is tender. Ladle into bowls and add 2 to 3 tablespoons (16 to 24 g) of Parmigiano-Reggiano to each bowl. Stir to combine and serve.

Nonna Romana Says

This can also be made with other cuts of pastina, such as ancini di pepe or even orzo, but the stelline are a favorite among bambini! Pastina is often used as baby food in Italy, and it was one of the first things I made for my granddaughter Rossella.

NONNA ROSA CARMELO'S

MINESTRONE

PREP TIME: 15 MINUTES • COOK TIME: 40 MINUTES • YIELD: 6 TO 8 SERVINGS

Zia Rosa is the minestrone queen! For as long as I can remember, my aunt Rosa has brought her famous minestrone over every week like clockwork. The vegetables change seasonally, but she always tosses them with oil and salt, drawing out their natural juices. As a result, she adds very little water, making it a true vegetable broth with tender veggies. *Perfetto!*

4 Roma tomatoes, cut into ½-inch (13 mm) dice

1 small onion, cut into ¼-inch (6 mm) dice

½ head cauliflower, cut into 1-inch (2.5 cm) pieces

¼ head cabbage, cored and cut into 1-inch (2.5 cm) strips

1 Idaho potato, peeled and cut into 1-inch (2.5 cm) chunks

1 red, yellow, or orange bell pepper, cored, seeded, and cut into 1-inch (2.5 cm) dice

1 small zucchini, cut into ½-inch (13 mm) dice

2 stalks celery, cut into ½-inch (13 mm) dice

1 small carrot, peeled and cut into ½-inch (13 mm) dice

1 small eggplant, cut into 1-inch (2.5 cm) cubes

1 cup (116 g) 1-inch (2.5 cm) chunks winter squash

2 tablespoons (8 g) minced fresh parsley

½ cup (120 ml) extra-virgin olive oil

2 teaspoons salt, or more if needed

1½ cups (350 ml) hot water

Crusty bread, for serving

Grated Parmigiano-Reggiano cheese, for serving

1. Put a 7- to 9-quart (6.6 to 8.5 L) stockpot over high heat. Add all the vegetables, parsley, olive oil, and salt, and cook, tossing with a wooden spoon, until the vegetables begin to break down, 15 to 20 minutes.

2. Add the hot water and reduce the heat to a simmer. Cover the pot and cook until all the vegetables are soft and tender, 15 to 20 minutes. Taste for seasoning and add more salt if needed. Serve with crusty bread and lots of grated Parmigiano-Reggiano.

Nonna Rosa Says

If you're making a big batch of minestrone for the week, I suggest undercooking it slightly so it doesn't get overcooked when it's reheated.

"I am married to a man who is passionate about food ... I've cooked every single day we've been married. We learn so much from each other."

When I take one step inside Zia Rosa's home in Bensonhurst, Brooklyn, it looks as if everything has been frozen in time. An antique Italian baroque sofa is covered in plastic, and in the kitchen, the small round kitchen table is covered with a hand-embroidered tablecloth with a vinyl covering on top of that for extra protection (of course). Even the dirt is clean in my Zia Rosa's home.

"Ciao Rosse'!" she says to me as I take a seat at the kitchen table. The aroma of fresh *taralli*—savory Italian biscuits—is still in the air from the early morning when she usually does most of her baking. My aunt is part of a dying breed of women who can cook, sew, and scrub things to perfection.

Considering how adept she is at cooking, it's surprising that it's a talent she developed later in her life. "I had been exposed to food, but I didn't start cooking until after I was married and in America. I asked my mother-in-law for suggestions sometimes, but mostly I taught myself."

In 1950s Italy, marrying an American was considered a path to prosperity and prestige. My great uncle Dominic was doing well as a waiter in Brooklyn, and came from a reputable family. After they married, they set off for a new country.

"When I arrived in America, I suffered. I didn't speak the language; I didn't know anyone." She quickly enrolled in night school and began learning English to pass her citizenship exam. "After three years, I became a citizen and petitioned for my mother. My sisters followed after that." That is when the realization hit me that without my aunt, none of my family would ever have been here.

Although she is my great-aunt, Zia Rosa has been like my "bonus" nonna for as long as I can remember. Because Zia Rosa is the only one of my nonna's sisters who settled in the States, she and my nonna have become a sort of dynamic duo over the years.

Today my aunt would call her life "a sacrificed life, but a happy life." Her marriage of nearly sixty years to my uncle, who is a veritable culinary master in his own right, has been one of the most inspiring and unforgettable relationships I have ever had the privilege of witnessing. Food is at the center of everything in their lives. "I am married to a man who is passionate about food, and I'll admit that I'm not half as passionate as he is . . . I've cooked every single day we've been married. We learn so much from each other."

To her four grandchildren, she is the kind of nonna they always count on for comfort. "Grandchildren are the greatest joy. Having them makes you realize that there is something greater than yourself in the world. You love them more than your children, and don't ask me why!" she says. "It's an instinctual thing."

MOZZARELLA WITH BROCCOLI RABE AND SUN-DRIED TOMATOES

Mozzarella alla Barese

PREP TIME: 10 MINUTES* • COOK TIME: 15 MINUTES • YIELD: 4 TO 6 SERVINGS

*REQUIRES AT LEAST 2 HOURS OF MARINATING

Neapolitans have *mozzarella alla Caprese*, and Pugliesi have *mozzarella alla Barese*, thanks to Nonna Romana. The flavors of Puglia are all present in this simple, delicious salad that is a twist on its Neapolitan cousin. I love the mix of creamy mozzarella and bitter broccoli rabe with the tanginess of sun-dried tomatoes.

½ cup (27 g) sun-dried tomatoes

1 tablespoon (6 g) chopped fresh mint

8 cloves garlic, sliced, divided

½ cup (120 ml) extra-virgin olive oil, divided, plus more for drizzling

10 cups (2.4 L) water

1 tablespoon (15 ml) salt

1 bunch broccoli rabe (about 1 pound/450 g), ends trimmed and washed

16 ounces (454 g) fresh mozzarella, cut into ½-inch (13 mm) thick slices

Nonna Romana Says

Be sure to buy good-quality fresh mozzarella in water, and never put it in the refrigerator before serving because it will dry out the cheese and make it chewy.

1. Place the sun-dried tomatoes in a small bowl with the mint, 3 cloves of the sliced garlic, and ¼ cup (60 ml) of the olive oil. Cover with plastic wrap and marinate for at least 2 hours or overnight.

2. Bring the water to a boil in a 6-quart (5.7 L) stockpot. Add the salt and mix well.

3. Drop the broccoli rabe into the boiling water and cook for 10 minutes. Drain in a colander and run under cold water.

4. Heat the remaining ¼ cup (60 ml) of olive oil in a large sauté pan over medium-high heat. Add the remaining 5 cloves of sliced garlic and cook and stir. When the garlic begins to color, 2 to 3 minutes, add the broccoli rabe. Cook and stir the broccoli rabe for another 2 to 3 minutes.

5. In a serving dish, layer the broccoli rabe, sun-dried tomato mixture, and mozzarella slices. Drizzle with more olive oil and serve at room temperature.

BEEF BROTH SOUP WITH CUT SPAGHETTI

Brodo di Carne con Spaghetti Spezzati

PREP TIME: 10 MINUTES • COOK TIME: 1 HOUR 35 MINUTES • YIELD: 4 TO 6 SERVINGS

This soup was traditionally eaten every Saturday night in Mola di Bari, where my Nonna Romana grew up. Her family would cook it low and slow for hours until the meat was falling off the bone and mix it with the most humble-cut spaghetti. Every time I make this, I imagine myself eating with them before a night out in the piazza.

2½ pounds (1.1 kg) beef short ribs, fat trimmed

12 cups (2.8 L) water

1½ pounds (680 g) russet potatoes (about 2 large potatoes), peeled and quartered

1 medium carrot, cut into ¼-inch (6 mm) dice

½ small onion, cut into ¼-inch (6 mm) dice

1 stalk celery, cut into ½-inch (13 mm) dice, plus a few leaves

2 plum tomatoes, cut into 1-inch (2.5 cm) dice

3 tablespoons (45 ml) extra-virgin olive oil

2 teaspoons salt

2 bay leaves

8 ounces (227 g) dried spaghetti

Grated Parmigiano-Reggiano cheese, for serving

1. Put a 6-quart (5.7 L) stockpot over high heat, add the water and short ribs, and bring to a boil. Skim any foam that floats to the surface with a spoon and discard.

2. Add the potatoes, carrot, onion, celery, tomatoes, olive oil, salt, and bay leaves. Reduce the heat to medium and cook, stirring occasionally, until the meat is tender and begins to separate from the bone, about 1½ hours. Remove and discard the bay leaves and bones.

3. When the soup has about 20 minutes to go, bring a medium pot of salted water to a boil. Break the spaghetti by hand into 2-inch (5 cm) pieces and drop them into the boiling water. Cook until al dente. Drain the pasta and add it to a bowl. Ladle the broth on top. Serve with lots of grated Parmigiano-Reggiano.

Nonna Romana Says

Short ribs work best with this dish, but if you cannot get them, you may substitute any beef with a bone, such as osso buco. In Italy, some people would only use a bone that they could get for free from the butcher to make the broth. The bone has all the flavor.

TUSCAN CABBAGE SOUP

Zuppa di Verza

PREP TIME: 15 MINUTES • COOK TIME: 1 HOUR 17 MINUTES • YIELD: 6 TO 8 SERVINGS

The mild and earthy flavor of the savoy cabbage in this soup is perfect against the richness of the sausage and pancetta. Instead of pasta, this soup is poured over a slice of crusty bread that is scooped up by the spoonful with the broth.

2 tablespoons (30 ml) extra-virgin olive oil

1 pound (454 g) sweet Italian sausage, casing removed

3 cloves garlic, minced

1 medium onion, cut into ¼-inch (6 mm) dice

1 cup (225 g) ¼-inch (6 mm) diced pancetta

3 quarts (96 ounces, or 2.8 L) chicken broth (about 12 cups)

2 large Idaho potatoes (about 1¼ pounds, or 568 g), peeled and cut into 2-inch (5 cm) chunks

½ small head savoy cabbage (about 1 pound, or 454 g), cored and cut into 2-inch (5 cm) strips

6 to 8 slices thick-crust Italian bread, 1 inch (2.5 cm) thick

Grated Parmigiano-Reggiano cheese, for serving

1. Heat the oil in a large skillet over medium-high heat. Add the sausage and cook and stir until browned, breaking it up with a wooden spoon, 6 to 8 minutes. With a slotted spoon, transfer the sausage to a plate, leaving the drippings in the skillet.

2. In the same skillet over medium heat, add the garlic and onion and cook and stir for 3 to 4 minutes. Raise the heat to high and add the pancetta. Cook and stir until the onions are very translucent and the pancetta is crisp, 8 to 10 minutes. Drain the oil from the skillet and set aside.

3. Put a 6-quart (5.7 L) stockpot over high heat. Add the broth, browned sausage, and potatoes. Add the sautéed pancetta with the onions and garlic to the stockpot, and bring to a boil. Reduce the heat to a simmer, cover, and cook, stirring occasionally with a wooden spoon, until the potatoes are cooked through, about 30 minutes.

4. Uncover the pot and add the cabbage. Cook just until the cabbage wilts, 3 to 5 minutes.

5. To serve, place a slice of bread in the bottom of a soup bowl and ladle the soup on top. Serve with lots of grated Parmigiano-Reggiano.

Nonna Nina Says
This is one of the most comforting dishes I remember from my own nonna, who was from Montepulciano. She loved this soup because the cabbage always maintained some bite even after you cooked it— so even if it was left over it didn't taste like leftovers!

CUCUZZA SQUASH SOUP

Zuppa di Cucuzza con Pasta

PREP TIME: 5 MINUTES • COOK TIME: 35 MINUTES • YIELD: 6 TO 8 SERVINGS

Cucuzza squash grows as wild here in the summer as it does back in Sicily. Nonna Michelina portions and freezes her summer squash so she can use it during the winter in many recipes, but especially in her favorite soup. The squash and pasta are cooked together in true Southern Italian style, and then, to make a rich broth, Michelina mixes in a simple, quick tomato sauce that most Sicilians call *picchi pacchi*. This soup works wonderfully when sprinkled generously with ricotta salata, a Sicilian sheep's milk cheese.

SAUCE

¼ cup (60 ml) extra-virgin olive oil

4 cloves garlic, minced

1 can (28 ounces, or 794 g) crushed
    tomatoes

½ teaspoon salt, plus more for
    the broth

¼ teaspoon red pepper flakes

BROTH

12 cups (2.8 L) water

2 pounds (907 g) cucuzza squash,
    cut into 1-inch (2.5 cm) cubes

8 ounces (227 g) dried pipette (ditalini
    or small shells can also be used)

¾ to 1½ cups (90 to 180 g) ricotta
    salata, for serving

1. **To make the sauce:** Heat the oil in a large saucepan over medium heat. Add the garlic and cook and stir until golden, 2 to 3 minutes. Add the tomatoes. Fill the can halfway with water. Swish it around to pick up the tomato stuck to the sides and then add the water to the sauce. Add the salt and red pepper flakes. Bring to a boil, reduce the heat, and simmer the sauce for 20 minutes, stirring occasionally with a wooden spoon.

2. **To make the broth:** While the sauce is simmering, in a 7- to 9-quart (6.6 to 8.5 L) stockpot, bring the water to a boil and add salt to taste. Add the cucuzza and cook until tender, 30 to 35 minutes. (If using frozen cucuzza, add it to cold water and bring to a boil.)

3. Drop the pasta into the water and cook together with the squash until the pasta is al dente.

4. Ladle the sauce into the pot with the pasta and cucuzza and stir to combine. Ladle into bowls and serve with 2 to 3 tablespoons (16 to 24 g) of grated ricotta salata.

Nonna Michelina Says

If you can't find the cucuzza in supermarkets or farmers' markets, you may substitute regular green squash. Just shave 10 to 12 minutes off the cooking time.

NONNA MARIA FIORE'S

CHICKEN SOUP WITH ORZO

Zuppa di Pollo con Orzo

PREP TIME: 10 MINUTES • COOK TIME: 1 HOUR 30 MINUTES • YIELD: 4 TO 6 SERVINGS

Nonna Maria's chicken soup is a feast for the soul, uniting the simplest of ingredients in a flavorful soup. She traditionally uses *capuntini*, which are tiny homemade *cavatelli*, but other small pastas may be substituted.

1½ pounds (680 g) skinless chicken
   thighs, fat trimmed

1½ pounds (680 g) skinless chicken
   drumsticks, fat trimmed

10 cups (2.4 L) water

1 tablespoon (15 ml) salt, plus more
   to taste

2 Roma tomatoes, cut into ½-inch
   (13 mm) dice

1 medium carrot, cut into ½-inch
   (13 mm) dice

1 small red onion, cut into ½-inch
   (13 mm) dice

1 stalk celery, cut into ½-inch
   (13 mm) dice

2 tablespoons (8 g) coarsely chopped
   fresh parsley

¼ cup (60 ml) extra-virgin olive oil

8 ounces (227 g) dried orzo

Crusty bread, for serving

Grated Parmigiano-Reggiano cheese,
   for serving

1. Add the water and 1 tablespoon (15 ml) of salt to a 6-quart (5.7 L) stockpot with the chicken and bring to a boil. Skim any foam that floats to the surface with a spoon and discard.

2. Add the vegetables, parsley, and olive oil. Bring to a boil once again. Once boiling, reduce the heat to a simmer, cover the pot, and cook, stirring occasionally with a wooden spoon, until the chicken is tender and separating from the bones, about 1 hour and 15 minutes. Taste for seasoning and add salt to taste.

3. Bring a medium pot of salted water to a boil, add the orzo, and cook until al dente. Drain the pasta and portion into bowls. Ladle the broth and chicken on top. Serve with crusty bread and lots of grated Parmigiano-Reggiano.

Nonna Maria Says
The soup can also be strained through cheesecloth for homemade chicken broth.

"First comes Jesus, then comes sauce!"

Originally from Altamura, Puglia, Nonna Maria Fiore might be tiny in stature (she is about 4'9"), but she has the stamina of someone half her age. A natural chatterbox, she leads me into her home with the energy of someone who has just had a double shot of espresso.

"When I came to this country, I didn't know how to do much. I was eighteen and I had to go to work, but I remember watching my mother and my sister, and how my father would wake me up early to help make the bread. I put my mind to it and I learned. Nobody is born knowing these things," she says. I watch her get to work making *capuntini*, a tiny handmade pasta she masterfully presses out by hand, her delicate fingers moving faster than my eyes can follow.

"My sister-in-law used to say I was a life-sized doll!" Nonna Maria says, laughing as she mixes cookie dough by hand on her basement kitchen table. Every single thing in the kitchen is spotless and looks brand-new, and it's almost as if we're in a life-sized dollhouse. Like so many nonne I know, the kitchen is where Nonna Maria feels most comfortable. It is a popular Italian-American custom—particularly in Brooklyn—to build a separate kitchen in the basement for the day-to-day cooking. The basement is usually where mass quantities of cookies, fresh pastas, and aromatic fried foods are prepared, leaving the upstairs kitchen to always be as tidy as possible, almost like a showroom. You know, in case company comes!

And company certainly comes to Nonna Maria's! With four children and seven grandchildren, Nonna Maria is the busiest doll in her dollhouse. "I try and still do all the traditions. I always make chicken cutlets and sauce on Sundays. I start early because I go to Mass first. I never miss Mass. First comes Jesus, then comes sauce!" She tells me this in a tone that implies she knows I haven't been to church in a while. "It's a lot of work sometimes but I love to cook; I love to make people happy!"

At the end of our visit, Nonna Maria brings me upstairs to show me her "upstairs kitchen," and I can't even believe my eyes: it's an adorable petite blue and white kitchen from the 1950s that looks so new it sparkles. I feel like I'm on the set of an old sitcom. As Nonna Maria steps in front of her perfect little kitchen, I can't help but think of the first words she said to me, and how the life-sized nonna doll looks so at home in her little dollhouse. "I'm a happy woman. I cry and I smile, but mostly smile!"

COLD BREAD SALAD

Cialledda

PREP TIME: 40 MINUTES • YIELD: 4 TO 6 SERVINGS

In Nonna Maria's native Altamura, *cialledda* was a way farmers would use hard leftover bread. Soaking the bread in water allows it to absorb all the flavors of the salad. The famous bread of Altamura, which is now made under strict guidelines in Italy, has a dense texture that holds its shape even after being soaked, but this dish can still work with almost any good crusty bread. It's a favorite during the warm summer months and can be a light but filling meal with the addition of a protein.

6 cups (690 g) 1-inch (2.5 cm) cubes stale Altamura or any good Italian bread

1 cucumber, thinly sliced

½ pound (227 g) cherry tomatoes, halved

3 stalks celery, cut into ½-inch (13 mm) dice

1 cup (235 ml) water

¼ cup (60 ml) extra-virgin olive oil

1 teaspoon dried oregano

½ teaspoon salt

1 navel orange, peeled and sectioned

1. In a large bowl, add all the ingredients except the oranges and toss well until all the water is absorbed.

2. Add the oranges on top. Cover the bowl with plastic wrap and refrigerate for 30 minutes, tossing occasionally. Serve.

Nonna Maria Says

Traditionally, farmers in Altamura made this salad with lemons instead of oranges. The addition of oranges would have made this a "rich" salad! But I love that the oranges give it some delicious sweetness. My grandchildren love it, too. You can also use blood oranges if they are available.

VEGETABLES AND SIDES

Verdure e Contorni

STUFFED ARTICHOKES

Carciofi Ripieni

PREP TIME: 15 MINUTES • COOK TIME: 47 MINUTES • YIELD: 6 SERVINGS

Toasting the bread crumbs takes these traditional Sicilian stuffed artichokes to the next level, while the chopped almonds give them a bit of crunch. Nonna Angelina uses her nonna super strength to wiggle them apart and get the stuffing all the way down to the edible base of the leaves. Yum!

½ cup (46 g) chopped unblanched almonds

6 medium artichokes (each 8 to 9 ounces, or 227 to 255 g)

Juice of 1 lemon

4 tablespoons (60 ml) extra-virgin olive oil, divided, plus more for drizzling

1 cup (108 g) plain bread crumbs

¼ cup (16 g) minced fresh parsley

3 cloves garlic, minced

½ cup (60 g) grated Pecorino Romano cheese

½ cup (60 g) grated Parmigiano-Reggiano cheese

½ cup (60 g) shaved Parmigiano-Reggiano cheese

Salt and black pepper, to taste

❚ Nonna Angelina Says

I actually cut off a little more of the sharp tips of the artichoke than most people do, because they're not edible. This also makes it easier to pull the artichoke apart and get the stuffing down to the base, where it really matters.

1. Preheat the oven to 350°F (175°C). Spread the almonds on an ungreased baking sheet in a single layer. Toast the almonds for 5 to 7 minutes, until golden and fragrant, keeping an eye on their color so they don't burn. Transfer to a plate and let cool.

2. Clean the artichokes by removing the outer leaves until you reach the light green part of the artichoke. Cut off the top part of the leaves (about ¾ inch, or 2 cm), trim ¼ inch (6 mm) of the stem, and peel the stem. Wiggle each artichoke apart with your thumbs and pull out the prickly purple leaves. Scoop out the fuzzy choke with a small spoon and discard. Place the artichokes in a bowl and completely cover with water. Add the lemon juice and let sit for about 10 minutes.

3. Heat 2 tablespoons (30 ml) of the olive oil in a medium sauté pan over medium heat. Add the bread crumbs and stir constantly with a wooden spoon until the bread crumbs just begin to turn lightly golden, 5 to 7 minutes. Remove from the heat and immediately transfer to a medium mixing bowl to prevent burning.

4. Add the parsley, garlic, grated cheeses, toasted almonds, and remaining 2 tablespoons (30 ml) of olive oil, and mix with a spoon until all of the oil is absorbed. Season with salt and black pepper, and mix well.

5. Wiggle each artichoke apart with your thumbs as much as you can, and pack the bread crumb mixture and a few shavings of the Parmigiano-Reggiano among the leaves. Place the artichokes in an large oven-safe skillet and drizzle with olive oil.

6. Add 1½ inches (4 cm) of water to the pan. Cover the pan with a lid or foil and place over medium heat. Cook until the artichokes are tender when pierced with a knife, 20 to 25 minutes. Meanwhile, preheat the oven to 400°F (200°C).

7. Uncover the skillet, transfer to the oven, and bake for 15 minutes, or until golden brown on top.

SAUTÉED BROCCOLI RABE

Cime di Rapa Saltate

PREP TIME: 5 MINUTES • COOK TIME: 15 MINUTES • YIELD: 4 TO 6 SERVINGS

The sight of fresh green broccoli rabe at a market is enough to send Nonna Romana into a tizzy! The dark, slightly bitter green almost always shows up on her table, whether mixed with pasta, steamed, or (my personal favorite) sautéed with lots of garlic and extra-virgin olive oil. It's so simple and delicious that you'll want it as a side with everything, as it complements a wide range of dishes.

10 cups (2.4 L) water

1 tablespoon (15 ml) salt, plus more to taste

1 bunch broccoli rabe (about 1 pound, or 454 g), ends trimmed and washed

¼ cup (60 ml) extra-virgin olive oil

5 cloves garlic, sliced

1. Add the water to a 6-quart (5.7 L) stockpot over high heat. Stir in the salt and bring to a boil.

2. Drop the broccoli rabe into the boiling water and cook for 10 minutes. Drain in a colander and run under cold water.

3. Heat the oil in a large sauté pan over medium-high heat. Add the garlic and cook and stir until it begins to color, 2 to 3 minutes. Add the broccoli rabe and cook and stir for another 2 to 3 minutes. Season with salt and serve.

Nonna Romana Says
After you boil the broccoli rabe, it can be wrapped in plastic and frozen. I do that whenever I buy it on sale!

"It wasn't until I was much older, probably around fifty years old, that I had the time to truly experiment with my cooking."

When I meet Nonna Rosa Iaccarino in a small village in the hills of the Amalfi Coast, I know immediately that she is going to be an unforgettable nonna. She is tall, slender, and dressed head to toe in white linen.

When we settle at a small bar near her apartment, Nonna Rosa orders us a *caffe freddo* (cold coffee) in the most lyrical Neapolitan dialect. "This is my home. I've never lived very far from Sant'Agata. I was in a boarding house in Rome when I was little and Napoli for university. The families I cook for all tell me, 'Rosa, we want to take you to America!' but I don't fly, so the only way I could go is by boat!" she exclaims.

Her English, which she mostly taught herself while cooking for vacationing families, is impeccable, but she still apologizes for it after every sentence. Despite her culinary talents, Nonna Rosa is perhaps the shiest and most modest nonna I've ever known. "I've never been

a proud person. There are people who tell me, 'Rosa you're a good cook,' but I think that all women are good cooks if they apply themselves."

Nonna Rosa describes her ardor for cooking as a dormant one. "My parents owned a hotel. I never thought much about cooking when I was little. I didn't want to bother my mother in the kitchen or the cooks at the hotel. I ate whatever they gave me," she says. "I suppose I became a good cook first by necessity, and then it developed into a passion. It wasn't until I was much older, probably around fifty years old, that I had the time to truly experiment with my cooking, and in 2002 I started to cook for families in villas. It really helped me come out of my shell!"

Rosa credits her mother and grandfather for being her main sources of inspiration when it comes to cooking. Her brother is the famed chef Alfonso Iaccarino, who owns the Michelin-starred eatery Don Alfonso 1890 just a few doors down from her home. "I am not a great chef like my brother. I'm a housewife who cooks!"

But when I taste her incredible dishes, there is no doubt in my mind that she is indeed a great chef. Her Flourless Almond Torte (page 200) can actually make you cry it's so good. Rosa's cooking style is simple and genuine. She makes dishes like spaghetti with clams and eggplant parmigiana for every family as if they were her own, using only the freshest local ingredients.

Nonna Rosa's only granddaughter, Sara, is already a tiny gourmand who, at age four, requests local specialties like floured and fried anchovies, and of course nonna's pizza. "Being a grandparent brings a happiness that I wish everyone could feel. It's a deeper love than you feel for your children. In Napoli they say children are pieces of your heart (*E' figli so' piezz 'e core*) but I think that saying applies more to grandchildren."

MUSHROOM-STYLE EGGPLANT

Melanzane a Funghetti

PREP TIME: 10 MINUTES • COOK TIME: 35 MINUTES • YIELD: 4 TO 6 SERVINGS

I lead culinary tours in Italy, and I first tasted this simple Neapolitan eggplant dish when Nonna Rosa came to cook for my guests during my first tour in Sorrento. She was a hit, and so was this amazing dish! The eggplant, which is cooked "mushroom style" in a light tomato and basil sauce, has a buttery quality that melts in your mouth.

2 pounds (907 g) eggplant (about 2 large), cut into 1-inch (2.5 cm) cubes

1¼ cups (300 ml) olive oil, for frying (or any frying oil you like), divided

2 tablespoons (30 ml) extra-virgin olive oil

2 cloves garlic, smashed

2 cups (300 g) cherry tomatoes, halved

½ teaspoon salt, divided

4 or 5 fresh basil leaves

🥄 **Nonna Rosa Says**
I sauté the garlic in oil very briefly and remove it. The idea is to just flavor the oil with the essence of the garlic, but you can mince it and leave it in if you prefer.

1. If desired, purge the eggplant by putting the cubes in a colander and sprinkling the eggplant generously with salt. Put a plate on top to weigh down the eggplant and place the colander over a bowl to catch the liquid. Let the water drain from the eggplant for 30 to 60 minutes. Rinse the eggplant under cold running water and pat dry with paper towels. (My nonna never did this and all her dishes turned out wonderfully!)

2. Heat ¾ cup (180 ml) of the olive oil in a large skillet over medium-high heat. Add the eggplant in 2 or 3 batches, adding more oil as needed, and fry until golden brown around the edges, 5 to 10 minutes per batch. Transfer the eggplant to a paper towel–lined plate to drain.

3. Heat the 2 tablespoons (30 ml) of extra-virgin olive oil in a large sauté pan over medium-high heat. Add the garlic and cook and stir until it just begins to brown, 1 to 2 minutes. Remove the garlic and discard.

4. Add the tomatoes and a dash of the salt to the garlic-infused oil. Cook, stirring with a wooden spoon, until the tomatoes have broken down into a chunky sauce, 5 to 7 minutes.

5. Add the fried eggplant and the basil to the sauté pan. Add the remaining salt and cook and stir for an additional 5 minutes.

NONNA ROSETTA RAUSEO'S
ROASTED POTATOES
Patate al Forno

PREP TIME: 10 MINUTES • COOK TIME: 1 HOUR 15 MINUTES • YIELD: 4 TO 6 SERVINGS

These are the ultimate roasted potatoes! They are a breeze to prepare, and with every crispy, flavorful bite, you will never believe they're baked instead of fried! The trick to these is the way Nonna Rosetta scrapes them from the pan in quick, fluid motions while they're still very hot, revealing the amazing crust! If you don't do it perfectly the first time, just remember that she's been doing this for a while.

¼ cup (60 ml) extra-virgin olive oil, plus more for brushing and drizzling

3 pounds (1.3 kg) russet potatoes, peeled and quartered

1 clove garlic, shaved

2 tablespoons (20 g) finely minced onion

2 tablespoons (8 g) grated Pecorino Romano cheese

¼ teaspoon dried oregano

1 teaspoon chopped fresh rosemary

½ teaspoon salt

¼ teaspoon black pepper

¼ cup (27 g) plain bread crumbs

Nonna Rosetta Says
For extra flavor, sprinkle a little more cheese over the top with the bread crumbs. My grandchildren love it!

1. Preheat the oven to 400°F (200°C). Brush a 13 × 9-inch (33 × 23 cm) baking pan with olive oil. Set aside.

2. Put the potatoes into a large mixing bowl, add the ¼ cup (60 ml) of olive oil, and toss well. Add the garlic, onion, cheese, oregano, and rosemary, and mix well to combine. Add the salt and black pepper, and mix well.

3. Spread the potatoes in a single layer in the pan. Sprinkle on the bread crumbs and drizzle some olive oil over the top. Cover with foil and bake for 30 minutes. Uncover and toss. Bake uncovered for an additional 45 minutes, or until browned and crisp on the edges.

4. Remove the pan from the oven. The potatoes will appear to be stuck to the bottom. While the pan is still very hot, take a flat spatula (pancake turner) and wedge it under the crust that has formed under the potatoes. Scrape the potatoes away from you, separating the crust from the pan.

5. Transfer to a serving platter and serve hot.

"I wanted to learn everything! Cookies, fresh pasta, taralli."

"I always liked to cook!" Nonna Rosetta says, as her eyes light up the minute I ask her about cooking. "I grew up in Aquilonia, a small town in the mountains of Avellino. There was nowhere to even buy bread, so everyone had to make it in their home."

My New York mind cannot even begin to process the idea of a town that doesn't sell bread! Even for Southern Italy, this was pretty extreme. Nonna Rosetta notices my surprise, but she goes on. "My mother was sick, and she would ask me to call my aunt to come make bread for us, but I would cry because I wanted to do it myself." At fourteen, she was told she was too young, but she insisted and was finally allowed to watch, and then eventually to help.

"The first time the bread didn't come out too great, but the second time it came out nice, and I proved myself." I can tell that this first loaf of bread sparked a passion and a talent for baking she enjoys to this day.

"I wanted to learn everything! Cookies, fresh pasta, *taralli*," she says. Rosetta parlayed her passion into a professional baking career that lasted more than two decades. Her speed and attention to detail set her apart from everyone else very quickly. "When I was sixteen, I left Italy to work in a clothing factory in Switzerland with my parents. I was happy to work and see a new place, but I missed baking. I used to daydream about decorating cakes."

Today, Rosetta is a veritable master of the pastry arts. You can try your hand at some of her coveted recipes like Soft Lemon Cookies with Limoncello Glaze (page 222) or Ricotta and Pinoli Tart (page 208) if you love baking too. Though she is retired from baking professionally, she focuses on passing on her passions and talents to her three young grandchildren, who are no less eager to learn than she was in her youth. "They're young, but not too young to learn. I still want to teach them. They always want to help me make cookies. They're the joy of my life."

Rosetta squeezes out buttercream flourishes and mixes dough by hand for a pie crust with lightning speed and the finesse of a renaissance painter. I am in shock as I watch how fast she moves, and I can't help but say, "Rosetta, you are so good! I mean, you're really talented!" She modestly smiles and says, "I know." Rosetta leads me to her freezer and shows me her buried treasure: a dozen beautiful delicious confections, all perfectly wrapped to maintain their freshness. "I make them just in case. I always like to bring something to someone's house." Now that's Italian!

PEASANT-STYLE ZUCCHINI

Zucchine alla Poverella

PREP TIME: 2 HOURS 15 MINUTES • COOK TIME: 50 MINUTES • YIELD: 4 TO 6 SERVINGS

Zucchine alla Poverella, or "poor lady's zucchini," is so named because of its humble ingredients. The deep flavor of these zucchini comes from frying and then marinating it in garlic, vinegar, olive oil, and fresh mint. This dish is never missing from a Pugliese family's table, and it makes the perfect side or antipasto. My great-grandmother Regina always made this recipe because it doesn't require refrigeration due to the oil-and-vinegar mixture. Or as Nonna Romana constantly reminds me, "These no need refrigerate!"

ZUCCHINI

Olive oil, for frying (or any frying oil you like)

2 pounds (907 g) unpeeled zucchini (about 3 large), cut into ¼-inch (6 mm) thick rounds

DRESSING

2 cloves garlic, minced

1 tablespoon (6 g) chopped fresh mint

⅓ cup (80 ml) red wine vinegar

3 tablespoons (45 ml) extra-virgin olive oil

Nonna Romana Says

This is a great dish to make the night before, because the longer the zucchini sits in the marinade, the better!

1. **To make the zucchini:** Heat about ½ inch (13 mm) of oil in a large skillet over high heat.

2. Add the zucchini and fry them in batches, turning occasionally with tongs, until dark golden in color, 6 to 8 minutes per batch.

3. Transfer the zucchini to a paper towel–lined plate to drain.

4. Let the zucchini cool to room temperature, and then transfer them to a 13 × 9-inch (33 × 23 cm) baking pan, spreading them into an even layer.

5. **To make the dressing:** In a small mixing bowl, whisk together the garlic, mint, vinegar, and olive oil. Spoon the dressing over the zucchini and cover the pan with plastic wrap.

6. Marinate the zucchini for at least 2 hours or overnight.

7. Serve at room temperature.

PAN-ROASTED ARTICHOKES

Carciofi Grigliati

PREP TIME: 30 MINUTES • COOK TIME: 20 MINUTES • YIELD: 4 TO 6 SERVINGS

Nonna Romana always told me stories of the artichoke season in Mola di Bari, including the fact that many farmers even tried to use them as currency. My own grandfather Leonardo once attempted to pay the midwife with a pallet of artichokes after the birth of one of his children! These pan-roasted beauties are incredibly simple to prepare and ready in minutes. Pan roasting adds a bit of char to the artichoke's subtle flavor, and the simple dressing makes it an easy dish to pair with a variety of meals.

10 baby artichokes

Juice of 1 lemon

¾ cup (180 ml) extra-virgin olive oil, divided

4 cloves garlic, minced

2 tablespoons (8 g) minced fresh parsley

Salt and black pepper, to taste

Nonna Romana Says

These will taste even better the next day, as the flavors from the garlic and parsley soak into the artichokes.

1. Clean the artichokes by removing the outer leaves until you reach the yellow or light green part of the artichoke. Cut off the top part of the leaves (about ¾ inch, or 2 cm), trim about ¼ inch (6 mm) of the stem, and peel the stem. Cut the artichokes in half lengthwise. Scoop out the fuzzy choke with a small spoon and discard.

2. Place the artichokes in a bowl and completely cover with water. Add the lemon juice and let sit for about 10 minutes.

3. Heat 1 tablespoon (15 ml) of the olive oil in a large cast-iron skillet over high heat and let it get very hot.

4. Brush each artichoke half, inside and out, with olive oil and put them in the pan face down.

5. Cook them in 2 batches, for 3 to 5 minutes on each side, or until they begin to turn brown. Transfer all the artichokes to a platter, facing up.

6. Add the garlic, parsley, and salt and black pepper to the remaining oil and mix well. Spread over the cut side of each artichoke.

7. Serve at room temperature.

EGGPLANT CAPONATA

Caponata di Melanzane

PREP TIME: 15 MINUTES • COOK TIME: 47 MINUTES • YIELD: 4 TO 6 SERVINGS

A Sicilian eggplant *caponata* recipe will vary from household to household. Nonna Angelina's has sugared almonds for a bit of crunch and a symphony of sweet and savory flavors.

½ cup (46 g) chopped unblanched almonds

3 cups (700 ml) water

2 stalks celery, cut into ½-inch (13 mm) dice

2 tablespoons (18 g) baby capers

½ cup (50 g) chopped green olives

2 pounds (907 g) eggplant (about 2 large), cut into 1-inch (2.5 cm) cubes

1¼ cups (300 ml) olive oil, for frying (or any frying oil you like)

¼ cup (60 ml) extra-virgin olive oil

1 medium onion, cut into ½-inch (13 mm) dice

½ cup (128 g) canned crushed tomatoes

½ cup (100 g) sugar, divided

½ cup (120 ml) red wine vinegar

Salt and black pepper, to taste

Nonna Angelina Says
When I have big parties, I always make this a day or two in advance because it holds up well. I think the taste gets better, too!

1. Preheat the oven to 350°F (175°C). Spread the almonds on an ungreased baking sheet in a single layer. Toast the almonds for 5 to 7 minutes, until golden and fragrant, keeping an eye on their color so they don't burn. Transfer to a plate and let cool.

2. Heat the water in a large saucepan over medium-high heat. Add the celery and bring to a boil. Cook until tender, 10 to 12 minutes. Turn off the heat and add the capers and olives. Let stand in the hot water for 3 to 4 minutes. Drain and set aside.

3. If desired, purge the eggplant (see step 1 on page 80 for instructions).

4. Heat the olive oil in a large heavy-bottomed skillet over high heat. Add the eggplant in 2 or 3 batches and fry until golden brown, adding more oil as needed, 5 to 6 minutes per batch. Transfer to a paper towel–lined plate to drain. Set aside.

5. Heat the ¼ cup (60 ml) of extra-virgin olive oil in a large sauté pan over medium-high heat. Add the onion and cook and stir until translucent, 5 to 7 minutes.

6. Add the tomatoes and cook, stirring with a wooden spoon, for 2 to 3 minutes. Add the boiled celery mixture and cook for 2 to 3 minutes longer. Add the fried eggplant and cook for 3 more minutes, stirring everything together with a wooden spoon.

7. Dissolve ¼ cup (50 g) of the sugar in the vinegar and add it to the pan. Cook for an additional 4 to 5 minutes. Taste for seasoning and add salt and black pepper.

8. Add the remaining ¼ cup (50 g) of sugar to the chopped almonds and mix to coat the almonds.

9. Transfer the caponata to a serving plate and garnish with the sugared almonds. Serve at room temperature.

PASTA AND FIRST COURSE

Paste e Primi

NONNA ROMANA SCIDDURLO'S

ORECCHIETTE WITH BROCCOLI RABE

Orecchiette con Cime di Rapa

PREP TIME: 5 MINUTES • COOK TIME: 15 MINUTES • YIELD: 4 TO 6 SERVINGS

This is quite possibly the most iconic recipe from the region of Puglia. The remarkable thing about it is how the broccoli rabe almost melts together with the pasta. This comes from the old Pugliese technique of boiling the pasta and vegetables together, and then sautéing them in garlic, oil, and anchovies. If you're not a big anchovy person, don't worry; once they're melted into the oil, the flavor is so subtle that you'll barely notice. If you're making this dish for people who don't love anchovies, don't even tell them they're in there! They'll never know!

16 ounces (454 g) dried or fresh orecchiette

1 bunch broccoli rabe (about 1 pound, or 454 g), ends trimmed, washed, and cut into bite-size pieces

6 tablespoons (90 g) extra-virgin olive oil

5 cloves garlic, sliced

4 anchovy fillets

¼ teaspoon red pepper flakes

Nonna Romana Says
My mother, Regina, would also add some sun-dried tomatoes to this dish to give it more color and flavor. You can chop them and add them to the oil when you are sautéing the garlic.

1. Bring a large pot of generously salted water to a boil.

2. If using fresh orecchiette, add the broccoli rabe first and boil for 5 to 7 minutes. Drop in the fresh orecchiette and continue cooking until the pasta is al dente, 4 to 5 minutes. If using dried orecchiette, add the pasta and broccoli rabe to the water together and boil until the pasta is al dente.

3. When the pasta has 4 to 5 minutes to go, heat the oil in a large skillet over medium heat. Add the garlic, anchovies, and red pepper flakes, and cook, stirring with a wooden spoon, until the garlic is golden and the anchovies have broken down, 2 to 3 minutes.

4. Scoop out about 1 cup (235 ml) of pasta water and set aside. With a large strainer or a spider, scoop out the pasta and broccoli rabe, letting the water drain out of each scoop, and add it directly to the skillet with the garlic and anchovies. Toss together quickly for 1 to 2 minutes, making sure you evenly coat the pasta with the garlic and oil. Serve in warm bowls.

FOUR-CHEESE LASAGNA

Lasagne ai Quattro Formaggi

PREP TIME: 20 MINUTES • COOK TIME: 1 HOUR 23 MINUTES • YIELD: 8 SERVINGS

People come from far and wide to taste Nonna Tina's famous lasagna at her son's restaurant, Trattoria L'incontro, in Astoria, Queens. Nonna Tina considers herself a bit of a lasagna master, as she has been making it regularly at the restaurant for over twenty years. The four cheeses melt together with her unique meat sauce to deliver the perfect piece of lasagna that cuts as beautifully as it tastes.

SAUCE

4 tablespoons (60 ml) extra-virgin
   olive oil, divided
2 small onions, cut into ¼-inch (6 mm)
   dice, divided
1 pound (454 g) ground beef
1½ teaspoons salt, divided
¼ cup (60 ml) dry white wine, such
   as Pinot Grigio or Sauvignon Blanc
2 cans (28 ounces, or 794 g, each)
   crushed tomatoes
2 or 3 fresh basil leaves, torn
Black pepper, to taste

LASAGNA

16 ounces (454 g) dried lasagna noodles
16 ounces (454 g) ricotta impastata
   or whole milk ricotta, drained
   (see Nonna Says on page 104)
½ cup (60 g) grated Parmigiano-
   Reggiano cheese, divided
¼ cup (30 g) shredded Asiago cheese
1 tablespoon (4 g) minced
   fresh parsley
Salt and black pepper, to taste
1 egg, beaten
16 ounces (454 g) fresh mozzarella,
   shredded

1. **To make the sauce:** Heat 2 tablespoons (30 ml) of the olive oil in a 6-quart (5.7 L) stockpot over medium-high heat. Add half of the onion and cook and stir until soft, about 5 minutes. Add the beef and ½ teaspoon of the salt. Cook, breaking up the meat with a wooden spoon into fairly big chunks, until all the meat is browned, 5 to 6 minutes.

2. Add the wine and cook until you can no longer smell the alcohol, 4 to 5 minutes.

3. Remove from the heat and transfer to a colander with a plate underneath. Drain for 10 minutes. Transfer to a bowl and set aside.

4. Heat the remaining 2 tablespoons (30 ml) of olive oil in a 5-quart (4.7 L) stockpot over medium heat. Add the remaining onion and cook and stir until translucent, 5 to 7 minutes. Add the tomatoes, remaining 1 teaspoon of salt, basil, and black pepper, and reduce the heat to a simmer. Cook, uncovered, for 15 to 20 minutes.

5. Add 2 cups (510 g) of the sauce to the meat and stir to combine. Set aside both sauces.

6. **To make the lasagna:** Preheat the oven to 400°F (200°C).

7. Bring a large pot of generously salted water to a boil and cook the lasagna noodles for half the time of the package instructions. Drain the pasta and run it under cold running water to stop the cooking process. Separate the lasagna sheets and lay them flat on a baking sheet to dry.

continued

Nonna Tina Says
Overlapping the lasagna sheets is key to crafting a lasagna that doesn't fall apart when you cut it. Lasagna is a delicate thing!

8. In a large mixing bowl, combine the ricotta, ¼ cup (30 g) of the Parmigiano-Reggiano, the Asiago, and the parsley. Mix well and season with salt and black pepper. Add the beaten egg and mix well. The mixture should be thick.

9. With your hands, form the ricotta mixture into 8 equal logs, each about 3 inches (7.5 cm) long. Place them on a plate. Refrigerate until ready to use.

10. Add about ½ cup (128 g) of the plain tomato sauce to the bottom of an 11 × 8-inch (28 × 20 cm) baking pan with high sides. Layer the lasagna sheets, overlapping them by one-third each.

11. Flatten the logs of ricotta with your hands and lay them on top of the lasagna sheets (this is so you don't disturb the pasta while trying to spread the ricotta, and it will also create a nice even layer of ricotta).

12. Add one-fourth of the shredded mozzarella and a sprinkle of the remaining Parmigiano-Reggiano.

13. Arrange another layer of the lasagna sheets. Spread all of the meat sauce in one layer over the pasta and cover with another one-fourth of mozzarella. Arrange one last layer of lasagna sheets and cover with the remaining tomato sauce and the remaining ¼ cup (30 g) of Parmigiano-Reggiano.

14. Cover with aluminum foil and bake for 30 minutes. Uncover and add the remaining mozzarella. Bake uncovered for an additional 10 minutes. Remove from the oven and let rest for 10 to 15 minutes before slicing.

"You gotta love the food like you love your boyfriend!"

When I first meet Nonna Tina Sacramone at her son Rocco's restaurant in Queens, her smile illuminates the entire room. She greets me with a warm "Hello, baby!" and I immediately feel special.

Her lovely blue eyes are delicately lined with a faint blue eyeliner that matches her blouse perfectly. "Where's the ring?" she asks me as she motions toward my bare left hand. Nonna Tina already had two of her three children by my age. She carefully inspects a ring I wear on my right hand and seems satisfied enough. "Okay, what I gotta say?" she asks. After a few moments, she begins to tell me her story.

Nonna Tina's culinary career began as a little girl cooking for her family after the death of her father in Orsogna, Abruzzo. "I was five years old when the war came. We would play in the street without shoes as the sound of the bombs sent us running back inside the house."

By age nine, Tina took on the role of head cook in her home while her mother worked to support the family. "In the beginning sometimes things came out good, other times not so good, but I kept trying till everything was perfect. Even then I did things with my whole heart." She tells me about the first time she cooked for her now husband when she was just fourteen. "He was coming over, and I wanted to do something special.

It wasn't the first time I had made fresh pasta, but I wondered what would happen if I tried to cook it in a soup. The whole time my heart was beating like crazy, worried I had made something inedible, but it was good! My husband turned to me and said, 'You are a chef!'"

Feeding a family proved difficult at times. "I would make the cheese meatballs. They were made of bread and cheese with no meat, but sometimes there was no cheese either!" In 1970, Tina made her way to America with her husband and children. When she arrived, she worked as a seamstress making ties for men. To help with her workload, she enlisted the help of Rocco, her oldest son. Later in life, they would switch roles, and Tina would help Rocco in his small pizzeria in Astoria, which eventually grew into the neighborhood institution that is now Trattoria L'incontro.

People come by in droves to taste her recipes, especially her lasagna, which she handcrafts herself. I am lucky enough to be allowed a peek as she cuts sheets of homemade pasta by hand. She delicately layers a blend of cheeses and sauce, cutting sheets of lasagna with the precision of an artist sculpting a masterpiece, and I know I am in the presence of genius. "These are secrets I no tell nobody! I only tell you because you a nice *ragazza*!" she exclaims.

When she's not in the restaurant kitchen, Nonna Tina is passing on the recipes to her four small grandchildren. "One day they wanted to help me make the pasta, and the baby goes, 'Nonna, I love this! Why don't you let me work?' But I told him, 'No baby, you gotta go to school, because you see Nonna no speak very well English. You need school.'" As I take one last sip of coffee, Tina offers me the most valuable advice about the importance of concentration in the kitchen: "Listen, when you touch the food, you gotta think and know when you gotta touch, because if you don't think about it, you'll ruin. You gotta love the food like you love your boyfriend!" In that moment, I knew exactly what she meant. Make love to the food, and it will love you right back.

MACCHERONI AND ORECCHIETTE WITH TINY MEATBALLS

Maritati con Polpettine

PREP TIME: 20 MINUTES • COOK TIME: 1 HOUR 5 MINUTES • YIELD: 4 TO 6 SERVINGS

Nonna Romana has been making this dish ever since I came back from a trip to Puglia and couldn't stop raving about it. A lovely nonna who was a chef at a winery in Salento served us this incredible platter of *maritati* pasta and tiny fried meatballs cooked in a gorgeous tomato and basil sauce, and it has been etched into my memory ever since. *Maritati* ("married couples" is the literal meaning) are a mix of *orecchiette* and *maccheroni*, so named because each pair of the two cuts of pasta represents a married couple. It was enough to make Nonna Romana blush!

MEATBALLS

½ pound (227 g) ground veal

1 egg, beaten

¾ cup (90 g) grated Pecorino Romano cheese

¼ cup (27 g) plain bread crumbs

2 cloves garlic, shaved

2 tablespoons (8 g) minced fresh parsley

¼ teaspoon black pepper

1½ cups (350 ml) olive oil, for frying (or any frying oil you like)

SAUCE

¼ cup (60 ml) extra-virgin olive oil

1 small onion, cut into ¼-inch (6 mm) dice

½ cup (120 ml) dry white wine

1 can (28 ounces, or 794 g) crushed tomatoes

2 fresh basil leaves, torn

½ teaspoon salt

Black pepper, to taste

PASTA

16 ounces (454 g) fresh semolina pasta dough, cut in half to make 8 ounces (227 g) each fresh orecchiette and maccheroni (you can substitute dried orecchiette and maccheroni or casarecce)

½ cup (60 g) grated Pecorino Romano cheese

1. **To make the meatballs:** Combine the veal, egg, cheese, bread crumbs, garlic, parsley, and black pepper in a large mixing bowl, and mix well, preferably with your hands.

2. Roll into meatballs about ½ inch (13 mm) in diameter (about 1 teaspoon per meatball).

3. Heat the frying oil in a medium heavy-bottomed saucepan over medium-high heat. Fry the meatballs in batches until browned on all sides, about 2 minutes per batch. Transfer to a paper towel–lined plate to drain. Set aside.

4. **To make the sauce:** Heat the extra-virgin olive oil in a large skillet over medium heat. Add the onion and cook and stir until translucent, 5 to 7 minutes.

5. Add the wine and cook until you can no longer smell the alcohol, 4 to 5 minutes. Add the tomatoes, basil, salt, and black pepper. Cover and cook for 15 minutes.

6. Uncover and reduce the heat to low. Add the meatballs and cook, uncovered, for an additional 10 minutes.

7. **To make the pasta:** Bring a pot of generously salted water to a boil, add the maritati, and cook until al dente, 6 to 7 minutes for fresh pasta. Drain and add the pasta to the skillet with the sauce and meatballs. Add the grated Pecorino Romano cheese and turn off the heat. Toss well for 1 minute. Serve in warm bowls with some more grated Pecorino Romano cheese.

RIGATONI WITH FRIED EGGPLANT

Rigatoni alla Norma

PREP TIME: 5 MINUTES • COOK TIME: 48 MINUTES • YIELD: 4 TO 6 SERVINGS

I'll never forget the day Nonna Michelina, or Zia Michelina, as I call her, came over to make this recipe on the *Cooking with Nonna* show. By the end of the day my face hurt so much from laughing, but this flavorful pasta made it all better. The eggplant takes on a creamy, almost buttery texture when fried, and it absorbs the light sauce beautifully. The nutty *ricotta salata*, which is a dried, salted ricotta, is the perfect topping to finish this Sicilian powerhouse dish.

4 baby Italian eggplant (you can substitute 2 medium eggplant)

1½ cups (350 ml) olive oil, for frying (or any frying oil you like)

3 tablespoons (45 ml) extra-virgin olive oil

4 cloves garlic, sliced

1 can (28 ounces, or 794 g) crushed tomatoes

2 fresh basil leaves, torn

½ teaspoon salt

Black pepper, to taste

16 ounces (454 g) dried rigatoni

Grated ricotta salata, to taste

Nonna Michelina Says

To save time, I usually fry the eggplant the night before and refrigerate it.

1. Cut the baby eggplant into round slices ½ inch (13 mm) thick. If using the larger eggplant, cut them into 1-inch (2.5 cm) strips. Do not peel.

2. Heat the frying oil in a large heavy-bottomed skillet over high heat. Fry the eggplant in batches until golden brown, 2 to 3 minutes per batch. Transfer the eggplant to a paper towel–lined plate to drain. Set aside.

3. Heat the 3 tablespoons (45 ml) of extra-virgin olive oil in a medium sauté pan over medium heat. Add the garlic and cook and stir until it begins to color, 1 to 2 minutes.

4. Add the tomatoes, basil, salt, and black pepper. Reduce the heat to low and cook for 15 minutes, stirring occasionally with a wooden spoon.

5. Set aside a few pieces of eggplant to decorate each bowl and add the rest to the sauce. Cook for an additional 10 minutes.

6. While the sauce finishes cooking, bring a large pot of generously salted water to a boil, drop in the rigatoni, and cook until al dente.

7. Drain the pasta and add it to the sauté pan with the sauce. Toss for 1 to 2 minutes and serve in warm bowls with a generous sprinkle of ricotta salata.

NONNA ROMANA SCIDDURLO'S

BAKED ZITI

Pasta al Forno

PREP TIME: 25 MINUTES • COOK TIME: 1 HOUR 25 MINUTES • YIELD: 4 TO 6 SERVINGS

There is truly no better dish to feed a small army of hungry people than a classic baked ziti. This recipe will have everyone fighting over the crispy, almost-burnt pieces of pasta—the best part! The secret is in adding the top layer of mozzarella during the last 10 minutes of cooking, so it browns perfectly.

SAUCE

3 tablespoons (45 ml) extra-virgin olive oil

1 small onion, cut into ¼-inch (6 mm) dice

2 cloves garlic, minced

3 bay leaves

¼ teaspoon red pepper flakes

½ pound (227 g) ground beef

½ teaspoon salt, divided

¼ cup (60 ml) dry red wine

1 can (28 ounces, or 794 g) crushed tomatoes

3 fresh basil leaves, torn

PASTA AND GARNISHES

16 ounces (454 g) dried ziti

½ cup (60 g) grated Parmigiano-Reggiano cheese

8 ounces (227 g) shredded fresh mozzarella

8 ounces (227 g) fresh mozzarella, cut into ½-inch (13 mm) cubes

Nonna Romana Says

Make sure you use fresh mozzarella that comes in water for this dish! It makes all the difference.

1. **To make the sauce:** Heat the olive oil in a 5-quart (4.7 L) stockpot over medium heat. Add the onion, garlic, bay leaves, and red pepper flakes, and cook, stirring with a wooden spoon, until the garlic turns golden and the onion is translucent, 5 to 7 minutes.

2. Add the ground beef and ¼ teaspoon of the salt. Cook, breaking up the ground beef with a wooden spoon, until it browns uniformly, 6 to 7 minutes.

3. Add the wine and cook until you can no longer smell the alcohol, 4 to 5 minutes.

4. Add the crushed tomatoes, the remaining ¼ teaspoon of salt, and the basil. Reduce the heat to a simmer and cook the sauce, uncovered, for 25 to 30 minutes, stirring occasionally with a wooden spoon. Remove and discard the bay leaves. Meanwhile, preheat the oven to 450°F (230°C).

5. **To make the pasta:** Bring a large pot of salted water to a boil and drop in the ziti. Cook for half the time on the package directions, about 5 minutes. The ziti must be harder than al dente. Drain, rinse the pasta under cold water, transfer to a bowl, and set aside.

6. Add 1 cup (255 g) of the sauce to the bottom of a deep 11 × 8-inch (28 × 20 cm) baking pan. Add half of the ziti and spread it evenly.

7. Spoon over another cup (255 g) of sauce, followed by a generous sprinkle of Parmigiano-Reggiano and then the shredded mozzarella. Add the other half of the ziti and cover it with the rest of the sauce and the remaining Parmigiano-Reggiano.

8. Bake the dish for 20 minutes. Remove from the oven, add the cubed mozzarella, and continue baking for another 10 minutes. If desired, you can place the pan under the broiler for 1 to 2 minutes to make the top nice and crispy! Let the dish rest for 15 minutes and serve.

SPAGHETTI WITH STRING BEANS

Spaghetti e Fagiolini

PREP TIME: 10 MINUTES • COOK TIME: 26 MINUTES • YIELD: 4 TO 6 SERVINGS

Every now and then, in late summertime, my Zia Rosa takes a short walk to my Nonna Romana's house with an overflowing bag of super-thin string beans that she and my Zio Domenico grow in their garden in Brooklyn. They grow so many that they risk the beans taking over the entire yard! Nonna Romana is more than happy to take them off her hands. My Zia Rosa's *spaghetti e fagiolini* is an ode to the dish she often prepared in Puglia, where she grew the very same string beans. I love the way they twirl perfectly around a fork with the spaghetti, picking up just the right amount of fresh tomato sauce and a hint of a pepper. *Cacioricotta*, a sharp, dry ricotta from the Salento area of Puglia, complements the flavors beautifully, and is traditionally paired with this dish. If you can't find Pinti string beans, you may substitute any thin string bean variety, such as snake beans (Chinese long beans) or haricot verts.

¼ cup (60 ml) extra-virgin olive oil

4 cloves garlic, sliced

1½ pounds (680 g) plum tomatoes, cut into ½-inch (13 mm) dice

1 yellow, red, or green bell pepper, seeded and cut into ¼-inch (6 mm) strips

3 or 4 fresh basil leaves, torn

½ teaspoon salt

1 pound (454 g) Italian Pinti string beans, trimmed on both ends and cut into 6- to 7-inch (15 to 18 cm) long pieces if necessary

16 ounces (454 g) dried spaghetti

Grated cacioricotta cheese, for serving

1. Bring a 6-quart (5.7 L) stockpot of generously salted water to a boil.

2. Heat the olive oil in a large skillet over medium heat. Add the garlic and cook and stir until lightly golden, 1 to 2 minutes.

3. Add the tomatoes, peppers, basil, and salt, and cook until the tomatoes break down and the peppers soften, 15 to 20 minutes. Do not overcook—you want to taste the fresh tomato flavor!

4. Drop the beans into the boiling water, and as soon as the water comes back to a boil, 2 to 3 minutes, add the spaghetti. Cook until al dente and drain.

5. Add the spaghetti and string beans to the skillet with the sauce and toss for 1 minute.

6. Serve in warm bowls with a generous grating of cacioricotta cheese.

Nonna Rosa Says

Wrap your cacioricotta *in paper towels when storing it in the refrigerator. The paper towels will absorb the humidity and keep the cheese fresh.*

FOUR-CHEESE TORTELLI WITH SWISS CHARD IN A BUTTER AND SAGE SAUCE

Tortelli con Bietole e Quattro Formaggi con Burro e Salvia

PREP TIME: 1 HOUR 30 MINUTES • COOK TIME: 12 MINUTES • YIELD: 4 TO 6 SERVINGS

It's always a big day when Nonna Rina makes her *tortelli*. I think the original recipe she gave me could make over two hundred! Tortelli are a type of ravioli from the Emilia-Romagna region that are usually filled with ricotta and herbs or vegetables. Each bite is an explosion of ricotta and Parmigiano-Reggiano. They can be served in a broth or in a delicate butter and sage sauce, like the one she makes here.

FILLING

1 bunch Swiss chard (about 1 pound, or 454 g), washed and white stalks trimmed

½ cup (125 g) ricotta impastata or whole milk ricotta, drained (see Nonna Says on page 104)

½ cup (120 g) mascarpone

½ cup (60 g) shredded fresh mozzarella

¾ cup (90 g) grated Parmigiano-Reggiano cheese

Dash of nutmeg

Salt, to taste

PASTA

1 pound (454 g) fresh egg pasta dough (page 21)

Flour, for dusting

SAUCE

½ cup (1 stick, or 120 g) salted butter

10 fresh sage leaves

½ cup (60 g) grated Parmigiano-Reggiano cheese

1. **To make the filling:** Bring a 5-quart (4.7 L) stockpot of lightly salted water to a boil. Add the Swiss chard leaves and give the pot a quick stir. Cover and cook for 5 minutes. Drain and let cool.

2. Once the chard is cool enough to handle, 10 to 15 minutes, squeeze out the excess water and roughly chop the leaves with a knife.

3. Add the ricotta, mascarpone, mozzarella, Parmigiano-Reggiano, and nutmeg to a food processor, and process for 10 to 15 seconds, until combined. Add the Swiss chard and process again until smooth. Taste for seasoning and add salt if desired. Transfer to a bowl and cover with plastic wrap. Refrigerate until ready to use.

4. **To make the pasta:** Cut the ball of dough into 4 equal parts. With a rolling pin or a pasta roller on its thinnest setting, roll out each piece of dough on a floured work surface into sheets as thin as possible. The dough should almost be translucent. Cover any pasta not being used with a clean towel.

5. With a knife or a ravioli cutter, trim the jagged ends into a clean square or a rectangle. Cut out 3-inch (7.5 cm) squares. Add any scraps to the rest of the dough to roll out.

continued

6. Add about 1 teaspoon of filling (about the size of a US quarter) to the center of each square.

7. Close the tortelli by folding one of the points over the filling to the opposite point to create little triangles. Press the outer dough around the filling closed with your fingers or a fork to seal them well. You may even re-trim them with the ravioli cutter to make them look pretty.

8. Rest the tortelli on a clean towel without touching each other.

9. Bring a large pot of generously salted water to a rolling boil and cook the tortelli until al dente, 3 to 5 minutes. Drain very carefully in a colander or scoop them out with a large strainer.

10. **To make the sauce:** Melt the butter in a large skillet over medium-high heat, stirring with a wooden spoon. Cook until the butter begins to turn a light brown color and smells nutty, 6 to 7 minutes.

11. Turn off the heat and add the sage leaves. Add the tortelli and toss in the butter and sage. Sprinkle the grated Parmigiano-Reggiano over the top and serve immediately.

"I don't stress out trying to be elaborate in the kitchen. For what? It's not worth it. Simplicity is always more chic!"

"Rossella *a' zia*, do you like my new dress? It's designer!" says my great aunt Caterina as she flings open the door to her third floor walk-up apartment in Mola di Bari, Italy. Fresh from the beauty parlor, I can still smell the perfume of hairspray on her teased blonde hair.

The aroma of battered, fried eggplant wafts in from the kitchen. "I fried it this morning before I went to the beach," says Aunt Rina, as we call her. She has always been the most resourceful and stylish of all my aunts. "I always manage to do it all!" Rina declares with pride.

Growing up, I was always amazed at how Rina was able to put together delicious lunches (the main meal of the day in Italy) and still have time for herself. It was a talent of hers I admired because she always seemed the happiest of her sisters (Rina is my Nonna Romana's younger sister, the third-born daughter). As a young girl, Rina was often tasked with doing the shopping.

"My mother would always send me to do her shopping. I would buy mussels from the fish vendor in Via Santa Chiara. We always had fruit from my uncles that had farmland. We had prosperity in our home."

Aunt Rina didn't always realize quite how good things were. "I was a difficult, finicky child when it came to eating. I would always complain about not liking anything. My big brother Vincenzo would sit next to me and nudge me telling me not to worry, that he would eat my portion. When my mother wasn't looking we would switch the plates under the table," she says with a loud cackle, her signature laugh.

Aunt Rina is a woman who loves the Italian lifestyle. She speaks of the town where she spent her youth with so much love. "Every night by 8 o'clock, we would be dressed and ready to go out in *piazza* (town square). We would buy a hot *panzerotto* and eat them all together in the street. Sundays we would go to mass in the mornings, and to the cinema in the evenings. It was simple, but beautiful."

When Rina left for America in 1963, she was excited, but ultimately left with a void in her heart. "In America, I dreamt of the *piazza* and of all my friends in Mola. America was all about work. I was fortunate to work at the sewing factory and make a nice salary, but it couldn't replace the Italian lifestyle that I missed so much." Luckily, a marriage proposal arrived for her via mail, and she returned to her beloved hometown. "I'm a happy person. My four grandchildren call me the happy nonna!" she says, laughing.

Aunt Rina is carefree and vivacious, especially when it comes to cooking. "I have always been different in character. I make things that are easy and that I know I do well; I don't stress out trying to be elaborate in the kitchen. For what? It's not worth it. Simplicity is always more chic!"

ZUCCHINI RISOTTO

Risotto con Zucchine

PREP TIME: 5 MINUTES • COOK TIME: 36 MINUTES • YIELD: 4 TO 6 SERVINGS

The summers spent at my great-aunt's villa in Puglia hold some of the greatest food memories for me. I remember my Zia Rina making this flavorful zucchini risotto often, and everyone would have at least two or three servings. She cautions to use *carnaroli* rice, which is starchier and will produce a creamier risotto, but if you have trouble finding it, *Arborio* will do just fine.

5½ cups (1.3 L) water

3 tablespoons (45 ml) extra-virgin olive oil

1 small onion, cut into ¼-inch (6 mm) dice

2 medium zucchini, quartered and sliced ⅛ inch (3 mm) thick

½ cup (120 ml) dry white wine, such as Pinot Grigio or Sauvignon Blanc

2 cups (370 g) carnaroli rice

2 vegetable bouillon cubes

½ cup (60 g) grated Parmigiano-Reggiano cheese

1. Add the water to a large saucepan and bring it to a boil on the stove. Reduce the heat to a simmer.

2. Put a 6-quart (5.7 L) stockpot over medium-high heat. Add the olive oil, onion, and zucchini, and cook, stirring with a wooden spoon, until the zucchini is soft, about 10 minutes.

3. Add the wine and cook for 1 minute.

4. Add the rice and bouillon cubes, and stir, coating the rice in the oil. Begin adding the boiling water little by little (about a ¼ cup, or 60 ml, at a time), stirring constantly, until the water is absorbed. The rice should be dry before adding more liquid.

5. Continue adding the water little by little until all the water is absorbed, 20 to 25 minutes. Taste the rice periodically to determine its doneness. The rice is cooked when the center is still al dente.

6. Remove from the heat and stir in the Parmigiano-Reggiano. Serve immediately.

DITALINI WITH ARTICHOKES AND PEAS

Ditalini con Carciofi e Piselli

PREP TIME: 45 MINUTES • COOK TIME: 35 MINUTES • YIELD: 4 TO 6 SERVINGS

Nonna Anna's super-simple pasta with peas and artichokes will turn anyone who's on the fence about this combo into a convert. *Ditalini con carciofi e piselli* is a lesser-known Italian comfort dish, but there's nothing more delicious on a rainy, chilly night. The frozen vegetables make it a snap to prepare, and the delicate flavors mingle beautifully. Don't even think about skipping the part where you rest the peas and artichokes for 40 minutes! Nonna Anna says that's when all the magic happens, and it will never taste the same if you don't. When nonna speaks, you listen!

16 ounces (454 g) frozen peas, thawed

1 medium onion, cut into ¼-inch (6 mm) dice

4 sprigs fresh parsley, minced

3 tablespoons (45 ml) extra-virgin olive oil, plus more for drizzling

¼ teaspoon salt

2 cups (475 ml) water

12 ounces (340 g) frozen artichoke hearts, thawed

16 ounces (454 g) dried ditalini

1. Put a 5-quart (4.7 L) stockpot over high heat and add the peas, onion, parsley, olive oil, and salt. Pour in the water and bring to a boil.

2. Add the artichokes and reduce the heat to medium. Cover and cook for 20 minutes. Turn off the heat and let stand, covered, for 30 to 40 minutes.

3. While the peas and artichokes are resting, bring a medium pot of generously salted water to a boil and cook the pasta until al dente. Drain and combine with the peas and artichokes. Serve in warm bowls with an extra drizzle of good-quality extra-virgin olive oil.

Nonna Anna Says

I wouldn't put cheese on this dish if you can help it. You don't want to overpower the flavors of the peas and artichokes.

NONNA ROSA CARMELO'S

STUFFED SHELLS

Conchiglioni Ripieni

PREP TIME: 15 MINUTES • COOK TIME: 1 HOUR 15 MINUTES • YIELD: 5 TO 7 SERVINGS

Three different cheeses make my Zia Rosa's stuffed shells melt-in-your-mouth incredible! She always knows exactly how to balance a baked pasta dish, and never overwhelms it with sauce. This dish is a must for holidays and big family meals because you can make it ahead and store it in the refrigerator!

SAUCE

3 tablespoons (45 ml) extra-virgin
  olive oil
1 small onion, cut into ¼-inch (6 mm)
  dice
3 bay leaves
¼ teaspoon red pepper flakes
½ pound (227 g) ground veal
¾ teaspoon salt, divided
¼ cup (60 ml) dry white wine
1 can (28 ounces, or 794 g) crushed
  tomatoes
3 fresh basil leaves, torn

FILLING

24 ounces (680 g) ricotta impastata
  or whole milk ricotta, drained
  (see Nonna Says on page 104)
6 ounces (170 g) fresh mozzarella,
  shredded or cut into very small
  pieces
¾ cup (90 g) grated Parmigiano-
  Reggiano cheese, plus more
  for sprinkling
2 tablespoons (8 g) minced
  fresh parsley
Salt and black pepper, to taste
2 eggs, beaten
1 box (12 ounces, or 340 g)
  jumbo shells

1. **To make the sauce:** Heat the olive oil in a 5-quart (4.7 L) stockpot over medium heat. Add the onion, bay leaves, and red pepper flakes, and cook, stirring with a wooden spoon, until the garlic turns golden and the onion is translucent, 5 to 7 minutes.

2. Add the veal and ¼ teaspoon of the salt, and cook, breaking up the meat with the spoon, until the meat browns uniformly, 6 to 7 minutes.

3. Add the wine and cook until you no longer smell the alcohol, 4 to 5 minutes. Add the tomatoes, basil, and remaining ½ teaspoon of salt. Reduce the heat to a simmer and let the sauce cook, uncovered, for 25 to 30 minutes, stirring occasionally. Remove and discard the bay leaves.

4. **To make the filling:** In a large mixing bowl, combine the ricotta, mozzarella, Parmigiano-Reggiano, and parsley. Season with the salt and black pepper. Add the eggs and mix until combined.

5. **To assemble:** Cook the shells according to the package instructions. Run them under cold running water to stop the cooking process.

6. Preheat the oven to 400°F (200°C).

7. Add 1½ cups (380 g) of sauce to a 15 × 10-inch (38 × 26 cm) baking pan. Spread the sauce across the bottom and around the sides of the pan with a wooden spoon.

8. Spoon the filling into each of the shells and place them in the baking pan. Spoon the extra sauce over each shell and top with an extra sprinkle of Parmigiano-Reggiano.

9. Cover the pan with aluminum foil and bake for 20 minutes. Uncover and sprinkle again with Parmigiano-Reggiano. Bake uncovered for an additional 10 minutes.

10. Remove from the oven and let rest for 10 to 15 minutes before serving.

"Make sure you ask your questions, because time goes on and people pass away, and you'll never know some things."

A dainty woman with a warm demeanor and kind eyes, Nonna Carmela D'Angelo is the picture of a classic Italian-American nonna. "You're pretty just like your photo!" she says to me. It isn't long before our conversation turns to food.

"I started to cook as soon as I got married. Small meals at first, because I was learning, but over time, the meals got bigger," she explains.

"My family was all in the same house in Middle Village, Queens. My parents upstairs and my aunt and uncle and my nonna downstairs. There was always someone home. I didn't realize until later that what a good feeling it was to never come home to an empty house," she says of her Italian-American upbringing. "I learned by watching. My grandmother Carmela, who lived downstairs, was always cooking. She made pasta almost every day. She only bought spaghetti from a store when she was in her eighties.

She barely ever left the house; she was always home and always cooking."

It's evident that as the matriarch of her family, Nonna Carmela is just as committed to maintaining the traditions that have been instilled in her. Her three children, five grandchildren, and great-grandchild depend on her to bring the family together. "All of my grandchildren cook. There's always something going on in their kitchens, and I'm learning from them too. They do things that I would never think to even do. A salad with raw Brussels sprouts! Can you imagine? But it's delicious."

When it comes to preserving her own recipes, Nonna Carmela leaves nothing to chance. Twenty years ago, she began handwriting recipe books to ensure her recipes live on. "I don't want them to lose everything my family had. I regret not watching everything my grandmother ever cooked." She hands me one of the small hardcover books, where all the recipes are organized by course.

As I flip through the pages, a photo of an eighteen-year-old Carmela falls to the table. "My kids say I looked like Ava Gardner!" Carmela says, half joking, but she's absolutely right.

Carmela cannot stress enough the importance of learning from family. "Make sure you ask your questions, because time goes on and people pass away, and you'll never know some things. Even though I lived in the same house with my family, there are some things I didn't ask and I'll never know," she says.

As she talks, though, I'm struck by Carmela's poise. Even as she hints at her own regrets, she projects only an abiding calmness, and I can't help but ask her what her secret is for being so centered. Without missing a beat, she says: "I'm old. When you're old, you're calm. What could happen?"

CAVATELLI WITH BROCCOLI

Cavatelli e Broccoli

PREP TIME: 5 MINUTES • COOK TIME: 15 MINUTES • YIELD: 4 TO 6 SERVINGS

I'm not sure there's a more beautiful sight than fresh golden garlic atop a bowl of cavatelli and broccoli. This dish is so easy to prep and cook that it's a breeze for Nonna Carmela to make for her gaggle of grandchildren. In true Southern Italian fashion, the vegetables and pasta are boiled together so that the pasta becomes infused with the broccoli flavor. This recipe uses some reserved broccoli and pasta water to make it a bit brothy, which you can adjust to your liking.

16 ounces (454 g) dried or fresh cavatelli

2 pounds (907 g) broccoli, cut into bite-size florets

6 tablespoons (90 ml) extra-virgin olive oil, plus more for drizzling

6 cloves garlic, sliced

¼ teaspoon red pepper flakes

¼ cup (30 g) grated Pecorino Romano cheese, plus more for sprinkling

Nonna Carmela Says
If you like your broccoli with a bit more bite, then scoop the florets out after 5 minutes and combine them when the pasta is ready.

1. Bring a large pot of generously salted water to a boil.

2. If using fresh cavatelli, add the broccoli first and boil until it is tender but still has a bit of bite, 5 to 7 minutes. Add the fresh cavatelli to the water and cook until al dente, approximately 4 to 5 minutes. If using dried cavatelli, add the pasta and vegetables to the water together and boil until the pasta is al dente.

3. Scoop out about 2 cups (475 ml) of pasta water and add to a large serving bowl. Transfer the pasta and broccoli to the serving bowl with the pasta water.

4. Heat the oil in a large skillet over medium heat. Add the garlic and red pepper flakes, and cook and stir until the garlic is golden and fragrant, 2 to 3 minutes.

5. Pour the sautéed garlic and oil over the cavatelli and broccoli in the bowl. Add the cheese and toss well. Serve in warm bowls with an extra sprinkle of cheese and a drizzle of olive oil.

SICILIAN TIMBALLO

Timballo di Anelletti

PREP TIME: 30 MINUTES • COOK TIME: 2 HOURS • YIELD: 6 TO 8 SERVINGS

I remember the first time I watched one of my favorite food movies, *Big Night*, with Stanley Tucci and Tony Shalhoub, who played the brothers Primo and Secondo. As I watched them cut into a big baked *timballo* in anticipation of Louie Prima coming to dinner, my eyes widened. Nonna Lydia's Sicilian timballo brings that dish to life for me. Timballo gets its name from the Italian word *timpano*, which means "drum." It is a drum-shaped pasta dish baked in a pastry crust and can be filled with many different ingredients. Nonna Lydia layers *anelletti*, a typical Sicilian ring-shaped pasta, with meat sauce, fried eggplant, and mozzarella for a showstopping dish fit for Louis Prima himself.

CRUST

3⅓ cups (400 g) all-purpose flour,
  plus more for dusting and the pan
Dash salt
1 cup (2 sticks, or 240 g) cold unsalted
  butter, cubed, plus more for greasing
2 eggs plus 1 egg for egg wash
¼ cup (60 ml) whole milk

PASTA AND SAUCE

3 tablespoons (45 ml) extra-virgin
  olive oil
4 cloves garlic, minced
1 pound (454 g) meatloaf mix (equal
  parts beef, pork, and veal)
½ cup (120 ml) dry white wine, such as
  Pinot Grigio or Sauvignon Blanc
2 bay leaves
20 ounces (567 g) canned crushed
  tomatoes (about 2¼ cups)
1½ cups (200 g) frozen peas, thawed
2 tablespoons (8 g) minced fresh parsley
Red pepper flakes, to taste
Salt and black pepper, to taste
12 ounces (340 g) dried anelletti or any
  other short pasta you prefer
16 ounces (454 g) mozzarella, thinly sliced

EGGPLANT

2 medium eggplant, peeled and sliced
  vertically into ¼-inch (6 mm) thick slices
1 cup (235 ml) olive oil, for frying (or any
  frying oil you like)

1. **To make the crust:** In the bowl of a stand mixer fitted with the dough hook attachment, combine the flour, salt, and butter. Mix on low speed first and then on high speed until all the butter is absorbed by the flour.

2. Switch to medium speed and add the eggs, one at a time, until they are fully incorporated. Add the milk and mix until a ball of dough forms (if the dough seems a bit dry, add another tablespoon, or 15 ml, of milk). Mix on medium speed for about 10 minutes, or until the dough is supple. Wrap the dough in plastic wrap and rest in the refrigerator for 30 minutes. In the meantime, get started on the sauce.

3. **To make the pasta and sauce:** Bring a large pot of generously salted water to a boil.

continued

4. Heat the olive oil in a 5-quart (4.7 L) stockpot over medium heat. Add the garlic and cook and stir until slightly golden, 1 to 2 minutes. Add the meat and brown, breaking it up with a wooden spoon, then add the wine and cook until you can no longer smell the alcohol, 4 to 5 minutes. Stir in the bay leaves, tomatoes, peas, and parsley. Add the red pepper flakes and salt and black pepper.

5. Cook the sauce for 5 minutes, stirring occasionally. Remove from the heat. Remove and discard the bay leaves. Transfer the mixture to a colander with a plate underneath and drain the liquid for about 10 minutes. You don't want the meat sauce to be too watery and leak through the crust!

6. Drop the anelletti into the boiling water and cook until very al dente. Drain and run under cold running water. Set aside.

7. **To make the eggplant:** Heat the olive oil in a large heavy-bottomed skillet over medium-high heat. Fry the eggplant slices in batches until golden brown on both sides, 2 to 3 minutes per batch. Transfer to a baking sheet lined with paper towels. Cool to room temperature.

8. **To assemble the timballo:** Preheat the oven to 350°F (175°C). Butter and flour a 9-inch (23 cm) springform pan.

9. Mix the anelletti into the meat sauce. Set aside.

10. Take two-thirds of the dough and place on a floured work surface. Wrap the other third of dough in plastic wrap and refrigerate until ready to use. Roll the dough into a ¼-inch (6 mm) thick circle at least 17 inches (43 cm) in diameter. You want this crust to come up the sides of the springform pan and hang over.

11. Roll the dough onto your rolling pin and unfurl it over the pan and up the sides. Leave 1 to 2 inches (2.5 to 5 cm) of excess dough hanging over the top.

12. Line the bottom and sides of the crust with the fried eggplant, letting the eggplant overhang the sides of the pan. Next, top the eggplant with one-third of the mozzarella slices.

13. Fill the pan halfway with the pasta and meat sauce mixture. Add another layer of eggplant and another layer of mozzarella. Fill the rest of the pan with the pasta and meat sauce mixture to form a little rounded dome.

14. Add the remaining mozzarella slices and fold the hanging eggplant slices over the top.

15. Roll out the remaining dough into a ¼-inch (6 mm) thick circle 12 inches (30 cm) in diameter and place it over the top of the pan to seal the timballo. Trim any excess dough hanging from the sides, and with your fingers, seal the bottom and top crusts together. You can also seal it with the tines of a fork. Roll any excess dough into thin ropes and make a cross over the top crust.

16. Beat the remaining egg and brush the top crust with the egg wash.

17. Bake for 60 to 75 minutes, until the top of the timballo is nicely colored. Let cool for 30 to 40 minutes before slicing.

"If something isn't perfect the first time, you can't give up. As an Italian woman, I'm persistent by nature."

"I live to eat and cook," the svelte Nonna Lydia Palermo tells me in the most elegant Queens accent I've ever heard. We are enjoying a homemade *cannolo* in her spacious Manhattan apartment. She tells me people don't often peg her for the traditional Italian-American woman that she is. "My mother was a very elegant woman. Always well-dressed but a fantastic cook. She taught me that a housewife doesn't have to be dowdy. It's about what you want."

As the granddaughter of a baker and the daughter of a restaurateur from Kew Gardens, you could say that food is in Lydia's blood. "My grandfather had a pastry shop in Italy, and then later opened one in America. My father owned a catering hall in Queens, and we had a big family and bigger family parties every other week. Until I was about twelve I had no idea other people existed. I just thought everyone was Italian!"

We both laugh as we think of how strong of an influence it is to grow up in an Italian family where tradition rules. "We always ate at a certain time. Even though my father was busy, he would make sure to come home for dinner, and if my friends came over they were always shocked by the kinds of food we ate at home. Lobster, traditional Sicilian dishes, and all different kinds of fish! I was exposed to so much," she says. Nonna Lydia's relationship to cooking didn't manifest itself until after she was married.

"My father told me to marry a doctor, so I did!" she says smiling as she refers to her late husband. "I was twenty-one when I got married, and although I had watched my mother, I didn't realize what went into cooking. I called her every five minutes. 'How do you do this? How do you make that?' But I learned." After all, having an Italian doctor as a husband came with certain duties. "My husband would be delivering a baby and he would call me at 2 a.m., and I would know to prepare something because an Italian man can't eat hospital food!"

Nonna Lydia shares with me the greatest lesson she has learned throughout her years in the kitchen: the power of experience. "If something isn't perfect the first time, you can't give up. As an Italian woman, I'm persistent by nature. If you really love something, you will be good. If you hate it, you won't be good. So learn to love it!"

Nonna Lydia is proud to have passed on her love of cooking to her daughter's twin boys. "My grandchildren are the joys of my life. They love helping me, and we have so much fun rolling meatballs. I want them to feel comfortable cooking because they're the future of the family. It's so important for a person to know how to cook; it brings in a lot of friends, and I tell the boys that when they grow up they'll get all the girls!" She winks, smiles, and knows she's totally right.

SPAGHETTI WITH MEATBALLS

Spaghetti alla Chitarra con Polpette

PREP TIME: 25 MINUTES • COOK TIME: 1 HOUR 30 MINUTES • YIELD: 4 TO 6 SERVINGS

A big bowl of spaghetti and meatballs isn't just delicious, it's iconic. It's always a party at Nonna Theresa's when she whips out her pasta guitar (*chitarra*) and lets all her grandchildren get in on the action. Her incredible Sunday sauce with meatballs cooked low and slow fills the entire kitchen with the most intoxicating aroma. You'll be ready to sit down and stay awhile.

SPAGHETTI

16 ounces (454 g) fresh egg pasta
    dough (page 21) or dried spaghetti
Semolina flour, for dusting

MEATBALLS

1 pound (454 g) meatloaf mix (equal
    parts beef, pork, and veal)
2 eggs, beaten
1 cup (120 g) grated Pecorino
    Romano cheese, plus more
    for serving
½ cup (54 g) plain bread crumbs
4 cloves garlic, shaved
2 tablespoons (8 g) minced
    fresh parsley
3 tablespoons (45 ml) extra-virgin
    olive oil
¼ teaspoon black pepper
Milk, as needed
2 cups (475 ml) olive oil, for frying
    (or any frying oil you like)

1. **To make the spaghetti:** On a clean work surface sprinkled with semolina flour, roll the dough into 7 × 10-inch (18 × 24 cm) rectangles that are ⅛-inch (3 mm) thick, depending on the size of your chitarra.

2. Flour the pan of the chitarra with semolina and place the rolled-out dough on top of the strings. With a rolling pin, roll the dough over the strings several times, pressing down. Swipe your fingers back and forth over the strings, "playing the guitar," as the spaghetti falls. Keep the rolled-out spaghetti in small mounds, each about the size of a fist, sprinkled with plenty of semolina flour until ready to use. The pasta will stick together if left in one big pile.

3. **To make the meatballs:** Add the meatloaf mix, eggs, cheese, bread crumbs, garlic, parsley, extra-virgin olive oil, and black pepper to a large mixing bowl, and mix well, preferably with your hands. If the mixture appears too dry, add milk, 1 tablespoon (15 ml) at a time, until the consistency improves.

4. Roll the mixture into meatballs about 1 tablespoon (15 g) in size. This should make 35 to 40 meatballs. You may have a few left over, but I've never heard anyone complain about extra meatballs before!

5. Heat the frying oil in a medium heavy-bottomed saucepan over medium-high heat.

continued

SAUCE

3 cloves garlic, peeled and halved

1 small onion, peeled and halved

6 tablespoons (90 ml) extra-virgin olive
    oil, divided

3 ounces (85 g) tomato paste
    (about 5 ½ tablespoons)

2 cans (28 ounces, or 794 g, each)
    crushed tomatoes

2 bay leaves

2 fresh basil leaves

1 teaspoon salt

Dash red pepper flakes

Dash black pepper

Nonna Theresa Says
*Whenever I roll the meatballs,
I always have a bowl of water
next to me so I can lightly wet my
hands between each one. It helps
you get a better grip and prevents
the meat from sticking to your
hands.*

6. Fry the meatballs in batches until browned on all sides, 3 to 4 minutes per batch. Transfer to a paper towel–lined plate to drain. Set aside.

7. **To make the sauce:** Add the garlic and onion to a food processor and process for about 10 seconds.

8. Heat 3 tablespoons (45 ml) of the extra-virgin olive oil in a medium sauté pan over medium heat, add the onion and garlic mixture, and cook and stir until the onions are soft and everything is golden, 6 to 7 minutes. Transfer to a small bowl and set aside.

9. Heat the remaining 3 tablespoons (45 ml) of extra-virgin olive oil in a 5-quart (4.7 L) heavy-bottomed stockpot over medium-high heat. Add the sautéed garlic and onion mixture and the tomato paste, and cook and stir for 2 to 3 minutes.

10. Add the tomatoes and stir to combine with a wooden spoon. Add the bay leaves, basil, salt, red pepper flakes, and black pepper, and stir to combine. Bring the sauce to a boil and cook for 5 minutes, stirring.

11. Add the meatballs to the sauce and reduce the heat to the lowest setting possible. Cover and cook for 45 minutes, stirring occasionally with a wooden spoon. Uncover and cook for an additional 15 minutes. Remove and discard the bay leaves.

12. Bring a large pot of generously salted water to a boil and cook the spaghetti until al dente, 4 to 5 minutes for fresh pasta. Drain and return to the pot.

13. Add about 2 cups (510 g) of the sauce to the pot with the pasta. Toss well to give the pasta a light coating of sauce. Portion into bowls and add more sauce to each bowl along with the meatballs. Serve with an extra sprinkle of Pecorino Romano.

"Don't get stressed out; make some pasta!"

"You must love to cook. If you think of it as a chore you will never make good food," says Nonna Teresa Petruccelli-Formato. "Cooking is like an art and you should treat every meal like you're creating a masterpiece," she tells me as we sit at her endless dining room table in her home in Flushing, Queens. Behind me is a newly renovated kitchen with immaculate, restaurant-grade stainless steel appliances, evidence that Nonna Teresa regards cooking as serious and important business.

"I was born in New York, but I've always felt more Italian than American. My parents came to America from San Cosma e Damiano, near Rome. I grew up going to Italy all the time. I remember one specific family trip back to Italy in the 1960s. We had decided to go by boat, and we took our station wagon and trunks of supplies for my family. At the time, people were still struggling after the war after being bombarded by Germans, Italians, and Americans. We brought sugar, coffee, flour, bolts of fabric. Everything! It was a different time."

While both her parents worked long hours in the hairdressing business during her childhood, Teresa spent her formative years being raised by her beloved nonna.

"Whenever I came home from school, my nonna would be cooking for my mother, and I would watch her closely. She was a short woman with huge breasts and her hugs would completely envelop you," she recalls.

"My nonna is definitely where my passion comes from, but my interests in cooking grew when I got married because I finally had my own house. Your cooking identity changes with marriage. When an Italian woman gets married, she takes on her husband's cooking influences. You want to cook the things your husband's mother made because let's face it, Italian men are all about the mother!"

Today, Nonna Teresa savors every moment of being a nonna. "It's like getting to relive your life. It's a second chance. My own nonna and aunt would watch my children while I worked, so they got to give them their first *pastina* and watch their first steps. So many times I would be in tears in my office. Now I make time to witness these things. When they want me to babysit, I'm always free. Even if they don't want me to babysit, I make sure they know I'm free. I do it because the love for your grandchildren is different than the love for your children. You're more relaxed and not as nervous. My children didn't come with a book of instructions, but when your grandchildren come, you can be the comforting presence to your children."

Nonna Teresa takes joy in preparing meals for her family whenever she can. "Food is important in an Italian family because it brings the family together. Sometimes just sitting for an hour and going over your day while eating can rejuvenate everyone. I used to worry about everything, except cooking!" she says. "Cooking has been the best therapy for me."

Over the years, Teresa even developed a mantra that can be applied to almost every situation: "Don't get stressed out; make some pasta!"

RIGATONI CARBONARA

Rigatoni alla Carbonara

PREP TIME: 5 MINUTES • COOK TIME: 10 MINUTES • YIELD: 4 TO 6 SERVINGS

Nonna Teresa's *carbonara* is a must-make on one of those lazy nights when you want something super quick and filling. Her version is rich and naughty, with half a dozen eggs and a pound of *pancetta* (bacon's sexier Italian cousin), but it will leave you with a full belly and a smile on your face, with very few ingredients and only 10 minutes cooking time!

2 tablespoons (30 ml) extra-virgin olive oil

1 pound (454 g) pancetta, cut into ¼-inch (6 mm) cubes

16 ounces (454 g) dried rigatoni

6 fresh eggs, at room temperature

⅔ cup (67 g) grated Pecorino Romano cheese

¼ teaspoon black pepper, plus more for sprinkling

Nonna Teresa Says

Always use the freshest ingredients possible when making carbonara. The ingredients are few and simple, so they should be the best!

1. Bring a pot of generously salted water to a boil.

2. Heat the olive oil in a large skillet over medium heat. Add the pancetta and cook and stir until crisp, 5 to 6 minutes. Turn off the heat.

3. Drop the pasta into the boiling water and cook until al dente.

4. Meanwhile, whisk together the eggs, cheese, and pepper in a mixing bowl.

5. Turn the heat back on to medium under the skillet. Scoop out about ¼ cup (60 ml) of the pasta water and add it to the skillet. Let the water evaporate for 1 to 2 minutes while stirring with a wooden spoon.

6. With a strainer, scoop out the pasta and add it to the skillet. Toss for 1 to 2 minutes. Remove from the heat and let the pan rest for 15 to 20 seconds.

7. Add the egg mixture to the hot pasta while stirring quickly with a wooden spoon to evenly coat the pasta. Serve immediately with an extra sprinkle of black pepper.

NONNA GIULIA ROTONDI

"If you tell me I can't do something, I have to show you that I can!"

As I sit with Nonna Giulia Rotondi in her Staten Island kitchen, I feel as though I'm the lucky ticket holder to an exclusive one-woman show. Giulia is not only a nonna and a longtime friend of my mother's, but she is also an accomplished theater actress, an unbelievable cook, and one hell of a storyteller!

Today, she is sitting with the ever-present cigarette in her right hand, while her large hoop earrings shine and brighten her face. In her youth, Giulia was never afraid to stand up for what she believed in, a personality trait she picked up from the nuns who raised her in an Italian boarding house in Molfetta.

After the death of her father when she was just eight, Giulia and her sister were sent to live in the church's paid boarding house, or *colleggio*, so they could receive an education. "It was supposed to be prestigious to be there because it meant your family could afford to pay, but the food took getting used to. They would give us the rinds of peas mixed with pasta. Bread without oil. Meat only once a week. And everyone received a different-sized portion of bread depending on how old you were."

"I noticed that sometimes the girls who got smaller pieces of bread were hungrier, and I couldn't bear it. I was entitled to more bread so I would break mine in half and pretend they gave me the wrong piece, and I would switch it for her."

Ironically, it was Giulia's brazen behavior in the boarding house that planted the first seeds of her incredible cooking skills. "As punishment for one of my tricks, I was told to make 140 pounds of bread, two to three times a week. I would be allowed to keep one loaf out of the batches," she said. "I learned how to cook because I was ambitious. In the boarding house we weren't allowed to cook with the nuns, because they didn't want us to see how they cut corners, but at eighteen I left the boarding house and was finally back at home with my family. Not being able to cook while I was in school lit a fire in me to learn. I'm that way: if you tell me I can't do something, I have to show you that I can!"

Over the years, Giulia has become a veritable master baker, specializing in classic Pugliese almond paste cookies. Every Christmas, she spends two weeks preparing over a dozen different varieties of cookies for her closest friends. She also enlists the help of her eight grandchildren, who she hopes will keep up the tradition after she's gone. "At this point, I know everyone expects them, and I want to keep doing it. Every year around Thanksgiving, people start asking me when I'm going to start. They ask, 'Are you going to make them this year?' and I say, 'Of course I am. Why wouldn't I? As long as there is life there is hope,'" she recounts, as she lights another cigarette.

BUCATINI WITH CAULIFLOWER

Bucatini Chi Vrocculi Arriminati

PREP TIME: 10 MINUTES • COOK TIME: 27 MINUTES • YIELD: 4 TO 6 SERVINGS

Nonna Liliana's *bucatini* dish delivers all the flavors of Sicily. The dried currants help create a wonderful balance of sweet and savory that you'll have to taste to believe.

7 tablespoons (105 ml) extra-virgin olive oil, divided

½ cup (54 g) plain bread crumbs

1 head cauliflower (about 2 pounds, or 907 g), trimmed into 1-inch (2.5 cm) florets

1 large onion, cut into ¼-inch (6 mm) dice

3 bay leaves

3 anchovy fillets, packed in oil

2 teaspoons tomato paste or Italian tomato concentrate

⅓ cup (50 g) dried currants or raisins

⅓ cup (45 g) pinoli (pine nuts)

Salt and black pepper, to taste

16 ounces (454 g) dried bucatini

Nonna Liliana Says

This is one of my favorite dishes that I can throw together very quickly, and it always impresses.

1. Add 2 tablespoons (30 ml) of the olive oil and the bread crumbs to a medium sauté pan over medium heat. Cook, stirring constantly with a wooden spoon, until the bread crumbs just begin to turn lightly golden, 5 to 7 minutes. Remove from the heat and immediately transfer them to a medium mixing bowl to prevent burning.

2. In a 6-quart (5.7 L) stockpot bring 4 quarts (3.8 L) of lightly salted water to a boil. Add the cauliflower florets and cook, covered, for 5 minutes. Scoop out the cauliflower and reserve the water to cook the pasta later.

3. Heat 4 tablespoons (60 ml) of the olive oil in a large sauté pan over medium heat. Add the onion and cook and stir for 8 to 10 minutes, or until the onion begins to color. Add the bay leaves, anchovies, tomato paste, currants, and pinoli. Give the pan a stir with a wooden spoon.

4. Add the cauliflower florets and cook and stir for 1 to 2 minutes. Add 2 to 3 ladles of the cauliflower water (about 1½ cups, or 350 ml). Stir with a wooden spoon until the tomato paste is fully incorporated and the florets are coated in the paste. Season with salt and black pepper.

5. Cover the pan and reduce the heat to low. Cook until the cauliflower is tender and most of the water has evaporated, about 10 minutes. Check the pan occasionally, adding more cauliflower water if the mixture seems dry.

6. Adjust the salt of the remaining cauliflower water and return the pot to a boil. Drop in the bucatini and cook until al dente. Drain the pasta and add it to the pan with the cauliflower. Add the remaining 1 tablespoon (15 ml) of olive oil and toss for 1 to 2 minutes. Serve in warm bowls with a sprinkle of the toasted bread crumbs.

ORECCHIETTE WITH BRACIOLE

Orecchiette con Braciole in Ragu

PREP TIME: 15 MINUTES • COOK TIME: 1 HOUR 25 MINUTES • YIELD: 4 TO 6 SERVINGS

On Sundays at Nonna Cecilia's house, there's always a big plate of fresh *orecchiette* with meat sauce and *braciole* waiting for you. Braciole are thin slices of beef that can be filled with different ingredients and rolled up and secured with toothpicks or twine. The tender meat of the braciole bursts with the simple flavors of garlic, parsley, and savory Pecorino Romano cheese. They slowly simmer in Nonna Cecilia's signature meat sauce and release all their beautiful flavors. Her family agrees that it just wouldn't feel like Sunday without them.

BRACIOLE

2 pounds (907 g) beef top round,
  cut for braciole

Salt and black pepper, to taste

2 to 3 ounces (57 to 85 g) Pecorino
  Romano cheese, cut into thin slices
  2 to 3 inches (5 to 7.5 cm) long (you
  should have about 24 slices)

¼ cup (16 g) finely minced fresh parsley

8 to 10 cloves garlic, finely minced

Red pepper flakes, to taste

SAUCE

¼ cup (60 ml) extra-virgin olive oil

1 small onion, cut into ¼-inch (6 mm) dice

1 small carrot, cut into ¼-inch (6 mm) dice

½ cup (120 ml) dry red wine, such as
  Cabernet Sauvignon or Merlot

2 cans (28 ounces, or 794 g, each)
  crushed tomatoes

3 bay leaves

1 teaspoon salt

PASTA

16 ounces (454 g) fresh orecchiette
  (page 18) or dried

Grated Pecorino Romano cheese,
  for serving

1. **To make the braciole:** Trim each slice of beef into 6 × 4-inch (15 × 10 cm) slices. If necessary, pound each slice between two pieces of plastic wrap until ¼ inch (6 mm) thick.

2. Season well with salt and black pepper.

3. Add 2 or 3 slices of the cheese and 1 teaspoon each of the parsley and garlic to each slice. Add a few red pepper flakes, if desired. Roll up the braciole and secure with toothpicks. Set aside.

4. **To make the sauce:** Heat the olive oil in a 6-quart (5.7 L) stockpot over medium-high heat. Add the onion and carrot, and cook and stir until soft, about 10 minutes.

5. Add the braciole and let them brown on all sides, 5 to 7 minutes. Add the wine and cook until you can no longer smell the alcohol, 4 to 5 minutes.

6. Add the tomatoes, bay leaves, and salt. Reduce the heat to a simmer, cover, and cook for about 1 hour, stirring occasionally with a wooden spoon.

7. **To make the pasta:** Bring a large pot of generously salted water to a boil. Drop in the orecchiette and cook until al dente, 4 to 5 minutes.

8. Drain and add the orecchiette to the pot of sauce. Toss for 1 to 2 minutes. Serve in warm bowls with a generous sprinkle of Pecorino Romano.

SPAGHETTI ALLA PUTTANESCA

PREP TIME: 5 MINUTES • COOK TIME: 18 MINUTES • YIELD: 4 TO 6 SERVINGS

There may be some debate as to the origin of the name of this famous dish, but there's no question that Nonna Gilda's version is delicious! It's ready in a snap and it hits the spot when you're craving something salty, spicy, and tangy all at once. Nonna Gilda's true Neapolitan *puttanesca* does not include anchovies. Truthfully, they are more of a Roman variation to the dish. You can add them if you like.

¼ cup (60 ml) extra-virgin olive oil

5 cloves garlic, sliced

6 anchovy fillets, packed in oil (optional)

2 tablespoons (18 g) capers

½ cup (50 g) pitted coarsely chopped Gaeta or Kalamata olives

¼ teaspoon red pepper flakes

1 can (28 ounces, or 794 g) crushed tomatoes

¼ teaspoon salt

16 ounces (454 g) dried spaghetti

Nonna Gilda Says
I always make this for big groups of people because it has few ingredients and everyone loves it. It's perfect for entertaining.

1. Heat the oil in a large skillet over medium heat. Add the garlic and cook and stir until golden brown, about 2 minutes. (You may also leave the garlic cloves whole and remove them after sautéing to just flavor the oil.)

2. Add the anchovies, if using, and cook, stirring with a wooden spoon, until the anchovies break down, about 1 minute.

3. Add the capers, olives, and red pepper flakes, and sauté for an additional 3 minutes.

4. Stir in the tomatoes and salt, and reduce the heat to low. Cook for an additional 10 minutes, stirring occasionally.

5. Bring a large pot of generously salted water to a boil, add the pasta, and cook until al dente. Drain the pasta, add it to the sauté pan with the sauce, and cook over medium heat, tossing, for 1 to 2 minutes. Serve in warm bowls.

NONNA GILDA TAORMINA

"Always use your imagination when you cook. If you want to substitute something just do it."

"I always loved being in the kitchen!" Nonna Gilda Taormina tells me in the dining area of her cozy Queens apartment. I feel a rush of nostalgia as I look around. Everything—from the embroidered curtains (that I'm certain came from Italy) to the china cabinet full of shimmery knick-knacks and fancy dishes—reminds me of home.

Born in Pollena Trocchia, a small city not far from Naples, Gilda always had a special passion for food. "I loved cooking since I was young. When I was a little girl, around eight or nine, and it was a holiday, I used to beg my mother to wait for me to come home from school before she started cooking and baking. She was really a great cook, and she never used measurements so I learned how to cook by watching and feeling instead of reading a recipe."

I listen closely as she explains her cooking philosophy. "Always use your imagination when you cook. If you want to substitute something just do it. Trust yourself enough to break the rules, because the little extras are what make things special."

In 1969, a whirlwind marriage to an American of Sicilian descent brought her to America when she was still a young girl. "I got married at St. Patrick's Cathedral in New York City . . . I wanted bridesmaids and the whole thing!" she tells me. "When I got married my cooking style changed because my husband wasn't used to eating the same things as I was. So I changed a few things and tried to make some dishes the same way his mother did. Now my cooking style is this Sicilian and Neapolitan fusion. I think he's used to the way I cook, and he likes it. It's only been forty-five years," she laughs.

Gilda recalls how strange it was adjusting to cooking in America. "All of a sudden there were all these big supermarkets and all new condiments like ketchup and mustard. I had no idea what to do with them! I missed the simple garlic and onions and the *carretto* (produce carts) that used to come through the streets in Pollena Trocchia, but over the years you learn how to keep your traditions alive."

Gilda shows me a large three-ring binder that reads *Gilda's Recipes*. "One of my daughters made this for me," she explains, as she shows me photos of her cooking. "My kids grew up with so many dishes that only I make. I didn't get them from the Internet or a cookbook; they were passed on to me. So I really hope they keep making the dishes and remember me," she says.

Of her four grandchildren, Gilda says: "Being a nonna means the world to me. I couldn't wait to become a nonna because I loved my nonna. My grandson feels so special that he has a nonna because most of the kids in his class don't. He brought me into his class to read aloud and he was beaming with pride and correcting the teachers when they called me grandma. 'She's not grandma, she's nonna,' he said!"

CHICORY WITH FAVA BEAN PUREE

Cicorie con Pure di Fave

PREP TIME: 10 MINUTES* • COOK TIME: 2 HOURS 19 MINUTES • YIELD: 4 TO 6 SERVINGS

*REQUIRES AT LEAST 8 HOURS OF SOAKING

Just looking at a dish of chicory with fava beans takes me back to my childhood summers in Mola di Bari. This dish is an acquired taste, so if you don't love bitter greens, then move along now! Chicory brings an earthy flavor to the smooth, almost buttery fava beans that magically puree themselves on the stove without being stirred. "If you start stirring them, they will stick and you will have to stir them the whole time," Nonna Anna warns.

1 pound (454 g) dried shelled fava beans

½ teaspoon salt, plus more to taste

6 to 7 cups (1.4 to 1.7 L) water, divided

4 tablespoons (60 ml) extra-virgin olive oil, divided, plus more for drizzling

2 pounds (907 g) chicory or dandelion greens, ends trimmed, washed, and cut into 4-inch (10 cm) pieces

Nonna Anna Says

The olive oil drizzle is very important in this recipe. Make sure you use the best quality extra-virgin olive oil you can find. It should pinch the back of your throat!

1. Place the fava beans, salt, and about 3 cups (700 ml) of the water, just enough to cover the favas by ½ inch (13 mm), in a 5-quart (4.7 L) heavy-bottomed stockpot and soak for at least 8 hours or overnight.

2. The fava beans will have absorbed most of the water, so add more water to just cover the favas, the remaining 3 to 4 cups (700 to 950 ml). Cover and cook over low heat, without stirring, until the favas are smooth, about 2 hours. It is very important to not stir the fava beans for the first 2 hours of cooking to prevent sticking. The fava beans will turn into a puree on their own as they boil. If you notice they look a bit dry, add some boiling water.

3. After 2 hours, add 1 tablespoon (15 ml) of the olive oil and stir with a wooden spoon until smooth. Taste for seasoning and add more salt to taste. Remove from the heat. If desired, you may beat the favas with an electric mixer or puree with an immersion blender to further smooth them out.

4. Fill a 7- to 9-quart (6.6 to 8.5 L) stockpot with generously salted water and bring to a boil. Add the greens, return the water to a boil, and cook for 10 to 15 minutes, until tender. Reserve 1 cup (235 ml) of the cooking water and drain.

5. Heat the remaining 3 tablespoons (45 ml) of olive oil in a large sauté pan over medium-high heat. Add the fava bean puree, stirring with a wooden spoon. Loosen with the reserved water if necessary. Add the greens and cook for 3 to 4 minutes, stirring until combined. Alternatively, spoon the fava beans into warm bowls and top with the chicory. Taste for seasoning and add more salt to taste. Serve with an extra drizzle of olive oil over the top.

SPAGHETTI WITH CLAMS

Spaghetti alle Vongole

PREP TIME: 10 MINUTES • COOK TIME: 16 MINUTES • YIELD: 4 TO 6 SERVINGS

The first time I guided a culinary tour in Sorrento, I was lucky enough to watch Nonna Rosa make this classic local dish. Traditionally, this dish is made with a variety of clams common to the Campania region of Italy. Known as *vongole veraci*, they are the tiniest baby clams you've ever seen, but they're absolutely bursting with flavor. They can be difficult to find Stateside, so super-fresh cockles or littleneck clams make a fine substitute. When it comes to ingredients, Nonna Rosa keeps it simple: garlic, olive oil, parsley, red pepper flakes, and the wonderful juice of the fresh clams. Even the tomatoes, which I thoroughly enjoy here, are optional. Nonna Rosa removes the seeds so their liquid doesn't overpower the clams. When making dishes with so few ingredients, freshness is paramount, so make good friends with your local fishmongers and they'll hook you up with the good stuff.

36 cockles or 24 littleneck clams

2 tablespoons (8 g) minced fresh
parsley, plus a few whole sprigs for
steaming the clams

5 tablespoons (75 ml) extra-virgin olive
oil, divided

16 ounces (454 g) dried spaghetti

3 cloves garlic, halved

15 cherry tomatoes, halved and seeded
(optional)

Red pepper flakes, to taste

Nonna Rosa Says

I leave the garlic quite large and let it flavor the oil. Then I remove it because many people don't like to eat large chunks of garlic. In this dish, the focal point is the flavor of the clams and you don't want people to be distracted.

1. Tap each of the clams and discard any that sound hollow. Wash the clams under cold running water to remove any sand.

2. Put a 6-quart (5.7 L) stockpot over high heat. Add the clams, whole sprigs of parsley, and 1 tablespoon (15 ml) of the olive oil. Cover and steam until all of the clams open, giving the pot a good shake every few minutes, 6 to 7 minutes.

3. Scoop out the clams and discard any that did not open. Reserve all the water in a glass for later use.

4. Bring a large pot of generously salted water to a boil and drop in the spaghetti. Cook until al dente.

5. Heat the remaining 4 tablespoons (60 ml) of olive oil in a large sauté pan over medium heat. Add the garlic and cook and stir until it just begins to turn golden, 1 to 2 minutes. Remove the garlic from the pan and discard.

6. Add the clams to the pan and toss with a wooden spoon for 1 to 2 minutes.

7. Add the tomatoes, if using, and carefully pour in the reserved water from the clams, first pouring it through a cheesecloth into a bowl to remove any grit.

8. Add the minced parsley and red pepper flakes. Toss together for another 2 to 3 minutes.

9. Add the drained spaghetti and toss together for another 1 to 2 minutes. Serve immediately.

SPAGHETTI WITH CHERRY TOMATOES, MOLA DI BARI STYLE

Spaghetti San Giuannidd' alla Molese

PREP TIME: 5 MINUTES • COOK TIME: 15 MINUTES • YIELD: 4 TO 6 SERVINGS

Spaghetti San Giuannidd', the name of this dish in my family's local dialect of Mola di Bari, is made differently all throughout Puglia. You will see some variations that contain olives, capers, and even anchovies. This recipe is in its simplest form but brings back some of the most vivid cooking memories for me. It was one of the first things my Nonna Romana ever taught me to make, and it's what my mother cooks whenever she needs to come up with something quick for dinner, because it's ready in just a few minutes and there's always an abundance of garlic, oil, parsley, and tomatoes in her house. This dish proves that you don't need to cook a tomato sauce for hours to get an explosion of flavor, as the fresh tomatoes barely need to be cooked at all to taste amazing.

¼ cup (60 ml) extra-virgin olive oil

5 cloves garlic, minced

1½ pounds (680 g) cherry tomatoes, halved

½ teaspoon salt

1 tablespoon (4 g) minced fresh parsley

16 ounces (454 g) dried spaghetti

Nonna Romana Says

Make sure your oil is very hot before you add the garlic, and don't let the garlic color past golden. This recipe is all about the garlic, so pay attention!

1. Bring a large pot of generously salted water to a boil.

2. Heat the olive oil in a large heavy-bottomed skillet over medium heat until it is almost smoking. Add the garlic and cook and stir until golden brown, 1 to 2 minutes.

3. Add the tomatoes and salt, and sauté until the tomatoes begin to break down, 5 to 6 minutes.

4. Drop the spaghetti into the boiling water and cook until it is slightly harder than al dente.

5. Add the parsley to the skillet and cook the sauce for another 4 to 5 minutes. Reduce the heat to a simmer and wait for the pasta to finish cooking.

6. Drain the pasta and add to the skillet. Toss for 1 to 2 minutes and serve.

MAFALDINE PASTA WITH ANCHOVIES

Lagane di San Giuseppe

PREP TIME: 5 MINUTES • COOK TIME: 15 MINUTES • YIELD: 4 TO 6 SERVINGS

For my Nonna Romana, the feast of St. Joseph on March 19 is particularly special. Geppino, her son and my uncle, is named for one of the many Italian variations on the name Giuseppe, or Joseph. When the big day approaches, she invites over Geppino and everyone else she knows who has a name derived from Joseph or Giuseppe to celebrate the feast of St. Joseph, Pugliese style! *Lagane di San Giuseppe* is the traditional Pugliese dish prepared only on St. Joseph's Day, and the ingredients are selected to honor St. Joseph's profession as a carpenter. The *Mafaldine*, which look like tiny lasagna noodles, represent curled wood shavings, while the toasted bread crumbs evoke sawdust. This dish is very simple but requires excellent timing, as adding water to hot oil and anchovies can be a bit explosive, but the aromatic pasta comes together quickly and is delicious when topped with the toasted bread crumbs. You'll want to make it more than once a year!

1 cup (108 g) plain bread crumbs

3 tablespoons (45 ml) plus ½ cup (120 ml) extra-virgin olive oil, divided

16 ounces (454 g) dried mafaldine

1 can (2 ounces, or 56 g) anchovies, drained and broken up into small pieces

Nonna Romana Says

The trick to this recipe is not letting the anchovies cook too much before adding the water. As soon as they begin to break apart, be ready with the ladle.

1. Put a high-sided large sauté pan over medium heat. Add the bread crumbs and 3 tablespoons (45 ml) of the olive oil to the pan together, stirring constantly with a wooden spoon until the bread crumbs just begin to turn lightly golden, 5 to 7 minutes. Remove from the heat and immediately transfer them to a medium mixing bowl to prevent burning. Bread crumbs will continue to cook if left in the pan.

2. Bring a large pot of generously salted water to a boil. Drop in the pasta and return to a boil.

3. When the pasta has 2 to 3 minutes to go before it is al dente, heat the remaining ½ cup (120 ml) of olive oil in a medium saucepan over medium-high heat. Once the oil is very hot, add the anchovies and stir carefully with a wooden spoon for about 5 seconds. There may be some spatter but it will calm down when you add the water in the next step.

4. Scoop out about 1 cup (235 ml) of the pasta water and add it to the sauté pan, stirring until the anchovies have dissolved.

5. Drain the pasta and transfer to a large serving bowl. Add the anchovy mixture and toss well to coat the pasta. Sprinkle with the toasted bread crumbs, reserving some for garnish. Serve the pasta in warm bowls and garnish with some extra bread crumbs on top.

RICE, POTATOES, AND MUSSELS

Riso Patate Cozze (Tiella Barese)

PREP TIME: 15 MINUTES • COOK TIME: 1 HOUR 10 MINUTES • YIELD: 6 TO 8 SERVINGS

This classic dish is typically baked in a terra-cotta (clay) pot and served as a hearty first course. Layers of al dente rice and fresh mussels play beautifully with the tangy salsa of tomatoes and onions. The recipe varies throughout the region of Puglia, and some variations include other summer vegetables, such as zucchini. Nonna Cecilia keeps hers classic, and serves it up during the warmer months.

1½ pounds (680 g) Idaho potatoes, peeled and cut into ⅛-inch (3 mm) slices

2 pounds (907 g) mussels, rinsed, scrubbed, and beards removed

½ cup (120 ml) dry white wine, such as Pinot Grigio or Sauvignon Blanc

5 tablespoons (75 ml) extra-virgin olive oil

6 cloves garlic, minced

1 medium onion, cut into ¼-inch (6 mm) half rings

1 pound (454 g) Roma plum tomatoes, cut into ½-inch (13 mm) dice

¼ cup (16 g) roughly chopped fresh parsley

Salt and pepper, to taste

3 cups (555 g) Arborio rice

¼ cup (30 g) grated Pecorino Romano cheese

4 cups (950 ml) boiling water

Nonna Cecilia Says

The mussels in this dish are served on the half shell, and opening them can be a bit tricky. If you can't get the hang of it, help them along by steaming them first, but make sure you save all the water that comes out of them.

1. Preheat the oven to 350°F (175°C). Place the potato slices in a bowl of cold water to prevent darkening.

2. Open all the mussels and leave the fruit on the half shell, discarding the other shell halves. Reserve the juice of the mussels in a glass. Set aside.

3. In a large mixing bowl, combine the wine, olive oil, garlic, onion, tomatoes, and parsley, and mix well. Season with salt and black pepper.

4. Cover the bottom of a deep 14 × 9½-inch (35 × 24 cm) baking pan with a layer of the onions and tomatoes. Next, add a layer of potatoes. Place a layer of mussels over the potatoes. Spoon about ½ tablespoon (5 g) of rice over each mussel, and then spread half the rice over the entire surface (about 1½ cups, or 278 g).

5. Repeat another layer each of onions and tomatoes, potatoes, mussels, and rice. Cover the top with the remaining potatoes and vegetables.

6. Add the liquid from the mixing bowl and the reserved juice of the mussels, being careful not to add any grit that settles at the bottom of the glass. Sprinkle with the grated cheese and add the boiling water, just enough to cover the potatoes.

7. Cover with foil and bake for 1 hour. Uncover and bake for an additional 10 minutes, until lightly golden. If desired, you can place it under the broiler for 1 to 2 minutes, or until the top is nicely colored.

8. Let rest for at least 20 minutes before serving.

PASTA WITH LENTILS

Pasta e Lenticchie

PREP TIME: 5 MINUTES • COOK TIME: 1 HOUR • YIELD: 4 TO 6 SERVINGS

This may seem like an odd comfort food for many, but this dish is perfect on a fall or winter day, and my Zia Chiara makes it at least once a week. It's full of simple ingredients you would usually keep in the kitchen, and it literally doesn't get any easier than this! Add all the ingredients to the pot and just let it do its thing.

1½ cups (338 g) dried brown lentils, rinsed

1 medium carrot, peeled and minced

1 small onion, minced

1 stalk celery, cut into ¼-inch (6 mm) dice

3 cloves garlic, whole

¼ pound (113 g) cherry tomatoes, diced

2 Idaho potatoes, cut into ½-inch (13 mm) chunks

3 tablespoons (45 ml) extra-virgin olive oil, plus more for drizzling

1 teaspoon salt

¼ teaspoon black pepper

8 ounces (227 g) any cut of dried small pasta, such as farfalline, soup shells, ditalini, or cut spaghetti

1. Add the lentils, carrot, onion, celery, garlic, tomatoes, potatoes, olive oil, salt, and black pepper to a 6-quart (5.7 L) stockpot. Add enough cold water so that the lentils are covered by 2 inches (5 cm). Bring to a boil.

2. Reduce the heat to low and cook until the lentils are tender and most of the water has been absorbed, 45 to 60 minutes.

3. Bring a large pot of generously salted water to a boil. Cook the pasta until al dente. Drain and add to the pot with the lentils. Toss for 1 to 2 minutes. Serve in warm bowls with a drizzle of extra-virgin olive oil.

Nonna Chiara Says

To cut down on the cooking time, I usually soak the lentils for at least 12 hours beforehand, making sure they're covered by 2 inches (5 cm) of water. The rest of the steps are the same.

"As a young girl, [my sister] Romana always cooked, and I watched. I was always interested as she would make something new every day."

I remember the first time I ever met Zia Chiara, who still lives in Puglia. My brother and I had just arrived in Bari to spend the summer in Italy. I had never met my grandmother's sister before, but I recognized her immediately. When she saw us, she flung her arms wide open and yelled "*Amore!*" so loudly that I was overcome with emotion and cried as I ran into her arms. It was a moment that I will never forget.

In every Italian family there is a boss, someone with whom you must clear all major decisions. While my grandmother, Nonna Romana, is without question the matriarch of my family, her youngest sister, Chiara, is the boss. "You know what you must do *a' zia*?" Even today, with an ocean between us, I can hear her voice in my head if I have a problem.

Although petite in stature, Chiara has a definite presence and confidence that always made me feel like she knew everything about everything. "I was four years old when my father, Leonardo, died. My mother, Regina, was mother and father to us all. She was busy in the family store while my sisters Romana and Rosa governed all seven children. Rosa would clean the house and Romana was always in the kitchen," she explains. I pour myself a refreshing glass of my favorite childhood drink, *Orzata*, a thick, sugary almond syrup that is mixed with water. "We really had a nice life all together," she recalls.

In 1963, after the death of my grandfather, Zia Chiara and five of her siblings boarded a train to join her sister Rosa and Nonna Regina in America. The train would arrive in Naples where they would then catch a boat to New York. "They either called it the blessed train or the godforsaken train because it was mostly understood that anyone that left wouldn't be coming back," Chiara explains.

Eventually, Chiara settled back in Italy with her husband, my uncle Cesare, and her two sons. It was there that she ran a successful shoe store. Zia Chiara managed the store, a husband, two children, and the marvelous lunches she pulled from her memories of watching her big sister Romana and her mother Regina. "As a young girl, [my sister] Romana always cooked, and I watched. I was always interested as she would make something new every day," says Chiara. I have fond memories of Chiara and her sisters at her summer villa making orecchiette like an assembly line.

Zia Chiara is about to become a nonna for the second time. "The first time I became a nonna I was fifty-two, now I'm almost seventy-two, and it's a completely different emotion. You realize that you're witnessing something phenomenal. With the technology and the photographs and the ultrasounds, I feel like I have already met my new granddaughter. It's incredible."

GNOCCHI WITH GORGONZOLA AND TOASTED HAZELNUTS

Gnocchi con Gorgonzola e Nocciole Tostate

**PREP TIME: 20 MINUTES • COOK TIME: 11 MINUTES • YIELD: 4 TO 6 SERVINGS
(MAKES ABOUT 16 OUNCES, OR 454 G, OF GNOCCHI)**

Nonna Rina's potato gnocchi are drenched in a dreamy, creamy Gorgonzola dolce sauce so rich that just one bite will send your taste buds into ecstasy. Crunchy, toasted hazelnuts top off this simple but luscious dish. When recipes call for just a few ingredients, quality is super important, so make sure you use a great Gorgonzola. It will make all the difference.

GNOCCHI

1 pound (454 g) russet potatoes, unpeeled
1 egg, beaten
1 teaspoon salt
Dash freshly grated nutmeg
Black pepper, to taste
1¾ cups (190 g) sifted all-purpose flour, plus more for dusting

SAUCE

¼ cup (30 g) chopped hazelnuts
1 cup (235 ml) heavy cream
5 ounces (142 g) Gorgonzola dolce cheese, rind removed

1. **To make the gnocchi:** Bring a large pot of water to a boil. Drop in the potatoes and cook for 30 to 40 minutes, or until easily pierced with a fork. Drain the potatoes and scrape the skins off with a knife once they are cool enough to handle but still hot. (Don't cool the potatoes too much before ricing!)

2. Put the potatoes through a potato ricer into a large bowl. Spread the potatoes on a plate and let them cool to room temperature, about 30 minutes. Transfer to a large mixing bowl.

3. Add the egg, salt, nutmeg, and black pepper. Sift the flour over the top to ensure there are no lumps. Mix together with a spoon until a ball of dough forms.

4. Turn the dough out onto a floured work surface. Flour your hands and knead the dough for 2 to 3 minutes, until smooth. If the dough seems soft, add a bit more flour until it is firm. Form the dough into a ball.

5. Cut the dough into 6 equal pieces and roll each piece into ½-inch (13 cm) thick ropes. Cut ropes into 1-inch (2.5 cm) pieces and roll each piece against a floured gnocchi board, floured tines of a fork, or floured cheese grater. You can also leave the gnocchi smooth. The choice is yours.

continued

6. Dust the gnocchi with flour and rest on a floured kitchen towel. Cook immediately.

7. To cook the gnocchi, bring 4 quarts (3.8 L) of generously salted water to a boil in a large pot and drop in the gnocchi. The gnocchi are done 30 seconds to 1 minute after they float to the top.

8. **To make the sauce:** Preheat the oven to 350°F (175°C). Spread the hazelnuts on an ungreased baking sheet in a single layer. Toast the nuts for 5 to 7 minutes, until golden and fragrant, keeping an eye on their color so they don't burn. Transfer to a plate and let cool.

9. Add the hazelnuts to a food processor and pulse 4 or 5 times, until finely ground. Set aside.

10. Put a large skillet over medium-high heat. Add the heavy cream and bring it to a simmer, making sure it doesn't boil. Lower the heat to medium, add the Gorgonzola cheese, and stir until it has melted completely. Reduce the heat to a simmer and cook the sauce for 3 minutes.

11. Add the gnocchi to the skillet and toss for 1 to 2 minutes over medium heat. Serve immediately in warm bowls with fresh black pepper and a sprinkle of the toasted hazelnuts.

"They asked me to come cook for them for two weeks, and I stayed fifteen years! Even God knew I was a great cook!"

"*Il dèstino e dèstino, cicciotta mia*" ("Destiny is destiny, my chubby girl"), Nonna Rina Mulazzi says to me as she sips her wine. At almost ninety, Nonna Rina is full of vitality. She wears a flowing floral skirt that is shorter than you would expect from any nonna, but it shows off her legs, which are still in unbelievable shape. "I like to dress up," she says unapologetically. "You never know where you're going to end up."

Nonna Rina's journey from Argentina to Italy to her cozy home in a Long Island suburb seems like a long fever dream. "I was born in Argentina. When I was four, me and my mother and my brother went back to Italy to help my uncles who were never married and served in the war. They needed my mother to cook for them. My father had to stay behind and work. My mother's job was to cook for my uncles, and every day she made something wonderful. I learned everything from her. I love cooking for people and that's why everything I make is delicious. Because I enjoy what I do," she says. Her four grandchildren and great-grandchild agree.

In Italy, Nonna Rina married at nineteen and described her life as simple but happy. "We worked very hard. I would pick tomatoes in the fields with my daughter. In the summers, my husband and I would go down to the vineyards from the mountains to work. We weren't hungry, but feeding a family was much harder then." Like many Northern Italians, Rina's home ran on rice and polenta. "Maybe there was a chicken for a holiday and never fish, unless it was *baccalà* (salt cod). We used to dream about meat! That's why I say God bless America, because you can have meat every day!"

In 1957, Rina and her family embarked on a harrowing journey to America. They settled in a tenement building. Though tenement living in New York City in Little Italy was very difficult at that time, Nonna Rina was happy with it. "It was the first time I felt heat in a building. It was the first time I saw electricity or running water. We shared a bathroom with the entire floor but I didn't care. It was beautiful," she smiles. While the years weren't the most glamorous of her life, Rina found joy in cooking the dishes she remembered from home, like tortellini and ravioli.

To her family, Nonna Rina's food has always had magical powers. Her grandchildren claim that her ravioli in broth could bring life to the dead. When the priest of her local parish in Little Italy heard about her prowess in the kitchen, he didn't think twice about hiring her. "They asked me to come cook for them for two weeks, and I stayed fifteen years! Even God knew I was a great cook."

SEAFOOD RISOTTO

Risotto alla Pescatora

PREP TIME: 10 MINUTES • COOK TIME: 1 HOUR 3 MINUTES • YIELD: 4 SERVINGS

Nonna Rosa keeps it simple when it comes to her seafood risotto. Don't feel tied to the ingredients she lists. Her recipe is all about the seafood, so it's imperative that whatever mix you use be super fresh. If something looks good at the fish market that day, then throw it in!

12 littleneck clams or 1 pound (454 g) cockles

6 cups (1.4 L) water

¼ teaspoon salt, plus more to taste

¼ pound (113 g) cuttlefish, washed and cut into ¼-inch (6 mm) rings, tentacles halved

12 mussels, rinsed, scrubbed, and beards removed

¼ pound (113 g) medium shrimp, washed, peeled, and deveined, tails removed, and cut into 1-inch (2.5 cm) pieces

¼ pound (113 g) bay scallops, washed

3 tablespoons (45 ml) extra-virgin olive oil

1 small onion, cut into ¼-inch (6 mm) dice

1 clove garlic, minced

2 cups (370 g) carnaroli or Arborio rice

Black pepper, to taste

Nonna Rosa Says

Fresh fish is the name of the game. You can substitute any of the seafood in this recipe with whatever is readily available at your local market.

1. Tap each of the clams and discard any that sound hollow. Wash the clams under cold running water to remove any sand.

2. Put a large saucepan over high heat. Add the water and ¼ teaspoon of salt and bring to a boil. Drop in the cuttlefish and cook, covered, for 20 minutes.

3. While the cuttlefish cooks, put a medium skillet over high heat and add the clams and mussels. Cover and steam until the clams and mussels have opened, 6 to 7 minutes. Discard any clams or mussels that did not open. Separate the fruit from all the shells and discard the shells. Reserve the water from the mussels and clams in a glass.

4. Scoop out the cuttlefish with a slotted spoon and transfer to a bowl. Drop the shrimp and scallops into the water and cook for 5 to 6 minutes. Remove with a slotted spoon and transfer to the bowl with the cuttlefish. Add the reserved water from the clams and mussels to the cooking water, first pouring it through a cheesecloth into a bowl to remove any grit. Reserve the water to cook the risotto.

5. Heat the olive oil in a 6-quart (5.7 L) stockpot over medium heat. Add the onion and garlic, and cook and stir until the garlic is golden, about 5 minutes. Stir in the rice with a wooden spoon and toast for 1 minute, stirring and coating the rice in the oil.

6. Begin adding the reserved fish stock in ¼-cup (60 ml) increments, stirring constantly, until the stock is absorbed. Continue adding the stock as soon as it is absorbed by the rice. After about 10 minutes of stirring, add in the cuttlefish, shrimp, scallops, and shelled clams and mussels. Continue stirring and adding broth until the rice is al dente, 10 to 15 more minutes. Taste for seasoning and add more salt and black pepper to taste. Serve immediately.

SECOND COURSE

Secondi

EGGPLANT PARMIGIANA, PUGLIESE-STYLE

Parmigiana di Melanzane alla Pugliese

PREP TIME: 20 MINUTES • COOK TIME: 1 HOUR 11 MINUTES • YIELD: 6 TO 8 SERVINGS

Every family seems to have an eggplant *Parmigiana* recipe that is almost an heirloom to them. Nonna Romana's famous Parmigiana has always been able to bring our family together at a moment's notice, because no one wants to miss the spectacular event. Layers of minty and cheesy, battered and fried eggplant come together with slightly sweet mortadella and creamy mozzarella for a powerhouse baked dish that hits that Italian comfort-food spot every time.

SAUCE

2 tablespoons (30 ml) extra-virgin
    olive oil

1 small onion, cut into ¼-inch
    (6 mm) dice

1 can (28 ounces, or 794 g) crushed
    tomatoes

4 or 5 fresh basil leaves, torn

½ teaspoon salt

PARMIGIANA

1½ cups (180 g) 00 or all-purpose flour

1¼ cups (150 g) grated Parmigiano-
    Reggiano cheese, plus 6 tablespoons
    (48 g) for sprinkling

6 cloves garlic, minced

½ cup (48 g) finely minced fresh mint

1 teaspoon salt

2 eggs, beaten

1½ cups (350 ml) plus 2 tablespoons
    (30 ml) water

1 to 2 large eggplant

Olive oil, for frying (or any frying oil
    you like)

12 ounces (340 g) fresh mozzarella,
    shredded

12 slices mortadella

1. **To make the sauce:** Heat the extra-virgin olive oil in a large saucepan over medium heat. Add the onion and cook and stir until translucent, 5 to 7 minutes.

2. Add the tomatoes, basil, and salt, and reduce the heat to low. Cook for 15 minutes, stirring occasionally with a wooden spoon. Remove from the heat and set aside. (This sauce does not require much cooking because it will be baked in the oven.)

3. **To make the Parmigiana:** In a large mixing bowl, combine the flour and 1¼ cups (150 g) of Parmigiano-Reggiano cheese with the garlic, mint, salt, eggs, and water. Whisk until you have a smooth batter. Set aside.

4. Peel the eggplant and slice them lengthwise, ¼ inch (6 mm) thick. You may also use a mandoline for greater precision. You will need about 20 large slices from the center of the eggplant. Use any of the smaller pieces to patch holes at the end if necessary.

5. Heat the frying oil, about 1½ inches (4 cm), in a large heavy-bottomed skillet over medium-high heat.

6. Dip the eggplant into the batter, allow the excess to drip off for a few seconds, and fry in batches until golden brown, 2 to 3 minutes per batch. Transfer to a paper towel–lined plate to drain.

7. Preheat the oven to 400°F (200°C).

continued

8. Spread about 1 cup (255 g) of the sauce on the bottom of a high-sided 11 × 8-inch (28 × 20 cm) baking pan.

9. Place a layer of the eggplant slices over the sauce. You should need about 4 slices per layer. Cut the pieces to fit the pan if necessary. Spoon another light layer of tomato sauce over each of the eggplant slices. Add about one-quarter of the shredded mozzarella and top with 2 tablespoons (16 g) of Parmigiano-Reggiano. Cover the cheese with a layer of 4 slices of mortadella.

10. Next, place another layer of eggplant slices. Spread another light layer of sauce and top with one-quarter of the mozzarella and 2 tablespoons (16 g) of Parmigiano-Reggiano. Add 4 mortadella slices. Repeat the process of layering the eggplant, sauce, cheeses, and mortadella once more.

11. Add one final layer of eggplant. Patch up any holes with either cut pieces of the eggplant or smaller pieces. Spread the rest of the sauce over the eggplant and sprinkle with the remaining 2 tablespoons (16 g) of Parmigiano-Reggiano.

12. Bake uncovered for 30 minutes. Sprinkle with the remaining quarter of mozzarella. Bake for 10 more minutes, until the sauce and cheese are bubbling.

13. Remove from the oven and let rest for 10 to 15 minutes before cutting.

CHICKEN IN LEMON SAUCE

Scallopine di Pollo al Limone

PREP TIME: 5 MINUTES • COOK TIME: 28 MINUTES • YIELD: 4 SERVINGS

This chicken in lemon sauce is a great way to use any leftover chicken cutlets (if such a thing even exists!), and it makes an easy, flavorful dinner that everyone will love. Nonna Nina has been making this dish for years, and it is highly requested by her family for the holidays and any family gathering.

All-purpose flour, for dredging

Salt and black pepper, to taste

1 cup (108 g) plain bread crumbs

1 tablespoon (8 g) grated Parmigiano-
Reggiano cheese

2 eggs, beaten

1 pound (454 g) chicken cutlets,
thinly sliced

Olive oil, for frying (or any frying oil
you like)

Butter, for greasing

1 cup (235 ml) chicken broth

½ cup (120 ml) dry white wine, such
as Pinot Grigio or Sauvignon Blanc

Juice of 1 lemon

1. Spread the flour in a shallow dish and season with salt and pepper.

2. In another shallow dish, combine the bread crumbs and cheese.

3. Add the beaten eggs to a shallow bowl and place the 3 bowls next to each other.

4. Dredge each of the cutlets in the flour, then dip into the egg, and finally coat in the bread crumbs. Transfer to a plate.

5. Heat the frying oil, about 1½ inches (4 cm), in a large heavy-bottomed skillet over medium-high heat. Fry the cutlets until golden brown on both sides, 1 to 2 minutes per side.

6. Preheat the oven to 350°F (175°C). Butter a 13 × 9-inch (33 × 23 cm) baking pan and arrange the cutlets in the pan.

7. Pour the chicken broth, wine, and lemon juice into the pan. Cover with aluminum foil and bake for 10 minutes. Uncover and flip the cutlets over, exposing the moist side. Bake uncovered for an additional 10 minutes. Spoon the pan sauce over the top and serve.

NONNA RINA PESCE'S

EGGPLANT ROLLATINI

Rollatini di Melanzane

PREP TIME: 20 MINUTES • COOK TIME: 1 HOUR • YIELD: 4 TO 6 SERVINGS

My Zia Rina's eggplant *rollatini* are a summertime favorite whenever I'm visiting with her. The fried eggplant in these little bundles takes on a buttery quality, and her simple mozzarella and bread crumb stuffing is a breeze to prepare.

SAUCE

2 tablespoons (30 ml) extra-virgin olive oil

1 small onion, cut into ¼-inch (6 mm) dice

1 can (28 ounces, or 794 g) crushed tomatoes

1 tablespoon (4 g) minced fresh parsley

½ teaspoon salt

ROLLATINI

1 medium eggplant

Olive oil, for frying (or any frying oil you like)

¾ cup (90 g) plus 2 tablespoons (16 g) grated Parmigiano-Reggiano cheese, divided

½ cup (54 g) plain bread crumbs

2 cloves garlic, minced

2 tablespoons (8 g) minced fresh parsley

1 tablespoon (6 g) minced fresh mint

8 ounces (227 g) fresh mozzarella, cut into ½-inch (13 mm) cubes

2 eggs, beaten

2 tablespoons (30 ml) extra-virgin olive oil

1. **To make the sauce:** Heat the olive oil in a large saucepan over medium heat. Add the onion and cook and stir until translucent, 5 to 7 minutes.

2. Add the tomatoes, parsley, and salt, and reduce the heat to low. Cook for 15 minutes, stirring occasionally with a wooden spoon. Remove from the heat and set aside. (This sauce does not require much cooking because it will be baked in the oven.)

3. **To make the rollatini:** Peel and vertically slice the eggplant into ¼-inch (6 mm) thick slices.

4. Heat the frying oil, about 1½ inches (4 cm), in a large heavy-bottomed skillet over medium-high heat. Fry the eggplant in batches until golden brown and pliable, 2 to 3 minutes. Transfer to a paper towel–lined plate to drain.

5. Preheat the oven to 375°F (190°C).

6. In a large mixing bowl, combine ¾ cup (90 g) of the Parmigiano-Reggiano, bread crumbs, garlic, parsley, mint, mozzarella, eggs, and olive oil. Mix well to combine.

7. Add about half the sauce to the bottom of a 13 × 9-inch (33 × 23 cm) baking pan.

8. Add about 1 tablespoon (15 g) of the stuffing to one end of each eggplant slice. Roll the slices tightly. Place seam-side down in the baking pan in 3 rows. Spoon the other half of the sauce over all the rollatini and sprinkle with the remaining 2 tablespoons (16 g) of Parmigiano-Reggiano. Bake for 30 minutes.

"I can't just make one pot of food for my family; I make enough for the whole block."

"It's a sin!" Nonna Theresa chastises when I tell her I can't possibly have another cookie. "Just one more," she says in a soft, sweet tone that makes it impossible to say no. Before I know it, several more appear on my plate, along with a refilled cup of coffee.

"When I was growing up in South Philly, people were always coming in and out of my house, and the first thing you would do is give them coffee and a piece of cake. I don't know how to be any other way," she says, with a big bright smile. Her smile is warm and welcoming. In fact it's impossible to be in a bad mood around Theresa, a petite, fiery redhead with a heart of gold. She buzzes about her kitchen, smiling as she fills another plate of food for me. It's clear that Theresa is at her happiest when she's cooking for people. "I just love to feed people. I'm the kind of person who gives things away. I can't just make one pot of food for my family; I make enough for the whole block. Life is nicer when you're that way; everyone knows to come over and have some coffee, and they always leave with something."

And she's not exaggerating. Theresa's doorbell rings several times during our visit, and each person is welcomed in and served a plate of her specialties.

"My personal cooking style isn't gourmet; it's just good, down-to-earth food! I concentrate on good, fresh ingredients and everyone loves it." Theresa's culinary journey didn't quite begin at an early age. She was born in South Philadelphia to immigrant parents from Reggio Calabria, and Theresa's mother was the queen of the kitchen during her formative years. "I wasn't allowed to cook when I was little. My father died when I was very young, and my mother would spend days working in a cigar factory, so she would come home from work and cook. Sometimes she would let me make a salad."

At nineteen, Nonna Theresa married her husband, Hank, whom she met when she was fourteen. Early on in their sixty-year marriage, she was handed a tool that really helped her shape her cooking skills. She pulls a small spiral notebook from a kitchen cabinet and opens it up to a page that says "Ravioli" in perfect cursive. "My mother-in-law was a great cook. When I got married, she gave me a handwritten book full of all her son's favorite recipes because she wanted to make sure her son ate well!" I laugh as I imagine this quintessential Italian mamma unable to bear the thought of her son having even one subpar meal.

In 1957, Theresa and her husband settled in southern New Jersey and went to work side by side at their very own butchery, G and M Super Market in Glendora, where they raised their three children and still live today. They were both young, ambitious, and passionate about bringing quality food to other Italian families. "Italian people care about good food above everything else. Food brings us all together and makes us a family."

Theresa's grandchildren come by during my visit, and I can see how much she loves being a nonna. "I never knew my nonna, but to me a nonna is someone who lives for her grandkids. I never say no; why should I? I leave that to their parents." As I watch them gather around her, I'm pretty sure her six grandchildren and one great-granddaughter wouldn't have it any other way!

SAUSAGE AND PEPPERS

Peperoni e Salsiccia

PREP TIME: 5 MINUTES • COOK TIME: 34 MINUTES • YIELD: 4 SERVINGS

Nonna Theresa's sausage and peppers is her simple go-to comfort food that can easily be whipped up in large quantities for her big family. Of course, this is a natural dish for Nonna Theresa, as she and her husband have owned a deli in southern New Jersey for many years and fresh sausage is available to her every day. This is wonderful on its own or on crusty Italian rolls as a sandwich.

4 tablespoons (60 ml) extra-virgin olive oil, divided

1 pound (454 g) Italian sweet and hot sausage links

1 large onion, quartered and sliced ⅛-inch (3 mm) thick

2 red bell peppers, seeded and cut into ¼-inch (6 mm) strips

2 yellow bell peppers, seeded and cut into ¼-inch (6 mm) strips

Salt and black pepper, to taste

¼ cup (60 ml) dry white wine, such as Pinot Grigio or Sauvignon Blanc

½ cup (120 ml) chicken stock

1. Heat 2 tablespoons (30 ml) of olive oil in a large heavy-bottomed skillet or a cast-iron pan over medium heat. Add the sausage and brown on all sides, 8 to 10 minutes. Remove the sausage from the pan with a slotted spoon and transfer to a cutting board. Slice into 2-inch (5 cm) chunks. Set aside.

2. Raise the heat to high. Add the remaining 2 tablespoons (30 ml) of olive oil to the pan along with the onion and peppers, and cook and stir until soft, about 20 minutes. Season with salt and black pepper.

3. Add the wine, chicken stock, and browned sausage to the pan. Cook until you can no longer smell the alcohol, 4 to 5 minutes. Serve.

Nonna Theresa Says

In case you double or triple this recipe, remember the peppers need their space! Make sure you use a large enough pan to sauté the peppers, or they won't cook correctly.

SEAFOOD BEATRICE

Zuppa di Pesce alla Beatrice

PREP TIME: 2 TO 4 HOURS • COOK TIME: 9 MINUTES • YIELD: 2 SERVINGS

If you're looking for an elegant entrée that comes together in minutes, then look no further than this incredibly easy *zuppa di pesce*. This was a favorite at Nonna Vivian's family restaurant in New York City, and it uses simple ingredients that really let the seafood shine. Serve it with chunks of crusty bread to soak up all of that magical seafood broth.

½ pound (227 g) sea scallops, washed

½ pound (227 g) calamari, washed and cleaned, bodies cut into ½-inch (13 mm) rings, tentacles left whole

8 littleneck clams, washed

8 mussels, rinsed, scrubbed, and beards removed

12 large shrimp, washed, peeled, and deveined

½ cup (120 ml) extra-virgin olive oil

½ cup (120 ml) dry white wine, such as Pinot Grigio or Sauvignon Blanc

3 cloves garlic, minced

¼ cup (16 g) minced fresh parsley

Juice of 3 lemons

Black pepper, to taste

1. Place all the cleaned seafood in a large mixing bowl. Add the olive oil, wine, garlic, parsley, lemon juice, and black pepper to taste and toss well. Cover the bowl with plastic wrap and marinate in the refrigerator for 2 to 4 hours.

2. Put a medium skillet over high heat and add all the marinated seafood and broth.

3. Cover the skillet and cook, stirring occasionally. Once the clams and mussels open, 6 to 7 minutes, uncover and cook for 1 to 2 minutes more.

4. Discard any clams or mussels that did not open. Serve immediately with crusty bread.

Nonna Vivian Says

To make this a red sauce, I add about 1 cup (255 g) of crushed tomatoes to the marinade.

"Sicilian cooking is all about layering flavors that contradict each other. Sweet and salty and crunchy. That's Sicily."

"There is only once in your lifetime that fortune knocks at your door, and if you are able to understand and embrace it, then you will succeed." I immediately recognize the old Italian proverb that Nonna Liliana Barone has translated for me with her own personal flair.

In many ways, Nonna Liliana is the quintessential voluptuous Italian woman, with a chic blonde bob and natural Sicilian charisma that makes me forget we barely know each other—a skill that would later serve her all too well in business.

Nonna Liliana came to the United States from Sicily when she was just sixteen, and by age twenty-two she was a wife, mother, and a businesswoman full of hope and ambition. "I was always a city girl. I was born in Palermo, so life was a bit different than in the country. I grew up in a family with seven siblings. I loved having a big family. My mother had a long table, and she would always set the table beautifully. I guess that's where my love for the table came from," she says.

"Cooking brings a lot of happiness to me. When I know company is coming, I put everything I have into it and I really enjoy sharing the food with everyone." That rings especially true when company includes Nonna Liliana's three children and eight grandchildren.

The flavors of Sicily are ever present in Nonna Liliana's kitchen. Crisp bread crumbs are paired with sweet raisins, earthy pine nuts, and salty anchovies. "Sicilian cooking is very simple but complex at the same time. It's all about layering flavors that contradict each other. Sweet and salty and crunchy. That's Sicily," she says. As I listen to her speak with such reverence about her passions for food, cooking, and family, I can't help but think about how driven she was as a businesswoman too. "I used to think I was weak, but I wasn't. Every girl has a sense of insecurity and slowly it disappears," she says confidently.

Before our meeting, all I knew of Nonna Liliana was that she was the *bomboniera* (party favor) queen of Bensonhurst. In 1972, she started a tremendously successful Italian wedding center, *La Casa Della Bomboniera*, specializing in party favors imported from Italy. She later also opened *Il Telaio*, which created custom wedding *trousseaus* (a *trousseau* was part of an Italian bride's dowry and included linens, tablecloths, bedclothes, undergarments, and nightgowns).

I vividly remember Liliana's ornate storefront in my old neighborhood on 18th Avenue and 72nd Street. Her business represented an era of Italy in America. A part of me begins to long for the old neighborhood of Nonna Liliana's time, when life was simpler and being traditional didn't take as much effort as it does today.

"I think in an Italian family it's incredibly important to sit down at a table every single night. It gives the warmth and the connection. A table is a place where you regroup, rewind, and express your feelings to one another. The ultimate expression of love!"

PALERMO-STYLE VEAL SKEWERS

Spiedini Palermitani

PREP TIME: 15 MINUTES • COOK TIME: 35 MINUTES • YIELD: 4 SERVINGS

The word *spiedini* translates to "skewers," or in this case, food that is cooked on skewers. Nonna Liliana recreates this famous *Palermitano* street food by filling tender, pounded veal with a savory-and-sweet bread crumb mixture that will explode in your mouth.

1 tablespoon (9 g) pinoli (pine nuts)

1½ teaspoons dried currants or raisins

¼ cup (60 ml) tepid water

¼ cup (30 g) grated Pecorino Romano cheese

1 cup (108 g) plain bread crumbs, plus more for sprinkling

2 tablespoons (8 g) minced fresh parsley

½ teaspoon sugar

¼ cup (60 ml) extra-virgin olive oil, plus more for brushing

2 large onions, 1 cut into ¼-inch (6 mm) dice plus 1 quartered and cut into 2-inch (5 cm) wedges to use on the skewers

25 bay leaves

1 pound (454 g) veal scallopini, pounded and cut into 4 × 2-inch (10 × 5 cm) fillets

2 ounces (57 g) provolone cheese, cut into ½-inch (13 mm) cubes

1. Soak 3 or 4 wooden skewers in water for at least 15 minutes to prevent burning. Soak the pinoli and currants in the tepid water in a glass for 10 minutes.

2. In a large mixing bowl, combine the Pecorino, bread crumbs, and parsley.

3. Drain the pinoli and currants and add them to a bowl along with the sugar. Toss to coat.

4. Heat the olive oil in a large sauté pan over medium heat. Add the diced onion and 2 or 3 of the bay leaves, and cook, stirring with a wooden spoon, until soft and golden, 13 to 15 minutes. Add the bread crumb mixture to the pan and cook for 1 to 2 minutes, just until all the oil has been absorbed by the bread crumbs. Remove from the heat.

5. Preheat the oven to 375°F (190°C). Line a 13 × 9-inch (33 × 23 cm) baking pan with parchment paper.

6. Fill each fillet of meat with about 1 tablespoon (15 g) of the bread crumb mixture, top with 1 or 2 cubes of the provolone, and roll lengthwise.

7. Prepare the wooden skewers by alternating an onion wedge, a bay leaf, and a veal roll, ending with a bay leaf and an onion wedge. You should be able to fit 6 veal rolls on each skewer.

8. Brush the veal rolls with extra-virgin olive oil and sprinkle with plain bread crumbs on all sides. Place the skewers in the baking pan and bake for 30 minutes.

9. Turn on the broiler to high and broil for 4 to 5 minutes, or until golden brown.

GRILLED SWORDFISH WITH TOMATOES AND OLIVES

Pesce Spada alla Pinucch'

PREP TIME: 5 MINUTES • COOK TIME: 33 MINUTES • YIELD: 4 SERVINGS

In Sicily, you will almost always find swordfish on the menu at any restaurant. My favorite way to cook this meaty fish is on the grill, and Nonna Giuseppa whips up a quick and tasty version featuring all the flavors of Sicily that's perfect for summertime cooking.

3 tablespoons (45 ml) extra-virgin olive oil, plus more for brushing

3 cloves garlic, crushed

1 cup (150 g) cherry tomatoes, halved

Dash salt, plus more to taste

¼ cup (60 ml) dry white wine, such as Pinot Grigio or Sauvignon Blanc

¼ cup (60 ml) water

Zest of 1 lemon

½ cup (96 g) pitted green olives

¼ cup (48 g) pitted Gaeta or Kalamata olives

½ teaspoon dried oregano

¼ teaspoon red pepper flakes

2 tablespoons (8 g) coarsely chopped fennel sprigs

Black pepper, to taste

4 swordfish fillets (6 to 7 ounces, or 170 to 198 g, each), 1 inch (2.5 cm) thick

1. Heat the olive oil in a medium heavy-bottomed skillet over medium heat. Add the garlic and cook for 1 minute. Add the tomatoes and a dash of salt, and cook and stir until the tomatoes begin to break down, 4 to 5 minutes. Add the wine and water and cook for 1 to 2 minutes.

2. Add the lemon zest, olives, oregano, red pepper flakes, and fennel sprigs, and cook for an additional 4 to 5 minutes. Season with salt and black pepper. Remove from the heat and set aside.

3. Season the swordfish with salt and black pepper on both sides.

4. Brush a two-burner grill pan with olive oil and place over high heat. Wait for the grill to get very hot and then add the swordfish fillets, 2 at a time. Grill for 4 to 5 minutes per side, until you have nice visible grill marks.

5. Spoon the sauce over each fillet and serve immediately.

STUFFED PEPPERS

Peperoni Ripieni

PREP TIME: 15 MINUTES • COOK TIME: 51 MINUTES • YIELD: 5 SERVINGS

Nonna Giulia stuffs her peppers with a meat and bread crumb mixture, and then simmers them slowly in a light tomato sauce. The sauce absorbs the juices of the meat and it blends beautifully with the tomatoes and peppers. The capers add a super-savory kick without overpowering.

SAUCE

¼ cup (60 ml) extra-virgin olive oil

1 medium onion, cut into ¼-inch (6 mm) dice

3 cloves garlic, minced

2 cans (28 ounces, or 794 g, each) crushed tomatoes

1 teaspoon salt

1 tablespoon (4 g) minced fresh parsley

PEPPERS

5 yellow bell peppers

5 tablespoons (75 ml) extra-virgin olive oil, divided

1 pound (454 g) ground beef

Dash salt

1 cup (120 g) grated Pecorino Romano cheese

½ cup (54 g) plain bread crumbs

5 cloves garlic, minced

1½ tablespoons (14 g) baby capers

3 eggs, beaten

Milk, as needed

Nonna Giulia Says

The extra sauce may also be served with pasta, making this a complete meal!

1. **To make the sauce:** Heat the olive oil in a 5-quart (4.7 L) stockpot, 10 inches (25 cm) in diameter, over medium heat. Add the onion and garlic, and cook and stir until the onion is soft and the garlic is golden, 5 to 6 minutes.

2. Add the tomatoes, salt, and parsley, and give the pot a good stir with a wooden spoon. Reduce the heat to low and cover the pot. Prepare the stuffing for the peppers while the sauce simmers.

3. **To make the peppers:** Cut the tops off of the peppers and remove the seeds and membranes. Discard. Rinse out the peppers to wash away any hidden seeds.

4. Heat 1 tablespoon (15 ml) of the olive oil in a medium heavy-bottomed skillet over medium-high heat. Add the meat and a dash of salt, and cook, breaking up the meat with a wooden spoon, until it is nicely browned, 5 to 6 minutes. Drain off any fat and set aside.

5. In a mixing bowl, combine the cheese, bread crumbs, garlic, capers, eggs, and browned meat. Mix well to blend. If the mixture seems dry, add a splash of milk.

6. Fill all the peppers with the stuffing until about ½ inch (13 mm) from the top. Place all of the peppers into the pot of sauce (don't worry if they tip over sideways a little). Spoon some of the sauce over the stuffing. Raise the heat to medium, cover the pot, and cook until the peppers are tender and the filling is cooked through, 35 to 40 minutes.

GRILLED CRUSTED OCTOPUS

Polpo con Mollica

PREP TIME: 5 MINUTES • COOK TIME: 12 MINUTES • YIELD: 4 TO 6 SERVINGS

Every year, Nonna Romana's hometown of Mola di Bari prepares for a three-day octopus feast called *La Sagra del Polpo*, where the area's special tenderized octopi are prepared in every way you can imagine and sold as delicious street food. My favorite variation is done on the barbecue after the octopus has been dipped in a delicious bread crumb mixture. You know it's perfectly grilled when the tentacles come out slightly charred and crispy. Aim for each octopus to be 5 to 6 ounces (142 to 170 g). If you cannot find the smaller variety of octopus, you may use a larger variety and cut it into pieces of two or three tentacles each, but not too big of pieces or it will be tough.

1 cup (108 g) plain bread crumbs

¼ cup (30 g) grated Parmigiano-
  Reggiano cheese

3 cloves garlic, minced

2 tablespoons (8 g) minced fresh
  parsley

Salt and black pepper, to taste

½ cup (120 ml) extra-virgin olive oil

2 pounds (907 g) tenderized octopus,
  washed and patted dry

Lemon wedges, for serving

1. In a mixing bowl, combine the bread crumbs, cheese, garlic, and parsley. Stir to blend. Season with salt and black pepper.

2. In another mixing bowl, add the olive oil.

3. Preheat a grill until it is very hot, about 500°F (250°C).

4. Dip each octopus into the oil and then coat the octopus in the bread crumb mixture until it is evenly coated. Immediately place each octopus on the grill, tentacle-side down, and cook until the tentacles have a nice char on them, 10 to 12 minutes. Turn frequently.

5. Serve immediately with a squirt of fresh lemon juice.

Nonna Romana Says

The octopus must go directly onto the grill as soon as it's breaded or the breading will turn to mush, so don't bread all of the octopi at once.

OVEN-BRAISED COD WITH SCALLIONS AND OLIVES

Merluzzo al Forno con Cipolle e Olive

PREP TIME: 5 MINUTES • COOK TIME: 15 MINUTES • YIELD: 4 SERVINGS

Nonna Romana has been making this tasty cod for years, and has converted many super-picky non-fish eaters. The flavors of the olives, scallions, and tomatoes soak into the mild fish like a dream, and it's so easy to prep, it's a perfect weeknight meal for busy families.

4 fresh cod fillets (about 6 ounces, or 170 g, each)

10 cherry tomatoes, halved

10 pitted Gaeta or Kalamata olives, halved

4 scallions, cut into 3-inch (7.5 cm) pieces (white and green parts)

½ cup (120 ml) water

½ cup (120 ml) dry white wine, such as Pinot Grigio or Sauvignon Blanc

2 tablespoons (30 ml) extra-virgin olive oil

Salt and black pepper, to taste

1. Preheat the oven to 400°F (200°C).

2. Place the fillets in a 13 × 9-inch (33 × 23 cm) baking pan. Add the cherry tomatoes and olives around the fillets, and add a few tomatoes on top of the fillets as well.

3. Place the scallions on top of the fillets in an X-shape.

4. Pour the water and wine into the pan and drizzle the olive oil on top of the cod. Season with salt and black pepper.

5. Bake for 15 to 20 minutes, until the cod flakes with a fork.

NONNA ANTOINETTE CAPODICCI'S

VEAL STEW IN A POLENTA BOWL

Spezzatino di Vitello con Polenta

PREP TIME: 10 MINUTES • COOK TIME: 1 HOUR 2 MINUTES • YIELD: 4 TO 6 SERVINGS

On a cold winter's day, Nonna Antoinette's veal stew warms you up like a blanket! Super-tender chunks of veal and slightly sweet peas come together in a luscious combination. The stew soaks into the polenta bowl, making every bite burst with flavor.

¼ cup (60 ml) extra-virgin olive oil

2 medium carrots, cut into ¼-inch (6 mm) dice

1 large onion, cut into ¼-inch (6 mm) dice

2 stalks celery, cut into ¼-inch (6 mm) dice

2 pounds (907 g) veal shoulder, cut into 1-inch (2.5 cm) cubes

All-purpose flour, for dredging

1 cup (235 ml) dry white wine, such as Pinot Grigio or Sauvignon Blanc

4 cups (950 ml) chicken broth

16 ounces (454 g) frozen peas

Salt and black pepper, to taste

1½ cups (240 g) polenta

1. Heat the olive oil in a 5-quart (4.7 L) heavy-bottomed stockpot or a Dutch oven over medium heat. Add the carrots, onion, and celery, and cook and stir until soft, 5 to 7 minutes.

2. Dredge the veal cubes in the flour, add to the pot, and brown the meat for about 5 minutes. Add the wine and chicken broth, and scrape up any bits stuck to the bottom of the pan. Raise the heat to medium-high and cook until you can no longer smell the alcohol, 4 to 5 minutes.

3. Reduce the heat to a simmer, cover the pot, and cook for 30 to 35 minutes, stirring frequently with a wooden spoon.

4. Stir in the peas. Continue to cook, covered, for 10 to 15 more minutes. Season with salt and black pepper.

5. Cook the polenta according to the package instructions. With a spoon, spread a layer of polenta around a soup bowl. Ladle in the stew and serve.

BARESE-STYLE STUFFED MEATLOAF

Polpettone Barese

PREP TIME: 20 MINUTES • COOK TIME: 1 HOUR 22 MINUTES • YIELD: 4 TO 6 SERVINGS

This cheese-stuffed meatloaf is the best you'll ever have, and the perfect one-pan dish for a chilly night. Just be sure and make the valley nice and deep when you place the filling inside or it will open up in the oven!

SAUCE

3 tablespoons (45 ml) extra-virgin olive oil

1 medium onion, cut into ¼-inch (6 mm) dice

1 can (28 ounces, or 794 g) crushed tomatoes

½ teaspoon salt

MEATLOAF

2 pounds (907 g) ground beef

3 cloves garlic, shaved

½ cup (54 g) plain bread crumbs

1 cup (120 g) grated Pecorino Romano cheese, plus more for sprinkling

6 eggs

3 tablespoons (45 ml) extra-virgin olive oil

½ teaspoon salt, plus more to taste

¼ teaspoon black pepper, plus more to taste

¼ pound (113 g) sliced mortadella

4 ounces (113 g) sharp provolone, cut into matchsticks

10 to 12 sprigs fresh parsley

3 medium potatoes, cut into wedges and placed in a bowl of water to prevent darkening

¾ cup (180 ml) water

1. **To make the sauce:** Heat the olive oil in a 3-quart (2.8 L) saucepan over medium heat. Add the onion and cook until it is translucent, 5 to 7 minutes.

2. Add the tomatoes and salt. Decrease the heat to low and cook for an additional 15 minutes, stirring occasionally with a wooden spoon. Remove from the heat and set aside.

3. **To make the meatloaf:** In a large mixing bowl, combine the ground beef, garlic, bread crumbs, Pecorino, eggs, olive oil, salt, black pepper, and 5 tablespoons (80 g) of the tomato sauce. Mix everything until well blended.

4. Spread a thin layer of tomato sauce in a 15 × 10-inch (38 × 25 cm) baking pan. Transfer the meat mixture to the baking pan and shape it into a log with a deep valley in the center.

5. Place the slices of the mortadella at the center of the valley followed by the provolone and several sprigs of the parsley.

6. With your hands, push the meat from either side toward the center to cover the mortadella and provolone.

7. Add the potato wedges to the sides of the meatloaf. With a small spoon, drizzle the potatoes with sauce. Spread any remaining sauce over the meatloaf.

8. Sprinkle the meatloaf and potatoes with more Pecorino and black pepper.

9. Pour the water into the side of the pan and bake for 1 hour, or until an inserted meat thermometer registers 160°F (71°C).

WHOLE STUFFED BRANZINO BAKED IN FOIL

Branzino in Cartoccio

PREP TIME: 10 MINUTES • COOK TIME: 25 MINUTES • YIELD: 4 TO 6 SERVINGS

Ever since I was a little girl, I have been able to fillet a whole fish by myself. (What do you want from me? I'm from a fishing village!) Nonna Romana and Zia Chiara pushed me to eat what they would refer to as "brain food" quite regularly. Cooking a fish whole is not only super easy, but it's also almost impossible to overcook. Why? Because everything from the skin to the bones adds moisture, and stuffing it with lemon zest and herbs packs in the flavor to the max. This recipe is very forgiving, so feel free to substitute the herbs and even the fish for varieties you enjoy.

2 whole branzini (about 1½ pounds, or 680 g, each), washed, cleaned, and gutted

2 tablespoons (30 ml) extra-virgin olive oil, plus more for brushing and drizzling

4 sprigs fresh rosemary

4 cloves garlic, sliced

6 sprigs fresh parsley

2 lemons, sliced

Salt and black pepper, to taste

Lemon wedges, for serving

1. Preheat the oven to 400°F (200°C). Prepare 2 pieces of aluminum foil. Each piece should be large enough to hold a fish, as well as be able to be closed up to make a pouch.

2. Brush each fish with some olive oil. Make sure there is enough oil to lubricate the fish so it does not stick to the foil. Lay each fish down on a piece of prepared foil.

3. Place 1 of the rosemary sprigs in the body of each fish and insert the remaining sprigs through each mouth. Insert 2 cloves of the sliced garlic and 3 of the parsley sprigs into each fish. Add the lemon slices and position them so they peek out slightly.

4. Drizzle 1 tablespoon (15 ml) of olive oil over each fish. Season the insides of the fish with salt and black pepper. Close up the foil to make a pouch and place the pouches on a baking sheet. Bake for 25 to 30 minutes, until the fish flakes with a fork.

5. To fillet the fish, run a thin-bladed knife along the backbone behind the head, cutting toward the tail. Gently lift up the top fillet with the knife or a fish spatula and transfer to a plate.

6. Using the knife, lift out the spine and separate it. Discard the spine and attached head. Use the knife to pick out any remaining small bones.

7. Drizzle with some extra-virgin olive oil and a fresh squirt of lemon juice and serve!

"When life gives you burnt lasagna, make some spaghetti with the extra sauce and move on!"

One of the first ladies to embark on the *Cooking with Nonna* adventure with me was Nonna Anna Buonsante from Mola di Bari, Italy, and over the years I have come to think of her as a member of my own family.

"I'm always happy! I'm Italian!" Anna says to me with a wave of her hand that makes her glittery nail polish sparkle in the sunlight. In fact, everything about Nonna Anna sparkles. At first glance, there's very little about her that seems nonna-esque. Clad in rhinestone leggings and crimped hair, you would never believe she's a mother of five and a grandmother of six, but her heart, on the other hand, is 100 percent nonna.

Almost all of Anna's children are in the food business and own several pizzerias across Pennsylvania. Many of them make recipes inspired by Anna's cooking when they were growing up. "You have to have heart when you cook; otherwise nothing comes out good," she says. She reminds her children constantly about her own childhood in Italy. "My father was a farmer in Mola di Bari. When it was

the season of potatoes, we had to eat potatoes every day. A lot of the things you would call *cucina povera* (poor people's food), but we were happy."

As I watch Anna juggle cooking for her children and grandchildren—who all seem to have different requests for the day's meal—I'm stunned that her bright smile never seems to leave her face. Given how long I have known her, I guess it shouldn't be that surprising.

Besides the incredible dishes she crafts, the most beautiful thing about Nonna Anna is her unbreakable spirit. Even when her marriage of nearly forty years ended, her happiness did not. With an ever-present smile on her face, Anna believes that we learn more in life from the mistakes we make, and this applies to learning to cook too. "Mistakes are important, in life and in cooking. The first time I made meatballs I only put meat in the meatballs and nothing else. They were so hard that my brother-in-law said he was going to use them to play ping-pong! But I learned!" I couldn't help laughing as I recalled my own culinary mishaps, and trust me, there have been a few.

As I help Anna clean up and we fold her sunny yellow tablecloth, she tells me something I'll never forget. "Don't be afraid in life. I went through a lot but I was never afraid. There will be days where everything goes wrong, but you just have to say to yourself that tomorrow will be better. When you have company coming and life gives you burnt lasagna, make some spaghetti with the extra sauce and move on!"

STUFFED EGGPLANT

Melanzane Ripiene

PREP TIME: 20 MINUTES • COOK TIME: 1 HOUR 42 MINUTES • YIELD: 4 SERVINGS

When meat was scarce in Puglia, eggplant provided a hearty, savory substitute for many families. These eggplant halves filled with cheese and bread are perfect for vegetarians, and Nonna Anna always serves them to her family during Lent and on most Friday nights.

SAUCE

2 tablespoons (30 ml) extra-virgin olive oil

1 small onion, cut into ¼-inch (6 mm) dice

2 cloves garlic, minced

1 can (28 ounces, or 794 g) crushed tomatoes

1 tablespoon (4 g) minced fresh parsley

½ teaspoon salt

EGGPLANT

4 russet potatoes

2 medium eggplant

¾ cup (180 ml) extra-virgin olive oil, plus more for drizzling

1 cup (120 g) plus 2 tablespoons (16 g) grated Parmigiano-Reggiano cheese, divided

½ cup (54 g) plain bread crumbs

1 tablespoon (6 g) minced fresh mint

3 tablespoons (12 g) minced fresh parsley, divided

2 cloves garlic, minced

¼ teaspoon black pepper

4 large eggs, beaten

1 cup (235 ml) water

1. **To make the sauce:** Heat the olive oil in a large saucepan over medium heat. Add the onion and garlic, and cook and stir until translucent, 5 to 7 minutes.

2. Add the tomatoes, parsley, and salt, and reduce the heat to low. Cook for 15 minutes, stirring occasionally with a wooden spoon. Remove from the heat and set aside.

3. **To make the eggplant:** Peel the potatoes and slice them into rounds, ¼ inch (6 mm) thick. Place them in a bowl of water to prevent darkening.

4. Cut off the stems of the eggplant and cut the eggplant in half lengthwise. With a knife or a spoon, scoop out the pulp of the eggplant, leaving a ¼- to ½-inch (6 to 13 mm) wall of pulp. Place the hollowed-out eggplant in a bowl of water to prevent darkening. Chop the pulp into ½-inch (13 mm) cubes.

5. Heat the olive oil in a medium heavy-bottomed skillet over medium heat. Add the eggplant cubes and cook, stirring constantly with a wooden spoon, until soft, 8 to 10 minutes. Drain the oil and set aside.

6. In a mixing bowl, combine 1 cup (120 g) of the cheese, bread crumbs, mint, 2 tablespoons (8 g) of the parsley, garlic, black pepper, and eggs. Mix well until blended. Add the sautéed eggplant and mix well.

7. Preheat the oven to 375°F (190°C).

8. Spread 1 cup (255 g) of the sauce in a 13 × 9-inch (33 × 23 cm) baking pan to completely cover the bottom. Add a layer of potatoes and sprinkle them with the remaining 1 tablespoon (4 g) of parsley, 1 tablespoon (8 g) of cheese, and a drizzle of olive oil.

9. Pat the hollowed-out eggplant dry with a paper towel and place them in the baking pan over the potatoes. Fill each eggplant with one-fourth of the filling. Pour the water into the bottom of the pan. Spread the remaining sauce over each eggplant and sprinkle with the remaining 1 tablespoon (8 g) of cheese.

10. Cover the pan with aluminum foil and bake for 1 hour. Uncover and bake for an additional 10 minutes. Serve immediately.

VEAL SALTIMBOCCA

Saltimbocca alla Romana

PREP TIME: 10 MINUTES • COOK TIME: 12 MINUTES • YIELD: 4 SERVINGS

Saltimbocca literally translates to "it jumps in your mouth," and this quintessential Roman dish is aptly named. The marriage of thinly pounded veal with prosciutto and sage in a wine and butter sauce is a match made in Italian food heaven. Many Italian-American variations add melted mozzarella on top, which Nonna Teresa includes when she's feeling a bit naughty, but the classic version *alla Romana* can't be beat. This dish is best served as soon as it's cooked, while still sizzling from the pan.

½ pound (227 g) veal leg, sliced for scaloppini and cut into 4 pieces

Salt and black pepper, to taste

8 thin slices prosciutto

8 fresh sage leaves

All-purpose flour, for dredging

2 tablespoons (30 ml) extra-virgin olive oil

2 tablespoons (30 g) unsalted butter

½ cup (120 ml) chicken broth

½ cup (120 ml) dry white wine, such as Pinot Grigio or Sauvignon Blanc

1. Pound each slice of veal between two pieces of plastic wrap until ¼ inch (6 mm) thick.

2. Lightly season each piece with salt and black pepper (the prosciutto may be salty, so you may not need much).

3. Lay 2 slices of prosciutto on each piece of veal and press firmly to adhere. Place 2 sage leaves atop the prosciutto and secure the layers with 2 toothpicks.

4. Place the flour in a shallow dish and dredge each of the slices, shaking off the excess. Set aside on a plate.

5. Heat the olive oil and butter in a large sauté pan over medium heat. Add the veal to the pan, prosciutto side down. Cook for 2 to 3 minutes on each side, until browned. Remove from the pan and transfer to a plate.

6. Raise the heat to medium-high, add the broth and wine, and cook until you can no longer smell the alcohol and the sauce is reduced slightly, 4 to 5 minutes. Deglaze while stirring with a wooden spoon and scraping up any bits from the bottom of the pan.

7. Add the veal back into the pan and cook for an additional 1 to 2 minutes, prosciutto side facing up. Transfer the veal to a serving platter, pour the sauce over the veal, and serve immediately.

PIZZA, BREADS, AND SAVORY BAKES

Pizza, Pane e Sfoglie Salate

NONNA ROMANA SCIDDURLO'S

FOCACCIA BREAD, BARESE-STYLE

Focaccia alla Barese

PREP TIME: 2 HOURS 20 MINUTES • COOK TIME: 35 MINUTES • YIELD: 4 TO 6 SERVINGS

You could say that Nonna Romana's basement apartment, located next to the boiler room of the house, is the ideal focaccia-making environment. The warm temperature helps the focaccia rise and produces a texture that is crispy on the outside and soft and pillowy on the inside. She seasons it simply every time with extra-virgin olive oil, fresh tomatoes, and a sprinkle of oregano and salt.

DOUGH

2 tablespoons (30 ml) extra-virgin olive oil, plus more for brushing

1 packet (¼ ounce, or 7 g) active dry yeast

¾ cup (180 ml) water

2 cups (240 g) 00 or all-purpose flour, plus more for dusting

1 teaspoon salt

TOPPING

6 tablespoons (90 ml) extra-virgin olive oil, divided

3 Roma tomatoes, cut into 1-inch (2.5 cm) wedges

½ teaspoon dried oregano

Salt, to taste

Nonna Romana Says
If your kitchen is a little cooler than normal, you can let the focaccia rise in the oven at 100°F (38°C).

1. **To make the dough:** In the bowl of a stand mixer fitted with the dough hook attachment, combine the oil, yeast, and water. Let stand until the yeast is dissolved, 5 to 8 minutes.

2. In another mixing bowl, whisk together the flour and salt. With the mixer running on low speed, slowly add the flour to the yeast mixture. Mix until a smooth, supple dough forms, 8 to 10 minutes.

3. Transfer the dough to a bowl brushed with olive oil. Brush the ball of dough with more oil. Cover with plastic wrap and set aside to rise for 1 hour, or until doubled in size. Punch down the dough.

4. **To make the topping:** Add 4 tablespoons (60 ml) of the olive oil to a 12-inch (30 cm) round pizza pan and spread it evenly, making sure you coat the bottom and sides of the pan.

5. Spread the dough to the edges of the pan with your fingers, starting from the center and working your way out.

6. Top with the tomatoes and drizzle the remaining 2 tablespoons (30 ml) of olive oil over them. Sprinkle the oregano over the entire surface of the focaccia, followed by a sprinkle of salt.

7. Cover with plastic wrap and set aside to rise in a warm place for 1 hour.

8. Preheat the oven to 475°F (240°C).

9. Bake for 30 to 35 minutes, until golden brown.

NONNA ROMANA SCIDDURLO'S
PIZZA RUSTICA

PREP TIME: 50 MINUTES • COOK TIME: 1 HOUR 15 MINUTES • YIELD: 6 TO 8 SERVINGS

Nonna Romana's *pizza rustica*, also known as *pizza chiena* (stuffed pizza), quickly became one of the most popular recipes on *Cooking with Nonna*. This rich, decadent recipe is the perfect mix of cheeses and meats baked together in a flaky pastry dough that Italians usually serve to break the Lenten fast for the Easter holidays.

CRUST

3⅓ cups (400 g) all-purpose flour,
   plus more for dusting and the pan

Dash salt

1 cup (2 sticks, or 240 g) cold
   unsalted butter, cubed, plus more
   for greasing

2 eggs plus 1 egg for egg wash

¼ cup (60 ml) whole milk

1 tablespoon (15 ml) water

FILLING

¼ pound (113 g) prosciutto, cut into
   ½-inch (13 mm) cubes

¼ pound (113 g) sopressata, cut into
   ½-inch (13 mm) cubes

¼ pound (113 g) mortadella, cut into
   ½-inch (13 mm) cubes

4 ounces (227 g) fresh mozzarella,
   cut into ½-inch (13 mm) cubes

4 ounces (227 g) sharp provolone,
   cut into ½-inch (13 mm) cubes

¼ cup (30 g) grated Pecorino Romano
   cheese

3 eggs

16 ounces (454 g) basket cheese,
   cut into ½-inch (13 mm) cubes

Black pepper, to taste

1. **To make the crust:** In the bowl of a stand mixer fitted with the dough hook attachment, combine the flour, salt, and butter. Start on low speed first and then switch to high speed and mix until all the flour is incoporated.

2. Add the 2 eggs, one at a time, until they are fully incorporated. Add the milk and mix until a ball of dough forms. (If the dough seems a bit dry, add another tablespoon, or 15 ml, of milk.) Continue to mix on medium speed for about 10 minutes, or until the dough is supple.

3. Wrap the dough in plastic wrap and let rest in the refrigerator for 30 minutes. Meanwhile, prepare the filling.

4. **To make the filling:** In a large mixing bowl, combine the prosciutto, sopressata, mortadella, mozzarella, provolone, and Pecorino Romano and mix well.

5. Add the 3 eggs and mix well, making sure the eggs evenly coat everything.

6. Add the basket cheese and mix gently so as not to break it apart too much. Season with fresh black pepper. Set aside.

7. **To assemble the pizza rustica:** Preheat the oven to 350°F (175°C). Butter and flour a 9-inch (23 cm) springform pan.

continued

8. Take two-thirds of the crust dough and put it on a floured work surface. Wrap the other third of dough in plastic wrap and refrigerate until ready to use. Roll it out to a ¼-inch (6 mm) thick circle at least 16 inches (41 cm) in diameter. You want this crust to come up the sides of the springform pan and hang over.

9. Roll the dough onto your rolling pin and unfurl it over the pan and up the sides. Leave some excess dough hanging over the sides.

10. Add the filling and spread it evenly. With a sharp knife, cut the excess dough from around the border of the pan.

11. Add the scraps to the remaining one-third of dough and roll it out to a ¼-inch (6 mm) thick circle. With a ravioli cutter, cut 1½-inch (4 cm) strips to create the lattice top.

12. Beat the remaining 1 egg in a small bowl with the tablespoon (15 ml) of water and brush the lattice with the egg wash.

13. Bake for 1 hour and 15 minutes, or until the center is set and the crust is nicely colored. Cool completely before serving.

PROSCIUTTO AND CHEESE-STUFFED BREAD

Pane Imbottito

PREP TIME: 1 HOUR 20 MINUTES • COOK TIME: 45 MINUTES • YIELD: 4 SERVINGS

Anyone who invites Nonna Antoinette over asks for her famous stuffed bread. She calls this her "clean-out-the-fridge bread," because it can literally be made with any leftover cold cuts and cheeses you have on hand and twisted into heavenly perfection.

DOUGH

1 tablespoon (15 ml) sugar

2 tablespoons (30 ml) extra-virgin olive oil, plus more for greasing and brushing

1 packet (¼ ounce, or 7 g) active dry yeast

¾ cup (180 ml) water

2 cups (240 g) all-purpose flour, plus more for dusting

1 teaspoon salt

FILLING

¼ pound (113 g) prosciutto, cut into ¼-inch (6 mm) dice

½ teaspoon garlic powder

¼ teaspoon black pepper

1 tablespoon (8 g) grated Pecorino Romano cheese

1 tablespoon (8 g) grated Parmigiano-Reggiano cheese

2 ounces (57 g) fresh mozzarella, shredded

2 tablespoons (16 g) shredded Asiago cheese

2 tablespoons (16 g) shredded provolone cheese

Nonna Antoinette Says
Optionally, you can brush the bread with egg wash to color it a bit more before baking.

1. **To make the dough:** In the bowl of a stand mixer fitted with the dough hook attachment, combine the sugar, olive oil, yeast, and water. Let stand until the yeast is dissolved, 5 to 8 minutes.

2. In another mixing bowl, whisk together the flour and salt. With the mixer running on low speed, slowly add the flour to the yeast mixture. Mix until a smooth, supple dough forms, 8 to 10 minutes.

3. Transfer the dough to a bowl brushed with olive oil. Brush the ball of dough with more oil. Cover with plastic wrap and set aside to rise for 1 hour, or until doubled in size.

4. Turn the dough out onto a floured surface and knead for 2 to 3 minutes.

5. **To make the filling:** Preheat the oven to 375°F (190°C). Grease a 18 × 13-inch (46 × 33 cm) baking sheet and a 9-inch (23 cm) round pan with olive oil.

6. Roll out the dough to fit the 9 × 13-inch baking sheet. Spread the prosciutto cubes over the dough. Sprinkle the dough evenly with the garlic powder and black pepper, followed by all of the cheeses.

7. Rolling from the long side closest to you, roll the dough away from you into a log.

8. Hold the dough by one end and twist the other until the log is completely twisted. Roll the log into a pinwheel shape and brush with olive oil. Transfer to the prepared round pan.

9. Bake for 40 to 45 minutes, or until the crust is golden brown.

NONNA CARMELA D'ANGELO'S
BACCALÀ PIE
Crostata di Baccalà

PREP TIME: 20 MINUTES* • **COOK TIME: 40 MINUTES** • **YIELD: 6 TO 8 SERVINGS**
*REQUIRES 1 TO 3 DAYS OF SOAKING

Once regarded as a fish for the poor, *baccalà*, or salt cod, is making a comeback on the food scene. Nonna Carmela's baccalà pie uses the traditional Pugliese dough and has a filling that is the perfect blend of sweet and savory. Her grandchildren have taken on the tradition of making the pies every year for Easter.

FILLING

1 pound (454 g) baccalà (salt cod)
2 tablespoons (30 ml) extra-virgin olive oil
1 medium onion, sliced
½ cup (75 g) raisins
½ cup (96 g) pitted green olives, coarsely chopped
¼ cup (36 g) capers
2 anchovy fillets, packed in olive oil
½ teaspoon black pepper

CRUST

⅓ cup (180 ml) extra-virgin olive oil, plus more for greasing and brushing
1 cup (235 ml) dry white wine, such as Pinot Grigio or Sauvignon Blanc
1 teaspoon salt
3 ⅓ cups (400 g) all-purpose flour, plus more for dusting
1 egg beaten with 1 tablespoon (15 ml) water (for egg wash)

1. **To make the filling:** Put the baccalà in a large bowl and cover with cold water. Place the bowl in the refrigerator and change the water 3 times a day. Soak for 1 to 3 days, depending on saltiness. Drain the baccala and shred by hand into bite-size pieces.

2. Heat the olive oil in a large sauté pan over medium heat. Add the onion and cook and stir until soft and transparent, 8 to 10 minutes.

3. Add the shredded baccalà to the pan along with the raisins, olives, capers, anchovies, and black pepper. Cook, stirring with a wooden spoon, for 3 to 5 minutes. Remove from the heat and set aside to cool to room temperature. In the meantime, make the dough for the crust.

4. **To make the crust:** In the bowl of a stand mixer fitted with the dough hook attachment, combine the olive oil, wine, and salt, and mix for 30 seconds on low speed.

5. Add the flour and mix until a smooth dough forms, 2 to 3 minutes.

6. **To assemble the pie:** Preheat the oven to 425°F (220°C). Grease a 9-inch (23 cm) round pie pan with olive oil.

7. Turn out the dough onto a floured work surface and cut the dough in half. Roll out half of the dough into a ¼-inch (6 mm) thick circle about 12 inches (30 cm) in diameter. Roll the dough up onto the rolling pin and unfurl it over the pie pan.

8. Add the cooled filling to the crust and spread into an even layer.

9. Roll out the other half of the dough to 10 inches (25 cm) in diameter and transfer to the top of the pie. Press the edges with your fingers to seal. Trim any excess dough and then press with the tines of a fork. Brush with the egg wash and dock with a fork.

10. Bake for 35 to 40 minutes, or until the crust is nicely colored.

"If someone is feeling a little down, they come and see me. They come in mooshad and leave laughing. This is who I am."

Come me, non c'è nessuno! Io sono unica al mondo! (Like me, there is no one. I am unique in the world!), Nonna Michelina Gagliardo sings to me. In true nonna fashion, she wears the classic *vestaglia*, or Italian cotton housedress, when I visit her in her Bronx home.

Her table is set with an iconic red-and-white checkered tablecloth and the cheese "smuggled in" from Italy is already on the table. "Taste this! This cheese arrived on Tuesday night in my cousin's suitcase from Sicily," she says. I take a bite of the sharp sheep's milk cheese and am overwhelmed with the incredible flavor. "I like to cook because I like to eat!" she says

Nonna Michelina tastes a sauce that's cooking on the stove. "Beautiful!" she declares. "In Corleone, all you could hope to eat was pasta with garlic and oil, pasta with vegetables, pasta with sauce. Meat when we were lucky, because it was expensive. Today everyone is rich compared to my time!"

Growing up in Sicily, Michelina was one of seven children.

"My father was a mason and my mother had a *bottega* (general store). I remember helping my mother and older sisters with the *sfincione*, *sfinci* (zeppole), and homemade pasta. We didn't have much, but we did things all together as a family.

"I got married at sixteen," she continues. "My husband would come with his horse carriage to my mother's *bottega* and buy one cigarette a day, just to see me. Today it seems crazy, but if you didn't get married by fifteen-sixteen, people thought you were old; no one would look at you anymore. It was different then; we were so much more mature."

Michelina's second marriage brought her to the United States, specifically the Bronx. "I'm used to my independence here...I have friends here for fifty years. If someone is feeling a little down, they come and see me. They come in *mooshad* (feeling "blah" or sad) and leave laughing. This is who I am."

A Gigi D'Alessio album starts playing, and Michelina begins to dance. "My youth is over, but in my old age I'm still dancing. When I was young, we weren't allowed to go dancing, so now I do it whenever I can." In fact, it's music that has had a hand in changing Michelina's life.

Michelina was introduced to social media by one of her nine grandchildren, Michael. He posted a video of her singing along to a rap song as she cooked up their family favorite, fried eggplant. The video was viewed more than 1.8 million times in a day and a half and drew many comments. "I miss my Nonna," read one. "Thank you for the memories," read another. Most people wanted to know who Michelina was.

Nonna Michelina relishes her newfound fame. "I like to make people smile. It's as simple as that. In this world, people either love you or they don't, but I'll be the same no matter what. The love of a nonna is unique. We teach you things your parents don't have time to pay attention to."

PIZZA WITH CHEESE, ONIONS, AND BREAD

Faccia di Vecchia

PREP TIME: 20 MINUTES* • **COOK TIME: 15 MINUTES** • **YIELD: 4 MINI PIZZAS**
*REQUIRES 24 HOURS OF REFRIGERATION

More than sixty years ago, a cousin of Nonna Michelina opened the restaurant U Zu Caliddu in Sicily and started serving the now-famous *faccia di vecchia*. This pizza gets its name from its irregular shape, which represents an old woman's face. Michelina traditionally flavors hers with onions, Pecorino Romano cheese, and *primo sale*, a semisoft sheep's milk cheese, which she tosses together with day-old bread soaked in an oregano-rich tomato sauce. If you have a hard time finding the primo sale, Michelina suggests substituting some sharp provolone. Please note that the dough has to be made 24 hours in advance, so plan accordingly.

DOUGH

1 tablespoon (15 ml) sugar

2 tablespoons (30 ml) extra-virgin olive oil, plus more for brushing

1 packet (¼ ounce, or 7 g) active dry yeast

¾ cup (180 ml) water

2 cups (240 g) all-purpose flour, plus more for dusting

1 teaspoon salt

FILLING

2 cups day-old Italian bread, crusts removed and broken into 1-inch (2.5 cm) cubes

1 can (28 ounces, or 794 g) crushed tomatoes

½ cup ½-inch (13 mm) cubes primo sale or provolone cheese

½ cup ½-inch (13 mm) cubes Pecorino Romano cheese

1 small onion, cut into ¼-inch (6 mm) dice

¼ cup (60 ml) extra-virgin olive oil, plus more for drizzling

1 tablespoon (15 ml) dried oregano

Salt, to taste

1. **To make the dough:** In the bowl of a stand mixer fitted with the dough hook attachment, combine the sugar, olive oil, yeast, and water. Let stand until the yeast is dissolved, 5 to 8 minutes.

2. In another mixing bowl, whisk together the flour and salt. With the mixer running on low speed, slowly add the flour to the yeast mixture. Mix until a smooth, supple dough forms, 8 to 10 minutes. Transfer the dough to a bowl brushed with olive oil. Brush the ball of dough with more oil. Cover with plastic wrap and refrigerate for 24 hours.

3. **To make the filling:** Place the bread cubes in a large bowl. Add the tomatoes and mix well, with your hands if you like.

4. Add the cheeses, onion, olive oil, and oregano. Season with salt. Mix all the ingredients well. Set aside.

5. **To make the pizza:** Preheat the oven to 500°F (250°C) with a pizza stone inside.

6. Turn the dough out onto a floured surface and knead for 2 to 3 minutes. Cut the dough into 4 equal pieces.

7. Flour a pizza peel and stretch the dough into an oblong shape or any shape that you like.

8. Spread about ¾ cup of filling onto the pizza, leaving a 1-inch (2.5 cm) border. Drizzle with some olive oil, slide the pizza onto the pizza stone, and bake for 14 to 15 minutes, or until the outer crust is golden. Repeat with the remaining dough and filling.

SAVORY ITALIAN BISCUITS

Taralli Baresi

PREP TIME: 1 HOUR 15 MINUTES • COOK TIME: 47 MINUTES • YIELD: 20 TARALLI

Taralli are Italian biscuits that are boiled and then baked to perfection at a high temperature. When I was little, Nonna Romana and Zia Rosa used to enlist me to crank the pasta roller by hand while they passed the dough through twenty times for each piece, until it was impossibly soft and supple. Together, they produce more taralli in one week than a professional bakery and give out bags of the crunchy, savory treats to all their friends.

½ cup (120 ml) olive oil

½ cup (120 ml) dry white wine, such as Pinot Grigio or Sauvignon Blanc

½ cup (120 ml) water

2 teaspoons salt

1 packet (¼ ounce, or 7 g) active dry yeast

4 cups (480 g) 00 or all-purpose flour

1. In the bowl of a stand mixer fitted with the dough hook attachment, combine the olive oil, wine, water, salt, and yeast. Mix on low speed for 1 minute.

2. Add the flour and continue mixing on low speed until a smooth ball of dough forms, about 10 minutes. If the mixture seems dry, add 1 tablespoon (15 ml) of wine at a time until it comes together.

3. Attach the pasta roller attachment to the mixer and set it to the largest setting possible.

4. With the mixer running on the highest speed, take a tennis ball–sized amount of dough and flatten it with your hands as much as possible.

5. Feed it through the pasta roller, holding the dough taut. The dough will have holes for the first passing. Pass the dough through the machine 20 more times. The dough is ready once it feels smooth, supple, and almost velvety in your hands.

6. Take the piece of dough to a clean work surface and roll it into a rope about ½ inch (13 mm) thick. Cut pieces from the rope about 8 inches (20 cm) long (a dinner knife is the perfect length!). Join the ends of the taralli to form a round shape. Place one end on top of the other and push down hard with your index finger to seal.

continued

7. Set the taralli aside, not touching one another, on a clean kitchen towel or tablecloth and repeat passing the dough through the machine and rolling it out until you have made all your taralli. (You will be able to make 2 or 3 taralli at a time. You must work in small batches passing the dough through the machine; it must be rolled out immediately or it will dry out.)

8. Once you have made all your taralli, let them rest for 15 minutes before boiling them.

9. Bring a 5-quart (4.7 L) stockpot filled with 3 quarts (2.8 L) of water to a boil. Drop the taralli in, 4 or 5 at a time, beginning with the first ones made. Stir the pot with a wooden spoon to prevent the taralli from sticking to the bottom. As soon as the taralli rise to the surface, scoop them out with a slotted spoon or spider and lay them back on the towel. Repeat with the remaining taralli.

10. Preheat the oven to 475°F (240°C).

11. Hold a boiled tarallo in your hand and with a sharp knife make an incision three-fourths of the way through all around the tarallo, rotating as you cut. Repeat to cut all the taralli.

12. Place 10 to 12 taralli at a time directly on the rack of the oven. These will puff up in the oven and require more space.

13. Bake for 7 minutes at 475°F (240°C), and then lower the temperature to 400°F (200°C). Bake for an additional 10 minutes, until golden, turning the taralli over with tongs halfway through.

14. Once fully baked, cool the oven down to 180°F (85°C). Place the taralli on a 13 × 9-inch (33 × 23 cm) baking sheet and bake for 30 minutes, until they are completely dry inside. This will remove all the humidity from the taralli and help them stay fresh much longer.

NONNA ANGELINA PURPURA'S

SICILIAN PIZZA

Sfincione Siciliano

PREP TIME: 1 HOUR • COOK TIME: 1 HOUR • YIELD: 6 TO 8 SERVINGS

Sfincione is a thick-crusted Sicilian pizza—or more of a *focaccia*, to be precise. Nonna Angelina prepares hers with a golden semolina crust and tops it with savory anchovies, Pecorino Romano cheese, and a delicious sauce with lots of oregano that builds incredible layers of flavor. The bread crumb topping melts into the cheese and creates a soft, creamy texture like no other. Although this dish is usually prepared between Christmas and New Year's in the Palermo area, Angelina makes two or three trays at a time for almost every holiday because it's that good!

DOUGH

2 packets (¼ ounce, or 7 g, each)
   active dry yeast

3 cups (700 ml) warm water

4 cups (668 g) semolina flour
   (semolina rimacinata; see
   page 10)

2 cups (240 g) all-purpose flour,
   plus more for dusting

1 tablespoon (15 ml) salt

2 tablespoons (30 ml) extra-virgin
   olive oil, plus more for greasing

SAUCE

2 tablespoons (30 ml) extra-virgin
   olive oil

1 medium onion, cut into ¼-inch
   (6 mm) dice

1 can (28 ounces, or 794 g) crushed
   tomatoes

½ teaspoon salt

½ teaspoon dried oregano

¼ teaspoon black pepper

1. **To make the dough:** Pour the yeast into the warm water in a small bowl and let dissolve for 5 minutes.

2. Grease a 18 × 13-inch (46 × 33 cm) baking sheet with olive oil.

3. In a large mixing bowl, whisk together the semolina flour, all-purpose flour, and salt. Slowly pour the yeast mixture into the bowl and stir until a sticky dough forms. Turn out the dough onto a floured work surface and knead for 7 to 10 minutes, until smooth. Add the olive oil to your hands and the dough and knead for another 2 to 3 minutes, until the oil has somewhat been incorporated.

4. Transfer to the baking sheet and press the dough out with your hands, pushing out from the center until it has spread into an even layer.

5. Cover the pan with a kitchen towel and set aside to rise for 1 hour in a warm, dry place. In the meantime, make the sauce.

6. **To make the sauce:** Heat the olive oil in a large saucepan over medium heat. Add the onion and cook and stir until translucent, 5 to 7 minutes.

7. Add the tomatoes, salt, oregano, and black pepper, and stir to combine. Reduce the heat to low and cook for 15 minutes, stirring occasionally with a wooden spoon. Remove from the heat and set aside.

continued

SFINCIONE

¼ cup (27 g) plain bread crumbs

2 tablespoons (16 g) grated
   Parmigiano-Reggiano cheese

1 teaspoon dried oregano

¼ teaspoon black pepper

18 anchovy fillets packed in olive oil,
   drained, fillets halved

1 cup (120 g) large-grated Pecorino
   Romano shavings

½ cup (120 ml) extra-virgin olive oil

Nonna Angelina Says
*When I let the dough rise,
I cover it with many blankets
or towels. Call me superstitious
or old-fashioned, but it works
for me!*

8. **To make the sfincione:** Preheat the oven to 400°F (200°C).

9. In a small mixing bowl, combine the bread crumbs, Parmigiano-Reggiano, oregano, and black pepper, and mix well.

10. Arrange the anchovy fillets over the dough. Top the anchovies with the Pecorino.

11. Spread the sauce over the sfincione, leaving a 1-inch (2.5 cm) border all the way around. Sprinkle the bread crumb mixture over the top and lightly press the entire sfincione with your fingers, creating indentations that will hold the olive oil. Drizzle the olive oil over the top of the sfincione, depositing it within the indentations.

12. Bake for 30 to 45 minutes, or until the bottom of the crust is golden brown.

SPINACH AND RICE PIE

Torta di Riso Genovese

PREP TIME: 1 HOUR • COOK TIME: 1 HOUR 7 MINUTES • YIELD: 4 SERVINGS

Torta di riso is a Ligurian specialty made with rice cooked in milk and water. When cut into squares, it makes a beautiful appetizer or passed hors d'oeuvre.

CRUST

2 cups (240 g) all-purpose flour,
  plus more for dusting
¼ cup (60 ml) extra-virgin olive oil,
  plus more for greasing
½ cup (120 ml) water
Dash salt

FILLING

1 cup (185 g) Arborio rice
1½ teaspoons salt, divided
1 cup (235 ml) water
1 cup (235 ml) whole milk
5 ounces (142 g) fresh baby spinach
  (about 4¾ cups)
3 tablespoons (45 ml) extra-virgin
  olive oil
1 large onion, cut into ¼-inch (6 mm)
  dice
4 cloves garlic, minced
¼ cup (16 g) minced fresh parsley
¼ teaspoon black pepper
3 eggs, divided
1 cup (120 g) grated Parmigiano-
  Reggiano cheese
Nutmeg, to taste

Nonna Vivian Says
If you're short on time, you can substitute the homemade crust with phyllo dough.

1. **To make the crust:** In the bowl of a stand mixer fitted with the dough hook attachment, combine all of the crust ingredients and mix on low speed until a smooth ball of dough forms. Wrap the dough in plastic wrap and let rest for at least 30 minutes.

2. **To make the filling:** In a medium saucepan, add the rice, ½ teaspoon of the salt, water, and milk, and bring to a boil over medium heat. Reduce the heat to low and cook until the rice is al dente, 10 to 12 minutes. Remove from the heat and let stand for about 30 minutes. All the liquid will be absorbed by the rice during this time.

3. Blanch the spinach in a large pot of lightly salted boiling water for 1 to 2 minutes. Drain and run under cold water. Squeeze out the excess water and finely chop the spinach.

4. Heat the olive oil in a medium sauté pan over medium heat. Add the onion, garlic, and parsley, and cook and stir until the onion is soft, 8 to 10 minutes. Add the spinach, black pepper, and remaining 1 teaspoon of salt, and cook and stir 1 to 2 minutes. Remove from the heat and let stand for 10 to 15 minutes.

5. In a medium mixing bowl, combine the spinach with the cooled rice. Beat 2 of the eggs in a small bowl, add to the spinach and rice mixture along with the cheese and nutmeg, and mix well.

6. **To assemble the pie:** Preheat the oven to 375°F (190°C). Grease a 9-inch (23 cm) round pan with 1½-inch (4 cm) high sides with olive oil.

7. On a lightly floured work surface, roll out the dough into a circle ¼ inch (6 mm) thick and about 12 inches (30 cm) in diameter. Roll the dough onto the rolling pin and unfurl it over the pan. Trim any excess that hangs over the pan. Spread the filling into the crust and fold the crust over the filling.

8. Bake for 30 to 35 minutes, or until the crust is nicely colored. Let rest for 15 minutes before cutting.

"I grew up cooking and eating. My cooking style is random and chaotic, but it gets done."

"Where's your housedress?" I jokingly ask Nonna Vivian Cardia, a dear friend of my mother's, as she opens her front door. "I don't wear housedresses, Rossella. I wear Jimmy Choo's!" she shoots back at me with a smile. We've played this game before. My very first memories of Vivian date back to when I was a little girl. I always admired her for being the sophisticated, raven-haired lady behind a restaurant hostess stand, smiling kindly and handing me crayons. At the time, I had no idea that she was such a dynamic woman. When I learned she was one of the first female traders on the floor of the New York Stock Exchange, I was inspired and full of hope that a woman could be mamma, nonna, and stock trader all at the same time.

Vivian, the daughter of Genovese immigrants, grew up in the West Village of New York City. Her mother, Elsie, or "ubiquitous Elsie" as Vivian likes to refer to her, was a regular on the Manhattan social scene. In 1955, with only $5,000, Vivian's parents opened the West Village landmark restaurant the Beatrice Inn, which became a neighborhood hangout for the likes of Charles Kurault and Woody Allen.

"I grew up cooking and eating. My cooking style is random and chaotic, but it gets done," Vivian says of her years at the Beatrice Inn. "We had many different chefs at various times and each one had their own style. One taught me how to make a perfect tomato sauce; another taught me about seafood. It was like an extended culinary education." For many Italian restaurant owners, eating never becomes any less important.

Vivian is the kind of nonna who cooks in high heels, a skill she developed while working at the Beatrice Inn for so many years. "My mother was fabulous; my grandmother was even more fabulous! That's how I was raised. In the restaurant business, you're always on. You couldn't turn my mother off! My mother would go around to each table talking to people. She made everyone feel like they were her best friend. She remembered everyone. We didn't close it until 2005 because we knew my mother wanted to be there for fifty years. If my mother was still alive, it would still be open!" she says.

Vivian passed on her love of cooking to her only grandson, Nick, whom she has raised since the age of four. "Being a nonna brings the most joy to your life. You feel like life will go on forever." Today, food and family remain the cornerstones of Vivian's life. "In an Italian family, everyone gets together over food. Even if it's all about outdoing the other. Did you taste Aunt Lucy's pasta? Isn't mine better? It's a little bit about rivalry, but a nice rivalry."

MOZZARELLA AND TOMATO FRITTERS

Panzerotti

PREP TIME: 1 HOUR 5 MINUTES • COOK TIME: 8 MINUTES • YIELD: 6 PANZEROTTI

Every summer I look forward to eating this special Pugliese street food, which is comparable to the Italian-American calzone. With every bite, gorgeous strings of fresh mozzarella ooze from the golden crust, which is light as a feather. Families from Puglia also make these for both New Year's and Christmas Eve.

DOUGH

2 tablespoons (30 ml) extra-virgin olive oil, plus more for brushing

1 packet (¼ ounce, or 7 g) active dry yeast

¾ cup (180 ml) water

2 cups (240 g) 00 or all-purpose flour, plus more for dusting

1 teaspoon salt

FILLING

6 ounces (170 g) fresh mozzarella, shredded

½ cup (60 g) grated Parmigiano-Reggiano cheese

½ cup (75 g) cherry tomatoes, cut into ¼-inch (6 mm) dice

1 tablespoon (9 g) capers (optional)

Black pepper, to taste

Olive oil, for frying (or any frying oil you like)

❯ Nonna Romana Says
Make sure you fry the panzerotti as soon as you finish making them or else you risk the dough drying out and splitting open in the oil.

1. **To make the dough:** In the bowl of a stand mixer fitted with the dough hook attachment, combine the olive oil, yeast, and water. Let stand until the yeast is dissolved, 5 to 8 minutes.

2. In another mixing bowl, whisk together the flour and salt. With the mixer running on low speed, slowly add the flour to the yeast mixture. Mix until a smooth, supple dough forms, 8 to 10 minutes.

3. Transfer the dough to a bowl brushed with olive oil. Brush the ball of dough with more oil. Cover with plastic wrap and set aside to rise for 1 hour, or until doubled in size.

4. Transfer the dough to a floured work surface and knead for 2 to 3 minutes. Cut the dough into six 2-ounce (56 g) pieces. Roll each piece into a ¼-inch (6 mm) thick round. (Don't worry if it isn't perfectly round; you will adjust the shape later with a ravioli cutter.)

5. **To make the filling:** Add 2 tablespoons (14 g) of mozzarella to the center of each piece of dough. Follow with 1 tablespoon (8 g) of Parmigiano-Reggiano and 1 tablespoon (10 g) of diced tomatoes. Add 4 or 5 capers, if using. Season with black pepper and fold the dough over to create a pocket.

6. Seal the edges around the filling by pressing with your fingers. You can also seal them with the floured tines of a fork. With a ravioli cutter, trim the edges, leaving a border about ½ inch (13 mm) wide. Add any scraps from the edges to a ball to make other panzerotti. Lay the panzerotti on a floured baking sheet and cover with a dish towel until they're ready to be fried.

7. Heat 1 inch (2.5 cm) of frying oil in a 5-quart (4.7 L) heavy-bottomed stockpot over medium-high heat. Fry the panzerotti in batches until golden brown, about 2 minutes per batch.

SAVORY SCALLION PIE

Scalcione

PREP TIME: 10 MINUTES · COOK TIME: 1 HOUR 15 MINUTES · YIELD: 4 TO 6 SERVINGS

Every Good Friday, families from Puglia enjoy a pie crust made with white wine, oil, and flour, and stuffed with an onion filling that varies from village to village. My Zia Rosa's is by far the best in the family. We all love it so much that she makes it throughout the year.

FILLING

6 bunches scallions (35 to 40 stalks)

¼ cup (60 ml) extra-virgin olive oil

½ cup (128 g) canned crushed tomatoes or 1 cup (150 g) cherry tomatoes, halved

1 cup (192 g) pitted Gaeta or Kalamata olives

½ cup (120 ml) dry white wine, such as Pinot Grigio or Sauvignon Blanc

5 anchovy fillets, broken up into small pieces (optional)

CRUST

⅓ cup (80 ml) extra-virgin olive oil, plus more for greasing and brushing

1 cup (235 ml) dry white wine, such as Pinot Grigio or Sauvignon Blanc

1 teaspoon salt

3 ⅓ cups (400 g) all-purpose flour, plus more for dusting

1. **To make the filling:** Trim the ends of the green and white parts of the scallions. With a paring knife, split the bulbs of the scallions in half lengthwise. Cut the scallions into 1½-inch (4 cm) pieces. Wash them well under cold water.

2. Heat the oil in a 5-quart (4.7 L) stockpot over medium-high heat. Add the scallions, tomatoes, olives, and wine. Give the pot a good stir with a wooden spoon. Cover and cook until the scallions are soft, about 15 minutes. Remove from the heat and transfer to a colander with a plate underneath to drain the juice. Set aside until cool. In the meantime, make the dough for the crust.

3. **To make the crust:** Preheat the oven to 400°F (200°C). Grease a 12-inch (30 cm) round pizza pan with olive oil.

4. Using a stand mixer fitted with the dough hook attachment, combine the olive oil, wine, and salt, and mix for 30 seconds on low speed. Add the flour and mix until a smooth dough forms, 2 to 3 minutes. Turn out the dough onto a floured surface. Cut the dough in half and roll one half into a circle, 14 inches (36 cm) in diameter. Roll the crust around the rolling pin and unfurl it over the pan. Smooth the sides and fit the crust into the corners of the pan, allowing the excess to come up the sides.

5. Add the scallion filling to the center of the crust and spread it evenly, leaving a border of about ½ inch (13 mm). Place the pieces of anchovy over the scallions.

6. Roll out the remaining dough into another circle 14 inches (36 cm) in diameter. Place it over the scallions and press the top and bottom crusts together with your fingers. Trim the excess dough from the top. Press the edges of the crust with the tines of a fork to create a seal. Brush the crust with olive oil and dock with a fork.

7. Bake for 1 hour, or until the crust has colored. Serve warm or at room temperature.

DESSERTS

Dolci

SICILIAN CANNOLI

Cannoli Siciliani

PREP TIME: 1 HOUR 30 MINUTES • COOK TIME: 24 MINUTES • YIELD: 24 CANNOLI

"A well-made *cannolo* just makes you feel better about life," Nonna Lydia tells me as she rolls out her family recipe for cannoli shells, perfected by her brother, a professional baker. A touch of cinnamon and white wine is added to the dough to create those iconic bubbles on the shells. Her ricotta filling is made with *impastata*, which produces a velvety, melt-in-your mouth texture. Keeping true to her Sicilian roots, she skips the chocolate chips, which are more of an Italian-American custom, instead opting for some colorful crushed pistachios, from Bronte, Sicily, if possible.

CANNOLI SHELLS

3 ⅓ cups (400 g) all-purpose flour,
 plus more for dusting

½ cup (100 g) lard

2 egg yolks plus 1 egg for egg wash

2 tablespoons (30 ml) granulated sugar

½ cup (120 ml) plus 2 tablespoons
 (30 ml) dry white wine, such as
 Pinot Grigio or Sauvignon Blanc

½ teaspoon vanilla extract

½ teaspoon ground cinnamon

Olive oil, for frying (or any frying oil
 you like)

1 cup (125 g) shelled pistachios

CREAM FILLING

32 ounces (907 g) ricotta impastata

3 cups (300 g) confectioners' sugar

¾ teaspoon ground cinnamon

1 teaspoon vanilla extract

½ teaspoon orange extract

1. **To make the cannoli shells:** In the bowl of a stand mixer fitted with the paddle attachment, combine the flour and lard, and mix on low speed until the lard has been absorbed in the flour.

2. Add the egg yolks and mix until combined. Add the granulated sugar, wine, vanilla extract, and cinnamon, and mix until the dough comes together. Shape the dough into a disk and wrap it in plastic wrap. Let rest for 1 hour at room temperature.

3. On a floured surface, roll out the dough into a sheet ⅛-inch (3 mm) thick. Cut out circles with a 4½-inch (11 cm) round cookie cutter or glass and wrap them around 1-inch (2.5 cm) metal cannoli tubes, overlapping the ends.

4. Beat the remaining egg in a bowl and brush the overlapping ends with egg wash, making sure you coat all the overlapping dough. Press the overlapping dough together to create a good seal.

5. Heat the oil, about 1½ inches (4 cm), in a large saucepan until it reaches 350°F (180°C). Fry the cannoli shells in batches of 2 until golden brown. Set aside to cool completely.

6. Place the pistachios in the bowl of a food processor. Process for about 1 minute, until fine. Set aside.

7. **To make the cream filling:** In a large mixing bowl, combine the impastata, confectioners' sugar, cinnamon, and extracts. Mix well and then pass through a strainer to smooth out the ricotta's texture.

8. Fill a disposable pastry bag with the cannoli cream and fill each cannolo with about 2 tablespoons (32 g) of the cream.

9. Dip each end of the cannolo into the crushed pistachios and serve.

FLOURLESS ALMOND TORTE

Torta Caprese

PREP TIME: 30 MINUTES • COOK TIME: 55 MINUTES • YIELD: 8 TO 12 SERVINGS

Nonna Rosa, who is my official nonna chef-instructor on my Sorrento culinary tour, teaches group after group how to make this moist, rich almond and chocolate cake spiked with whiskey. Caprese cake, common on the island of Capri, is a fudgy masterpiece with a bit of crunch and texture. The whipped egg whites give the cake an airiness that complements the richness of the chocolate. All it needs is a dusting of powdered sugar.

10 tablespoons (150 g) unsalted butter, softened, plus more for greasing

All-purpose flour, for the pan

9 ounces (255 g) unblanched almonds (about 1¾ cups)

5 ounces (142 g) bittersweet chocolate

1 teaspoon potato starch

1 tablespoon (15 ml) unsweetened cocoa powder

2 teaspoons baking powder

Dash salt

1 cup (200 g) granulated sugar

5 eggs, separated, at room temperature

3 to 4 tablespoons (45 to 60 ml) rum or whiskey (or to taste), for drizzling (Nonna Rosa prefers whiskey)

Confectioners' sugar, for dusting

1. Preheat the oven to 325°F (170°C). Butter and flour a 9-inch (23 cm) springform pan.

2. Add the almonds to the bowl of a food processor and process for about 1 minute, until fine. Transfer to a bowl. Next, add the chocolate to the food processor and process for about 30 seconds, until fine. Transfer to the bowl with the almonds and mix the two together. Set aside.

3. In a small bowl, sift together the potato starch, cocoa powder, baking powder, and salt. Set aside.

4. In the bowl of a stand mixer fitted with the paddle attachment, beat the butter and granulated sugar together on medium speed until fluffy, about 5 minutes. Turn the speed down to low and add the egg yolks, one at a time, letting each one become fully incorporated before adding the next. Add the chocolate and almonds, and mix until combined. Add the dry ingredients and mix until just combined.

5. In a separate mixing bowl, beat the egg whites with an electric mixer until stiff peaks form. Gently fold the egg whites into the batter.

6. Pour batter into the prepared pan and bake for 55 minutes, or until a toothpick inserted in the center comes out clean.

7. When the cake is still warm, drizzle the whiskey over the top. When the cake is cooled completely, sprinkle with confectioners' sugar and serve.

NONNA ROMANA SCIDDURLO'S

WEDDING CAKE

Torta Nunziale con Pasta Reale

PREP TIME: 55 MINUTES • COOK TIME: 47 MINUTES • YIELD: 10 TO 12 SERVINGS

When my Nonna Romana got married in 1952, a feast of *panini*, almond cookies, and this cake was prepared in honor of the newly married couple. Fast-forward to over half a century later and she still makes it for every special family occasion. A simple *pan di Spagna*, Italian sponge cake, is leavened with only beaten eggs, and the baked caked is soaked in rum. It is then filled with layers of custard cream and the quintessential Pugliese *pasta reale* (royal almond paste), topped with Amarena cherries, and frosted with lightly sweetened whipped cream. Traditionally, the cake was iced in a simple *glassa*, or glaze, but in America, whipped cream was used, reflecting newfound abundance. Fresh strawberries are always used to decorate, as they were a bit of a luxury at the time. If you cannot find Amarena cherries, you may use any sour cherries in syrup or cherry preserves.

CAKE
Butter, for greasing
1 cup (200 g) granulated sugar
6 eggs, at room temperature
Zest of 1 lemon
Dash salt
¾ cup (90 g) 00 or all-purpose flour
¾ cup (90 g) cornstarch
¾ cup (180 ml) rum
¾ cup (180 ml) water

CUSTARD CREAM
¾ cup (150 g) granulated sugar
6 tablespoons (45 g) cornstarch
2 cups (475 ml) whole milk
2 tablespoons (30 ml) heavy cream
5 egg yolks, beaten
½ teaspoon vanilla extract
Whole peel of 1 lemon

ALMOND PASTE FILLING
1¼ cups (181 g) blanched almonds
½ cup (120 ml) water
¼ cup (50 g) granulated sugar
Zest of 2 lemons

1. **To make the cake:** Preheat the oven to 350°F (175°C). Butter a 9-inch (23 cm) springform pan.

2. In a stand mixer fitted with the paddle attachment, beat together the granulated sugar, eggs, lemon zest, and salt on medium speed for about 30 seconds. Raise the speed to high and beat until the mixture is pale yellow, has doubled in volume, and ribbons form, 15 to 20 minutes minimum.

3. In a mixing bowl, sift together the flour and cornstarch 3 times. Sift the dry ingredients on top of the sugar and egg mixture little by little, folding it in very carefully so you don't deflate the egg mixture.

4. Pour into the prepared pan and bake for 40 minutes, or until the center is springy. Do not open the oven for the first 30 minutes of baking or you risk deflating the cake.

5. Cool completely and run a knife along the inner edge of the pan before opening the spring.

6. **To make the custard cream:** In a mixing bowl, whisk together the granulated sugar and cornstarch. Set aside.

7. In another mixing bowl, combine the milk, cream, beaten egg yolks, and vanilla extract, and whisk until blended.

continued

WHIPPED CREAM

2½ cups (600 ml) heavy cream

3 tablespoons (32 g) confectioners' sugar

ASSEMBLY

¾ cup (180 ml) rum

¾ cup (180 ml) water

8 ounces (227 g) Amarena cherries, drained, syrup reserved, cherries halved

Sliced fresh strawberries, for decorating (about 2 pints)

Nonna Romana Says

It may feel like you are adding too much rum to the cake, but the cake must be adequately moistened. You can change the quantity of the rum if it's too strong for you, but keep the amount of liquid (1½ cups, or 360 ml) the same. You can also substitute orange juice for the rum for a non-alcoholic version.

8. Put a large saucepan over medium heat and add the milk mixture and the sugar and cornstarch. Stir continuously with a wooden spoon. Add the lemon peel and continue stirring until the mixture thickens, 7 to 8 minutes. Remove from the heat. Scoop out the lemon peel and discard, and continue to stir for another 30 seconds.

9. Cool the custard by spreading it in a shallow baking dish. Cover it with plastic wrap, pushing the plastic against the cream. This will prevent a skin from forming. Place the baking dish in the refrigerator or freezer until cooled.

10. **To make the almond paste filling:** Place the almonds in the bowl of a food processor and process for about 2 minutes, until very fine. Transfer to a plate.

11. Put a medium saucepan over medium-high heat. Add the water and sugar, and bring to a simmer. Add the almonds and stir for about 10 seconds with a wooden spoon until the almonds have absorbed all the liquid. Stir in the lemon zest and remove from the heat. Set aside to cool.

12. **To make the whipped cream:** In a mixing bowl, combine the heavy cream and confectioners' sugar. Beat with an electric mixer until stiff peaks form. Refrigerate.

13. **To assemble the cake:** Slice the cake into 3 equal layers.

14. In a small bowl, mix the rum and water together. With a brush or a squeeze bottle (a squeeze bottle works better), moisten the bottom layer with about one-third of the mixture.

15. Using your fingers, crumble the almond paste evenly over the first layer, bringing it to the edge of the cake. Add the cherries over the almond paste in an even layer. Drizzle with 2 tablespoons (30 ml) of reserved syrup from the cherries.

16. Add the middle layer of the cake and moisten it with another one-third of the rum mixture. Spread the custard cream evenly over the layer. Add the top cake layer and moisten it with the remaining third of rum mixture.

17. Spread the whipped cream over the entire cake and decorate with sliced fresh strawberries.

"The way I tell if someone is a good cook is from their pasta. If the pasta is good, then they're a good cook."

Nonna Angelina Purpurra—a Sicilian, blonde, blue-eyed bombshell of a nonna—is waiting outside her Long Island home when I arrive. Sporting her *Cooking With Nonna* apron, she gives the somewhat formidable impression of being the boss. In fact, Nonna Angelina became the boss of her family's kitchen in Carini, Sicily, when she was only fourteen years old. Once Angelina's older sister was married off, her mother set out to teach her everything she would need to know to be a good wife and cook someday.

"I loved to cook and clean. I cooked every day for forty-six years," she says lovingly, referring to her wonderful marriage. "The best years of my life were when my husband was alive. In Carini, we lived across the street from each other, and we liked each other since we were eleven years old," she says.

Her big blue eyes begin to tear, and it's impossible to understand just how hard it must be to lose someone you have been with nearly your entire life. It's why Sunday dinner is so important to Angelina and her family.

"You never know when it's going to be the last Sunday. I remember the last one we spent together. All our children and grandchildren came, and for some reason we took pictures with everyone. He passed three days later, but I know that last Sunday was special."

When Nonna Angelina arrived in Brooklyn in 1950, she dreamed of working hard, making money, and going back to Italy as soon as she could. Today, Nonna Angelina has seven grandchildren and five great grandchildren. "Becoming a great-grandmother was beautiful. It made me feel reborn." She speaks about her great-grandchildren with the love and wonder of a brand new mother, as if she's totally aware of how lucky she is to bear witness to their incredible journey in this world. "I just want to be remembered as the nonna that made delicious food," she says with a laugh.

Nonna Angelina's stamina amazes me. She tells me careful planning is the secret to seamless execution in the kitchen. "I have parties for eighty people, and I cook everything! You gotta plan and think what dishes can last, so you make those a few days before. Don't go crazy." Her only exception is pasta, which has to be made at the very last minute to be good. "The way I tell if someone is a good cook is from their pasta. If the pasta is good, then they're a good cook."

I asked her the most important thing she learned about cooking over the years. "You have to experiment. I always tried to do new things; every Christmas I wanted to make new dishes. I would ask all my friends, 'How do you do this? How do you make that?' Before I knew it, they were asking *me* how to cook," she says.

SICILIAN MILK PUDDING

Biancomangiare

PREP TIME: 1 HOUR 30 MINUTES • COOK TIME: 10 MINUTES • YIELD: 4 TO 6 SERVINGS

Having been around since the Middle Ages, this dessert has definitely stood the test of time. Nonna Angelina still remembers when the milkman would bring his cow through the streets of Carini and her mother would buy fresh milk—and I mean *fresh* milk—to make this super-easy treat. This delicious milk pudding can be poured into ramekins for single servings or, as here, poured over ladyfinger cookies to create a creamy, makeshift cake.

3 ounces (85 g) ladyfinger cookies (about 12)

4 cups (950 ml) whole milk

¾ cup (150 g) sugar

½ cup (60 g) cornstarch

2 teaspoons vanilla extract

¼ teaspoon almond extract (optional)

Ground cinnamon, for sprinkling

Nonna Angelina Says

A few of the ladyfingers may decide to float when you pour the biancomangiare over them. You can push them down, but if they keep floating, just leave them alone and they should settle as it sets.

1. Line a 11 × 7-inch (28 × 18 cm) baking pan with ladyfinger cookies.

2. Put a large saucepan over medium heat and combine the milk, sugar, cornstarch, and extracts. Cook, stirring constantly, until the mixture thickens, about 10 minutes. The mixture will be thick and smooth.

3. Remove from the heat. Ladle mixture over the cookies and sprinkle with cinnamon. Some of the cookies may float to the top—not to worry.

4. Refrigerate for at least 1½ hours or overnight before serving.

RICOTTA AND PINOLI TART

Crostata della Nonna

PREP TIME: 15 MINUTES • COOK TIME: 1 HOUR • YIELD: 6 TO 8 SERVINGS

It's unbelievable how quickly Nonna Rosetta puts together this beautiful tart with a rich, lemony ricotta filling. To save time, she presses the crust directly into the pie plate with her hands and it comes out perfectly. When she's feeling creative, she chills the leftover dough and rolls out pieces to cut out and create designs.

FILLING

1 pound (454 g) whole milk ricotta

2 large eggs

⅔ cup (130 g) sugar

¾ cup (102 g) plus 3 tablespoons
    (25 g) pinoli (pine nuts), divided

CRUST

6 tablespoons (90 g) unsalted butter,
    softened, plus more for greasing

1½ cups (180 g) all-purpose flour, plus
    more for dusting

½ teaspoon baking powder

Dash salt

½ cup (100 g) sugar

1 egg, at room temperature

1 teaspoon lemon zest

1. Preheat the oven to 350°F (175°C). Grease a 9½-inch (24 cm) pie plate with butter.

2. **To make the filling:** In a mixing bowl, combine the ricotta, eggs, sugar, and ¾ cup (102 g) of the pinoli, and mix well until combined. Set aside.

3. **To make the crust:** In a mixing bowl, whisk together the flour, baking powder, and salt. Set aside.

4. In the bowl of a stand mixer fitted with the paddle attachment, combine the butter, sugar, egg, and lemon zest. Mix on medium speed until fluffy, about 5 minutes. Reduce the speed to low.

5. Add the flour mixture and mix until all the flour is incorporated.

6. Press three-fourths of the dough into the prepared pie plate. Trim the excess dough around the edges. Spoon in the ricotta filling.

7. On a well-floured surface, roll out the remaining one-fourth of dough into an ⅛-inch (3 mm) thick circle. If the dough is too soft and breaks apart, wrap it in plastic wrap and refrigerate for 10 to 15 minutes. With a ravioli cutter, cut out strips about 1 inch (2.5 cm) wide and place them in a lattice pattern over the top of the filling. Press the edges lightly to adhere.

8. Sprinkle the tart with the remaining 3 tablespoons (25 g) of pinoli, pressing them into the ricotta.

9. Bake for 1 hour, or until the lattice has colored nicely.

WHEAT PIE

Pastiera Napoletana

PREP TIME: 1 HOUR • COOK TIME: 1 HOUR 55 MINUTES • YIELD: 8 TO 10 SERVINGS

Nonna Gilda makes these classic grain pies two at a time for the Easter holidays. An old Neapolitan tradition mandates that the *pastiera* be made a few days before the Easter holidays—but no later than the Thursday or Good Friday of Holy Week—so that all the flavors have a chance to meld.

CRUST

2½ cups (300 g) all-purpose flour, plus more for dusting

½ cup (100 g) sugar

3 large eggs

2½ (36 g) tablespoons vegetable shortening, plus more for greasing

Dash salt

Zest of 1 lemon

FILLING

2 ounces (44 g) hulled wheat (spelt)

2 cups (475 ml) cold water

2 eggs, separated

12 ounces (340 g) whole milk ricotta

1 cup (200 g) sugar

2 teaspoons vanilla extract

½ teaspoon orange extract

¼ cup (36 g) citron or candied fruit (optional)

1. **To make the crust:** In a large mixing bowl, combine the flour, sugar, eggs, shortening, salt, and lemon zest. Mix with your hands until a firm dough forms. Flatten the dough into a disk. Wrap in plastic wrap and refrigerate for at least 1 hour or overnight.

2. **To make the filling:** Rinse the hulled wheat under cold water. Pour the water into a small saucepan over low heat. Add the rinsed wheat and cook until tender, stirring occasionally with a wooden spoon, 30 to 40 minutes. Drain and set aside until cool.

3. In the bowl of a stand mixer fitted with the paddle attachment, beat the egg yolks on medium speed until fluffy and lemon colored, about 5 minutes. Add the ricotta, wheat, and sugar, and mix until combined. Add the extracts and citron, if using, and mix until incorporated.

4. In a separate mixing bowl, beat the egg whites with an electric mixer until soft peaks form. Gently fold the egg whites into the ricotta mixture. Set aside.

5. **To assemble the pie:** Preheat the oven to 350°F (175°C). Grease a 9-inch (23 cm) round pie pan with vegetable shortening.

6. Roll out the dough on a lightly floured surface into a 12-inch (30 cm) circle about ¼ inch (6 mm) thick. Roll the dough up onto the rolling pin and unfurl it over the pie pan, allowing the excess to hang off the sides. Pour the filling into the crust and trim the excess dough. On a lightly floured surface, roll out the excess dough into a ⅛-inch (3 mm) thick circle. With a ravioli cutter, cut out 1-inch (2.5 cm) strips and place them in a lattice pattern over the filling, pressing the edges slightly to adhere. Trim the excess dough.

7. Bake for 1 hour and 15 minutes, until crust has colored and the filling has set. Let cool before serving.

NONNA ANTOINETTE CAPODICCI'S

STRUFFOLI

PREP TIME: 1 HOUR • COOK TIME: 15 MINUTES • YIELD: 8 TO 10 SERVINGS

Classic Neapolitan *struffoli* have made their way onto almost every Italian-American family's Christmas dessert table. The deep-fried golden marbles glistening with honey and decorated with festive sprinkles are usually presented piled high in large mounds or in the shape of a wreath. Keeping true to her family tradition back in Italy, Nonna Antoinette always makes large quantities every holiday season to give away to friends and family. She never worries about anyone re-gifting them: "People treat them like gold!"

STRUFFOLI

3 cups (360 g) all-purpose flour, plus
    more for dusting and the pan

½ teaspoon baking powder

Pinch salt

2 tablespoons (30 g) unsalted butter,
    softened

2 tablespoons (25 g) sugar

4 eggs, room temperature

1 tablespoon (15 ml) dry white wine

1 teaspoon vanilla

Zest of ½ lemon

Zest of ½ orange

Olive oil, for frying (or use any frying oil
    you like)

Rainbow jimmies or nonpareils,
    to decorate

HONEY SYRUP

1½ cups (510 g) honey

½ cup (100 g) sugar

2 tablespoons (30 ml) water

1. **To make the struffoli:** In a mixing bowl, whisk together the flour, baking powder, and salt. Set aside.

2. In the bowl of a stand mixer fitted with the paddle attachment, beat the butter and sugar on medium speed until combined. Reduce the speed to low and add the eggs, one at a time, making sure each is fully incorporated before adding the next. Add the vanilla, wine, and zest. Add the dry ingredients and mix until a slightly firm dough comes together, about 3 to 4 minutes.

3. Flour your work surface and a baking sheet. Take a small chunk of dough, and with your hands, roll it into a long rope, about ½ inch (13 mm) thick. With a knife, cut the rope into ¼-inch (6 mm) pieces. Roll the pieces into balls and place them on the prepared baking sheet. Repeat with the rest of the dough.

4. Place a large saucepan over medium-high heat and heat the oil, about 1½ inches (4 cm), until it reaches about 350°F (175°C). Fry the struffoli in small batches until light golden brown, 2 to 3 minutes. Transfer to a paper towel–lined plate to drain.

5. **To make the honey syrup:** Place a second large saucepan over a medium heat and bring the honey, sugar, and water to a boil.

6. Drop in the struffoli in small batches, just as you did when you fried them. With a slotted spoon, stir them in the honey until they are completely coated, then transfer them to a serving plate.

7. Allow the honey to become a bit tacky before molding the struffoli into a mound or a ring shape. Decorate with sprinkles.

APPLE BUNDT CAKE

Torta di Mele

PREP TIME: 10 MINUTES • COOK TIME: 1 HOUR • YIELD: 8 TO 10 SERVINGS

I can't tell you how many times I would come home from school as a little girl and follow the intoxicating aroma of Nonna Romana's apple cake downstairs into her little basement apartment. I would cut a big piece and pick the apple slices that had been caramelized with sugar off the top and eat them one by one before I would take a bite of the moist, olive oil–based cake. Whenever Nonna has a get-together with her girlfriends, this cake is usually their first request.

Butter, for greasing

3⅓ cups (400 g) all-purpose flour

4 teaspoons baking powder

Dash ground cinnamon

1 cup (200 g) sugar, plus more for
    sprinkling

5 eggs

1 cup (235 ml) olive oil

Zest of 1 lemon

4 Granny Smith apples, peeled,
    sliced ¼ inch (6 mm) thick, and
    tossed with lemon juice to prevent
    darkening

Nonna Romana Says
*The apples can also be cut into
small cubes and mixed into the
batter instead of in a layer. It's
up to you!*

1. Preheat the oven to 400°F (200°C). Grease a 10-inch (25 cm) tube pan with butter.

2. In a mixing bowl, whisk together the flour, baking powder, and cinnamon. Set aside.

3. In the bowl of a stand mixer fitted with the paddle attachment, beat together the sugar and eggs on high speed for 2 to 3 minutes, until frothy. Reduce the speed to medium, add the olive oil and lemon zest, and mix until combined.

4. Reduce the speed to low and add the flour mixture a little at a time until fully incorporated. Scrape down the sides of the bowl if necessary. The batter will be thick. Do not overmix.

5. Pour half the batter into the prepared pan and spread evenly. Using half the apples, arrange the apple slices around the ring of the pan. Pour the remaining batter over the apples and spread evenly to cover them.

6. Arrange the remaining apple slices on top, overlapping one another. Sprinkle with sugar.

7. Carefully transfer to the oven and bake for 40 to 45 minutes, until an inserted toothpick comes out clean and the top apples are golden brown.

ITALIAN BUNDT CAKE

Ciambella

PREP TIME: 5 MINUTES • COOK TIME: 35 MINUTES • YIELD: 8 TO 10 SERVINGS

When I spent my summers with my Nonna Romana's youngest sister, Chiara, a massive ring of vanilla-scented *ciambella* would always be on her kitchen table. It would be made on Sunday mornings and eaten for the next two or three days with coffee. On the first day, it is incredibly moist, and as it dries up, it becomes perfect for dipping into *caffè latte*, making it the ultimate breakfast cake.

½ cup (1 stick, or 120 g) unsalted butter, softened, plus more for greasing

3⅓ cups (400 g) 00 or all-purpose flour

2 teaspoons baking powder

1½ cups (300 g) sugar

Zest of 1 lemon

2 teaspoons vanilla extract

4 eggs, at room temperature

½ cup (120 ml) whole milk

1. Preheat the oven to 425°F (220°C). Butter a 10-inch (25 cm) tube pan.

2. In a mixing bowl, whisk together the flour and baking powder. Set aside.

3. In the bowl of a stand mixer fitted with the paddle attachment, beat the sugar and butter on medium speed until fluffy, about 5 minutes. Turn the speed down to low and add the lemon zest, vanilla extract, and eggs, one at a time, letting each egg become fully incorporated before adding the next.

4. Add about one-third of the flour, then add milk. Keep alternating with the flour and milk, making sure you end with the flour. The batter will be somewhat thick.

5. Pour the batter into the prepared pan and bake for 5 minutes at 425°F (220°C). Lower the temperature to 400°F (200°C) and bake for an additional 25 to 30 minutes, until an inserted toothpick comes out clean.

RICOTTA CHEESECAKE

Torta di Ricotta

PREP TIME: 10 MINUTES • COOK TIME: 1 HOUR 10 MINUTES • YIELD: 8 TO 10 SERVINGS

If you're dreaming of a smooth, citrusy ricotta cheesecake that's fuss-free, then look no further. Nonna Romana skips the crust business and gets right to the point by whipping all the ingredients together at once and baking the cake until it's set and golden.

Butter, for greasing
All-purpose flour, for the pan
48 ounces (1.4 kg) whole milk ricotta
8 large eggs
1 cup (200 g) sugar
Zest of 2 large oranges

1. Preheat the oven to 425°F (220°C). Butter and flour a 10-inch (25 cm) springform pan.

2. In the bowl of a stand mixer fitted with the paddle attachment, combine all the ingredients, and mix on medium speed until well blended, about 10 minutes.

3. Pour into the prepared pan and bake for 30 minutes on the second from bottom rack. Lower the temperature to 375°F (190°C) and continue baking for an additional 40 minutes, until the filling is set and the top is golden brown.

4. Let cool completely before opening the spring and cutting.

NONNA CHIARA TAPINO'S

CUSTARD-FILLED PASTRIES WITH CHERRIES

Pasticciotti con Amarena

PREP TIME: 1 HOUR 40 MINUTES • COOK TIME: 16 MINUTES • YIELD: 10 PASTRIES

Pasticciotti are little cream-filled tarts typical of the Lecce area of Puglia. My Zia Chiara has been slightly obsessed with them for as long as I can remember, and she has made many variations over the years. This one, filled with a classic pastry cream and topped with Amarena cherries, is highly addictive! If you cannot find Amarena cherries, you may use any sour cherries in syrup or cherry preserves.

DOUGH

2 cups (240 g) all-purpose flour,
    plus more for dusting and the pan
1 teaspoon baking powder
Dash salt
½ cup (100 g) sugar
1 large egg
¼ cup (50 g) lard
¼ cup (½ stick, or 60 g) unsalted
    butter, at room temperature, plus
    more for greasing
1 teaspoon vanilla extract
¼ cup (60 ml) whole milk

CUSTARD FILLING

¾ cup (150 g) sugar
6 tablespoons (45 g) cornstarch
2 cups (475 ml) whole milk
2 tablespoons (30 ml) heavy cream
5 egg yolks, beaten
½ teaspoon vanilla extract
Whole peel of 1 lemon

1. **To make the dough:** In a mixing bowl, whisk together the flour, baking powder, and salt. Set aside.

2. In the bowl of a stand mixer fitted with the paddle attachment, beat the sugar and egg on medium speed until smooth. Add the lard, butter, and vanilla extract, and mix until combined. Add the dry ingredients and mix until crumbly. Add the milk and mix until a dough forms. The dough will be soft.

3. Divide the dough into 2 equal disks. Wrap each disk in plastic wrap and refrigerate for 1 hour or overnight.

4. **To make the custard filling:** In a mixing bowl, whisk together the sugar and cornstarch. Set aside.

5. In another mixing bowl, combine the milk, heavy cream, beaten egg yolks, and vanilla extract, and whisk until combined.

6. Put a large saucepan over medium heat and add the milk mixture and the sugar and cornstarch. Stir continuously with a wooden spoon.

7. Add the lemon peel and continue stirring until the mixture thickens, 7 to 8 minutes.

8. Remove from the heat. Scoop out the lemon peel and discard, and continue to stir for another 30 seconds.

ASSEMBLY

16 ounces (454 g) Amarena cherries,
  drained

1 egg yolk

1 tablespoon (15 ml) whole milk or
  heavy cream

9. Cool off the custard by spreading it in a shallow baking dish. Cover it with plastic wrap, pushing the plastic against the cream. This will prevent a skin from forming. Place the baking dish in the refrigerator or freezer until cooled.

10. **To assemble the pastries:** Preheat the oven to 425°F (220°C). Butter and flour ten 3-inch (7.5 cm) fluted round molds.

11. On a well-floured surface, roll out one of the disks to a ¼-inch (6 mm) thick sheet. Using a 4½-inch (11 cm) round cookie cutter or a glass, cut out 10 rounds. Re-roll any scraps, flouring your surface in between, until you have finished the disk of dough.

12. Fit each round piece of dough into the molds and press the sides to remove any air bubbles. Place 2 Amarena cherries at the bottom of each mold. Fill each of the molds with about 3 tablespoons (42 g) of the custard. Top each with 3 Amarena cherries.

13. Roll out the second disk and cut out another 10 rounds. Place each round on top of the molds and press down to adhere. Trim any excess dough.

14. Whisk the egg yolk with the milk and brush the tops of each pastry.

15. Place all the molds on a 18 × 13-inch (48 × 33 cm) baking sheet and bake for 15 to 18 minutes, until tops are golden.

COOKIES

Biscotti

RICOTTA COOKIES

Biscotti di Ricotta

PREP TIME: 45 MINUTES • COOK TIME: 15 MINUTES • YIELD: ABOUT 50 COOKIES

Few things in life make me happier than seeing a big plate of ricotta cookies covered in their dreamy glaze. It's no wonder these quickly became the most popular recipe on the *Cooking with Nonna* website. The recipe is very versatile and can be adapted to almost any flavor, but Nonna Romana's classic version is my favorite because it showcases the rich ricotta flavor.

COOKIES

2 cups (240 g) all-purpose flour

1 teaspoon baking powder

½ teaspoon salt

½ cup (100 g) granulated sugar

½ cup (1 stick, or 120 g) unsalted butter, softened

8 ounces (227 g) whole milk ricotta

1 teaspoon vanilla extract

1 egg

ICING AND DECORATION

1 cup (100 g) confectioners' sugar

2 teaspoons whole milk or lemon juice

Rainbow nonpareils, for decorating

1. **To make the cookies:** Preheat the oven to 350°F (175°C).

2. In a mixing bowl, whisk together the flour, baking powder, and salt. Set aside.

3. In the bowl of a stand mixer fitted with the paddle attachment, beat the sugar and butter on medium speed until fluffy, about 5 minutes. Add the ricotta, vanilla extract, and egg, and mix until combined. Reduce the speed to low and add the dry ingredients, mixing until incorporated.

4. Drop by level tablespoons (15 g) about 2 inches (5 cm) apart onto an ungreased baking sheet. Bake for 15 minutes. Transfer to a wire rack to cool.

5. **To make the icing and decorate the cookies:** In a small bowl, mix together the confectioners' sugar and milk. Drizzle over the cookies and top with the sprinkles. Allow the icing to dry completely before serving.

Nonna Romana Says

To make the cookies more uniform, I usually roll the dough into little balls before baking. If the dough sticks to your hands, wet your hands with a bit of water. Then they'll bake up perfectly round and pretty!

NONNA ROSETTA RAUSEO'S

SOFT LEMON COOKIES WITH LIMONCELLO GLAZE

Dolci Morbidi al Limone

PREP TIME: 30 MINUTES • COOK TIME: 15 MINUTES • YIELD: ABOUT 34 COOKIES

These super-moist lemon cookies are a favorite among Nonna Rosetta's children and grandchildren. The fragrant lemon zest and silky mascarpone make these cookies soft and rich, while the limoncello glaze is the perfect sweet and tart combination.

COOKIES

2½ cups (300 g) all-purpose flour

1 teaspoon baking powder

½ teaspoon salt

¼ cup (½ stick, or 60 g) unsalted
    butter, softened

1 cup (200 g) granulated sugar

½ cup (120 g) mascarpone cheese,
    at room temperature

Zest of 1 lemon

½ teaspoon lemon extract

2 eggs

LEMON GLAZE

1 cup (100 g) confectioners' sugar

1½ (23 ml) tablespoons limoncello or
    fresh lemon juice

½ tablespoon (8 ml) whole milk

Zest of 1 lemon

1. **To make the cookies:** Preheat the oven to 350°F (175°C).

2. In a mixing bowl, whisk together the flour, baking powder, and salt. Set aside.

3. In the bowl of a stand mixer fitted with the paddle attachment, beat the butter and sugar on medium speed until fluffy, about 5 minutes. Add the mascarpone, lemon zest, lemon extract, and eggs, and mix until smooth.

4. Decrease the speed to low and add the flour mixture. Mix until the flour is fully incorporated. Do not overmix.

5. Drop by level tablespoons (15 g) about 2 inches (5 cm) apart onto an ungreased baking sheet and bake for 15 minutes. Transfer to a wire rack to cool with aluminum foil underneath.

6. **To make the glaze:** In a bowl, combine the confectioners' sugar, limoncello, milk, and lemon zest, and mix until smooth. Drizzle over the cookies. Allow the glaze to dry completely.

Nonna Rosetta Says
For my younger grandchildren, I omit the limoncello from the glaze and I use lemon juice or lemon extract.

NONNA ROMANA SCIDDURLO'S

SUGAR-COATED EGG TARALLI

Taralli all'Uovo

PREP TIME: 2 HOURS 15 MINUTES • COOK TIME: 17 MINUTES • YIELD: ABOUT 30 TARALLI

In contrast to their savory counterpart (page 185), these *taralli* have a sweet airiness to them, and are traditionally made for the Easter holidays and weddings. Their size and shape are unique to the village of Mola di Bari, and Nonna Romana says that the sugar glaze can take even the most expert bakers many tries to master. My great-aunt Maria was so adept at the glaze that people in town would call her to come over and glaze their freshly baked taralli. If you get really good at making them, people will ask you to come and glaze theirs, too!

TARALLI

4 ⅔ (560 g) cups all-purpose flour

½ teaspoon baking powder

6 large eggs

¼ cup (60 ml) olive oil

¼ cup (60 ml) dry white wine, such as
   Pinot Grigio or Sauvignon Blanc

ICING

2 cups (400 g) granulated sugar

¾ cup (180 ml) plus 2 tablespoons
   (30 ml) water

Nonna Romana Says

The first taralli you glaze will have a bit of shine to them. As the sugar begins to dry and turn white, the shine will disappear, but the sugar is still good. You must try to work fast. After seventy years, I'm still not fast enough to beat the sugar!

1. **To make the taralli:** In a mixing bowl, whisk together the flour and baking powder. Set aside.

2. In the bowl of a stand mixer fitted with the dough hook attachment, beat together the eggs, olive oil, and wine on low speed. Add the flour mixture and increase the speed to medium. Mix until a dough forms, about 10 minutes.

3. Attach the pasta roller attachment to the mixer and set it to the largest setting possible. With the mixer running at the highest speed, take a tennis ball–sized amount of dough and flatten it with your hands as much as possible. Feed it through the pasta roller, holding the dough taut. The dough will have holes for the first passing. Pass the dough through the machine 20 more times. The dough is ready once it feels smooth, supple, and almost velvety in your hands.

4. Take the piece of dough to a clean work surface and roll it into a rope about ½ inch (13 mm) thick. Cut pieces from the rope about 8 inches (20 cm) long (a dinner knife is the perfect length). Join the ends of the taralli to form a round shape. Place one end on top of the other and push down hard with your index finger to seal. Set the taralli aside, not touching each other, on a clean kitchen towel or tablecloth.

continued

5. Repeat passing the rest of the dough through the pasta roller and rolling it out until you have made all your taralli. (You will be able to make 2 or 3 taralli at a time. You must work in small batches passing the dough through the machine; it must be rolled out immediately or it will dry out.)

6. Once you have made all your taralli, let them rest for 15 minutes before boiling them.

7. Bring 3 quarts (2.8 L) of water to boil in a 5-quart (4.7 L) pot. Drop the taralli in, 4 or 5 at a time, beginning with the first ones made. Stir the pot with a wooden spoon to prevent the taralli from sticking to the bottom. As soon as the taralli rise to the surface, scoop them out with a slotted spoon or spider and lay them back on the towel. Repeat with the remaining taralli.

8. Preheat the oven to 475°F (240°C).

9. Hold a boiled tarallo in your hand and with a sharp knife make an incision three-fourths of the way through all around the tarallo, rotating as you cut. Repeat to cut all the taralli.

10. Place 10 to 12 taralli at a time directly on the rack of the oven. These will puff up in the oven and require more space.

11. Bake for 7 minutes and then lower the temperature to 400°F (200°C). Bake for an additional 10 minutes, until golden, turning the taralli over with tongs halfway through.

12. Once fully baked, cool the oven down to 180°F (85°C). Place the taralli on a 13 × 9-inch (33 × 23 cm) baking sheet and bake for 30 minutes, until they are completely dry inside. This will remove all the humidity from the taralli and help them stay fresh much longer.

13. **To make the icing:** Add the water and sugar to a 2-quart (1.9 L) saucepan over medium-high heat and bring to a boil, stirring constantly with a wooden spoon. Boil for 5 minutes, then turn off the heat.

14. In a large metal mixing bowl, add about ½ cup (120 ml) of the sugar mixture and 7 or 8 taralli. Tumble them with a wooden spoon so they become coated with the icing. As soon as they're nicely coated, turn them out onto a wire rack with aluminum foil underneath. You must do this quickly because the sugar will begin to dry and harden. Repeat with the remaining taralli. If the sugar in the pot hardens, add 1 tablespoon (15 ml) of water and melt it over medium heat until the mixture becomes liquid again.

15. Allow the taralli to dry completely, 30 to 40 minutes.

TOASTED ALMOND SPICE COOKIES

Paste di Mandorle

PREP TIME: 1 HOUR • COOK TIME: 15 MINUTES • YIELD: ABOUT 36 COOKIES

Every *nonna* I know from Mola di Bari makes a variation of this toasted almond cookie, but some of them are so hard they can leave you needing dental work! Nonna Giulia's take on this classic Pugliese cookie is soft and moist without sacrificing the traditional spice.

COOKIES

Butter or nonstick cooking spray, for greasing

16 ounces (454 g) whole almonds

3⅓ cups (400 g) all-purpose flour

2½ tablespoons (14 g) unsweetened cocoa powder

½ teaspoon baking powder

½ teaspoon ground cinnamon

½ teaspoon ground cloves

2 large eggs

1¾ cups (350 g) granulated sugar

¾ cup (180 ml) olive oil

Zest of 2 lemons

2 tablespoons (30 ml) sambuca liqueur

6 tablespoons (90 ml) brewed espresso, at room temperature

GLAZE

1 cup (100 g) confectioners' sugar

2 tablespoons (30 ml) whole milk

¼ teaspoon fresh lemon juice

Nonna Romana Says

You can also use blanched almonds for this recipe.

1. **To make the cookies:** Preheat the oven to 375°F (190°C). Grease 2 large baking sheets with butter or nonstick cooking spray.

2. Place the almonds in a food processor and process for 15 to 20 seconds, until the almonds are coarsely chopped.

3. Spread the almonds on one of the prepared baking sheets and toast for 7 to 10 minutes, until lightly golden. Transfer to a plate and let cool.

4. In a large mixing bowl, whisk together the flour, cocoa powder, baking powder, cinnamon, and ground cloves. Set aside.

5. In the bowl of a standing mixer fitted with the paddle attachment, beat together the eggs, granulated sugar, oil, lemon zest, sambuca, and espresso on medium speed until combined. Reduce the speed to low and add the dry ingredients. Mix until fully incorporated. Add the almonds and mix until fully incorporated.

6. On a lightly floured surface, roll a handful of the dough into a 1½-inch (4 cm) thick rope. Lightly press the rope with the floured tines of a fork to create ridges. Cut the dough into 2-inch (5 cm) pieces on the diagonal to create a rhomboid shape. Place the cookies about 1 inch (2.5 cm) apart on the second prepared baking sheet. Repeat with remaining dough.

7. Bake for 15 minutes. The cookies may appear soft out when they come of the oven but will harden as they cool. Transfer to a wire rack with aluminum foil underneath to cool completely.

8. **To make the glaze:** In a bowl, combine the confectioners' sugar, milk, and lemon juice and mix until smooth. Brush each of the cookies with the glaze and allow the glaze to dry.

JAM-FILLED OLIVE OIL COOKIES

Paste con Marmellata

PREP TIME: 20 MINUTES • COOK TIME: 18 MINUTES • YIELD: 16 COOKIES

For as long as I can remember, Nonna Romana's pantry was always lined with jars of homemade jam. Sometimes she would leave jam to cook on the stove at the lowest heat possible . . . overnight! (Do not try this at home, kids! Nonna is a professional.) You can try your hand at making the jam yourself or swap it for any fruit preserve you like.

COOKIES

Butter, for greasing

2¼ cups (270 g) all-purpose flour, plus more for dusting

1½ teaspoons baking powder

2 eggs plus 1 for egg wash

½ cup (100 g) sugar, plus extra for sprinkling

6 tablespoons (90 ml) olive oil

Zest of 1 lemon

½ cup (160 g) Nonna's Grape Jam (below) or preserve of your choice

NONNA'S GRAPE JAM

Yield: About 3 cups (960 g)

5 pounds (2.3 kg) seedless red grapes

1 cup (200 g) sugar

Nonna Romana Says

You can omit the sugar from the jam recipe if you prefer. I personally think the fruit is sweet enough, but the sugar acts as a preservative, so it keeps a bit longer. If you don't add sugar, make sure you consume the jam within 2 weeks.

1. **To make the cookies:** Preheat the oven to 375°F (190°C). Grease a baking sheet with butter.

2. In a mixing bowl, whisk together the flour and baking powder. Set aside.

3. In the bowl of a stand mixer fitted with the paddle attachment, beat the 2 eggs and the sugar on medium speed until lemon colored and foamy, about 5 minutes. Add the olive oil and lemon zest and mix until fully incorporated. Add the flour mixture and mix until fully incorporated. The dough will be rather soft.

4. Flour your hands well. Take a rounded tablespoon (16 g) of the dough and flatten it into a disk. Add about 1 teaspoon of jam to the center and fold the dough around it to seal. Place the cookies about 2 inches (5 cm) apart on the prepared baking sheet.

5. Beat the remaining egg in a bowl. Brush each cookie with the egg wash and sprinkle with sugar. Bake for 18 to 20 minutes, or until the cookies are golden brown on top. Cool on a wire rack.

6. **To make the jam:** Put a 6-quart (5.7 L) heavy-bottomed stockpot over the lowest heat possible. Add the grapes and sugar and stir to coat the grapes. Cover and cook until the mixture is bubbling, about 1 hour.

7. Uncover the pot and cook until the grapes have cooked down, about 3 hours. Do not stir the pot at all during cooking. This will make the grapes stick and you will have to stir constantly.

8. The grapes will break down and become a jam on their own. Cool completely and transfer the jam to a jar. Keep refrigerated for up to 6 months.

ANISE COOKIES

Biscotti all'Anice

PREP TIME: 30 MINUTES • COOK TIME: 10 MINUTES • YIELD: ABOUT 25 COOKIES

These soft and simple anise cookies make an appearance at every holiday table in my family. If you've never made icing with heavy cream instead of milk before, then you just haven't lived! These will melt in your mouth, and the touch of sambuca liqueur gives them a little kick.

COOKIES

3 eggs
2½ cups (300 g) all-purpose flour
1 cup (100 g) confectioners' sugar
1 tablespoon (15 ml) plus ½ teaspoon
    baking powder
½ cup (1 stick, or 120 g) unsalted
    butter, softened
1 tablespoon (15 ml) anise extract,
    or to taste
1 teaspoon vanilla extract

ICING AND DECORATION

1½ cups (150 g) confectioners' sugar
3 tablespoons (45 ml) heavy cream
½ teaspoon whole milk
½ teaspoon anise extract or sambuca
    liqueur
1 drop any food color
White nonpareils, for decorating

1. **To make the cookies:** Preheat the oven to 350°F (175°C).

2. In a large mixing bowl, beat the eggs with an electric mixer until foamy. Set aside.

3. In the bowl of a stand mixer fitted with the paddle attachment, combine the flour, confectioners' sugar, and baking powder. Mixing on low speed, gradually add the butter and extracts until the mixture resembles crumbs.

4. Add the beaten eggs and mix until a stiff dough forms.

5. Roll dough into balls, about 1 tablespoon (15 g) in size, and place about 2 inches (5 cm) apart on an ungreased baking sheet.

6. Bake for 10 to 12 minutes. The cookies will be slightly cracked on top. Transfer to a wire rack to cool completely.

7. **To make the icing and decorate the cookies:** In a small bowl, mix together the confectioners' sugar, heavy cream, milk, anise extract, and food color. If you prefer a thinner icing, you can thin it out with more cream or milk. Spoon over the cookies and decorate with the nonpareils. Allow the icing to dry completely before serving.

Nonna Romana Says
Everyone will love the texture of the heavy-cream icing, but make a note that the icing will always remain a little soft. If you're going to travel with them and prefer an icing that will dry all the way through, substitute the heavy cream with 2 tablespoons (30 ml) of whole milk.

SESAME SEED COOKIES

Biscotti Reginella

PREP TIME: 15 MINUTES • COOK TIME: 25 MINUTES • YIELD: ABOUT 60 COOKIES

One whiff of these cookies and I'm transported to an Italian bakery in Brooklyn where little old couples buy them by the pound. Although they are Sicilian in origin, my Pugliese great-grandmother Regina took a tremendous liking to these mild anise-flavored cookies coated with sesame seeds. My Nonna Romana carries on the tradition of making them because she considers them worthy of her highest compliment when it comes to desserts: "Not too sweet!" The shapes and flavorings of these cookies are different depending on who makes them, but these are my great-grandmother's *Reginella* cookies.

3 cups (360 g) all-purpose flour,
    plus more for dusting

2 teaspoons baking powder

3 large eggs

1 cup (200 g) sugar

1 cup (190 g) vegetable shortening

2 teaspoons anise extract

1 cup (235 ml) whole milk

1½ cups (215 g) raw sesame seeds

1. Preheat the oven to 375°F (190°C).

2. In a mixing bowl, whisk together the flour and baking powder. Set aside.

3. In the bowl of a stand mixer fitted with the paddle attachment, beat together the eggs, sugar, shortening, and anise extract on medium speed until fluffy, about 5 minutes. Reduce the speed to low and add the flour mixture. Mix until the flour is incorporated and a dough forms.

4. Pour the milk into a bowl and spread the sesame seeds on a plate. On a floured work surface, take a tennis ball–sized piece of dough and roll it out to a 1-inch (2.5 cm) thick rope. Cut 2-inch (5 cm) long pieces and dip each piece into the milk with a slotted spoon. Roll in the sesame seeds. Repeat until all of the dough is used.

5. Place the cookies about 1 inch (2.5 cm) apart on an ungreased baking sheet. Bake for 20 to 25 minutes, until the seeds are toasted. The cookies may be slightly cracked on top.

"I still cook every day for my husband, Rocco, of fifty-four years. He only started making his own coffee recently."

I call Giuseppa to confirm our meeting at her home, and she responds in true nonna fashion, "Okay, see you then! Unless, God forbid, anything happens." I'm immediately reminded of my own nonna's frequent response, *se Dio vuole*, or if God wants.

At Giuseppa's beautiful home in Connecticut, she offers me a tour and a coffee with sambuca. "See these curtains?" she asks, stopping at a window. "I made them myself," she says, beaming. "I always liked to cook and sew. I made my first dress at ten, and I became a certified seamstress at thirteen before coming to America." This is a talent she later developed into a successful custom drapery business.

"I love this country to death, but the memories of home live in my heart." Giuseppa says. "I remember the fresh fruit of Sicily. Fresh figs and almonds. *Granita* (an Italian ice slush) made from real Sicilian citrus. I remember the sweet aroma of *Zagara* (orange blossom flower) as I would walk through the streets. Everything you cooked was wonderful because of the ingredients of the island. The best!"

There's something very no nonsense about

Nonna Giuseppa, especially when she talks about her homeland. "My father was a farmer. We weren't the poorest people or the richest people, but we were very happy," she says. Even though she has been an American citizen for nearly sixty years, Sicily is still very much a part of her identity and a place she credits with developing many of her talents. "My fascination with cooking started when I was young, maybe eight or nine. I had two brothers and I would always try to help Mamma around the house. My mother would be doing housework, and she would yell, 'Pinucch' (put the salt) in the pasta. Stir the sauce!' She was tough, but she wanted to make sure I learned in case life got hard," she explains. "With time my style became very creative. If I find a recipe, I have to change it, and I rarely make something the same way twice."

She recalls her arrival in America with emotion. "At thirteen, my mother and brothers and I got on the ship bound for New York. We were finally going to join my father who had already been there for almost three years. We arrived at pier number 9 on Ellis Island, and as soon as I saw my father I ran and jumped over several chains into his arms. The security men tried to chase after me, but I heard one guard saying, 'Let her go; she's in her father's arms.'"

Today Giuseppa finds all her happiness in her family. "Being a nonna is a blessing. I'm blessed to be able to share and teach my grandchildren our traditions." She still cooks for them regularly and relishes their appreciation. "It's all worth it when they say, 'Nonna, nobody does it like you.' She even still cooks every day for her husband, Rocco, of fifty-four years. "He only started making his own coffee recently," Nonna Giuseppa laughs.

When I return home, I think warmly about my visit with Nonna Giuseppa and her husband who went a half-century without knowing how to make coffee. But before I turn in for the night, I make good on my promise to call Nonna Giuseppa to let her know I made it back in one piece.

PINOLI COOKIES

Biscotti con Pinoli

PREP TIME: 45 MINUTES • COOK TIME: 15 MINUTES • YIELD: ABOUT 44 COOKIES

Nonna Giuseppa keeps the flavors of Sicily with her in these soft, chewy *pinoli* cookies. The pinoli on the bottom become nice and toasted, while the ones on top seem to melt together with the almond paste when you eat them. These are super easy to make, and always disappear quickly from the cookie tray.

Butter, for greasing
1 pound (454 g) almond paste
¼ cup (30 g) all-purpose flour
1 teaspoon baking powder
Zest of 1 lemon
3 egg whites, at room temperature
½ cup (100 g) sugar
2 cups (272 g) pinoli (pine nuts)

Nonna Giuseppa Says
If you like your cookies with a bit more crunch, just cook them 3 to 5 minutes longer. It's up to you!

1. Preheat the oven to 350°F (175°C). Grease a baking sheet with butter.

2. In a large mixing bowl, grate the almond paste with a large cheese grater. Add the flour, baking powder, and lemon zest.

3. In another bowl, beat the egg whites with an electric mixer while adding the sugar a little at a time until glossy and soft peaks form.

4. Fold the almond paste mixture into the egg whites until combined. Beat until smooth, about 1 minute.

5. Spread the pinoli on a plate. With a small ice cream scoop, take a scoop of dough at a time and roll it in the pinoli, covering all sides. Place the cookies on the prepared baking sheet about 2 inches (5 cm) apart.

6. Bake for 15 minutes, or until slightly golden. Transfer to a wire rack to cool.

ALMOND COOKIES WITH CHERRIES

Bocche di Dama

PREP TIME: 1 HOUR • COOK TIME: 15 MINUTES • YIELD: 24 COOKIES

In my family, every big event sends my Nonna Romana and her sisters into a cookie-baking frenzy. Together, they craft dozens of homemade almond-cookie trays that guests either take home or immediately open and enjoy at the event with their coffee and desserts. These cherry-filled almond-paste cookies are always the centerpiece of all their cookie trays. Their name, *bocche di dama*, translates to "lady's mouth" because they resemble a little kiss. This version utilizes the classic *pasta reale* almond paste and is filled with Amarena cherries. You may also substitute with any sour cherries in syrup or cherry preserves.

COOKIES

Butter, for greasing
16 ounces (454 g) blanched almonds
1 cup (200 g) granulated sugar
2 egg whites
Zest of 2 lemons
4 ounces (113 g) Amarena cherries, drained

ICING

1 cup (100 g) confectioners' sugar
1 tablespoon (15 ml) plus ½ teaspoon whole milk
4 ounces (113 g) semisweet chocolate

Nonna Romana Says
You can also add just a little bit of rum to the cherries and soak them before you fill the cookies!

1. **To make the cookies:** Preheat the oven to 350°F (175°C). Grease a baking sheet with butter.

2. Add the almonds to a food processor and process for 2 minutes. Transfer to a large mixing bowl and add the granulated sugar, egg whites, and lemon zest. Mix well with your hands until a paste forms.

3. Take a walnut-sized amount of paste and roll it into a ball. With your index finger, press a deep indentation into the center of the ball and insert 2 cherries. Roll the ball closed, adding a bit more paste to patch the hole if necessary. Repeat with the remaining dough.

4. Place the cookies on the prepared baking sheet and bake for 15 to 16 minutes. The cookies will seem soft when they come out of the oven but will harden as they cool. Transfer to a wire rack with foil underneath.

5. **To make the icing:** In a small bowl, mix together the confectioners' sugar and milk until smooth.

6. Dip each of the cookies into the icing, letting the excess run down the cookies. Alternatively, you can just dust the cookies with confectioners' sugar.

7. Melt the chocolate in a double boiler or microwave. Cool for 5 minutes and transfer to a small zipper-top plastic bag. Snip a tiny corner off of the bag and create a swirl design over each cookie. Let dry completely on the wire rack.

NONNA CECILIA DEBELLIS

"I had never seen so much food in my life. There was seafood, and meatballs, and lasagna, and things we couldn't even dream about in Italy!"

At just shy of five feet tall, Nonna Cecilia is short and sweet. As I pull up to the Staten Island home she shares with her family, I see her smiling and waving to me through a second-floor window. Inside, she offers me a cup of coffee and a sweet cake.

As I look around, I notice the walls are covered in photos of her three daughters, six grandchildren, and great-grandchild. Cecilia cooks up a storm for her them every Sunday, and relishes her role as a nonna. "There are never less than ten people here every week. I love bringing them all together. I'm seventy-eight now, but as long as I can do it, I do it. If I stopped, they'd all be too hungry!" she says.

Cecilia was born in Mola di Bari, Puglia, to very humble beginnings. "Things were very hard. My father was already in America when I was born, and they had closed the passage so he couldn't send any money to us. I remember my mother selling all her jewelry and at times making an entire meal out of anchovies and chili flakes. We would all worry if my uncle decided to join us for dinner because he would eat all our food. My brother was also very sick. My mother would go to buy fava beans on the black market and risked being shot!"

After the death of her brother, Cecilia and her mother decided to join her father in America. "When we got to Brooklyn, my *commara* (godmother) had made dinner, and I had never seen so much food in my life. There was seafood, and meatballs, and lasagna, and things we couldn't even dream about in Italy! We lived around all Italians. In the summertime, we would all sit outside together and watch people play in the open johnny pumps. It was like being in Italy, except here we could work!"

When Cecilia's mother started working, Cecilia began her love affair with cooking. "When my mother went to work, she would leave me notes and instructions on how to cook things so they would be ready when she came home. Sometimes I didn't do too good, but I learned."

By nineteen, Gino, a young man also from Mola di Bari, had set his sights on her. "His father was a friend of the family, and he always said that I should marry his son. One day I came home from church, and he was in my house. My father said he liked me and I had to decide if I wanted to marry him."

Cecilia pauses to show me her wedding portrait. "But I married him, and the love came after and lasted for forty-four years." Cecilia smiles warmly. As I left her home that day, it was with respect, admiration, and a second piece of cake.

COFFEE PUFFS

Dolci di Caffe e Cannella

PREP TIME: 30 MINUTES • COOK TIME: 10 MINUTES • YIELD: 32 COOKIES

The aroma of these chocolate-and-spice-and-everything-nice cookies fills Nonna Cecilia's apartment and lures everyone into the kitchen. The light lemon glaze on these airy coffee, chocolate, and cinnamon cookies makes them the perfect complement to a cup of espresso.

COOKIES

3 ⅓ cups (400 g) all-purpose flour

4 teaspoons baking powder

6 tablespoons (32 g) unsweetened cocoa powder

1½ teaspoons ground cinnamon

¼ cup (½ stick, or 60 g) unsalted butter, softened

1 cup (200 g) granulated sugar

Zest of 1 orange

2 eggs

¼ cup (60 ml) brewed espresso coffee, at room temperature

ICING

1 cup (100 g) confectioners' sugar

2 tablespoons (30 ml) whole milk

¼ teaspoon lemon extract

Nonna Cecilia Says

For some extra coffee flavor, you can dust the icing with a dash of espresso powder.

1. **To make the cookies:** Preheat the oven to 375°F (190°C).

2. In a mixing bowl, whisk together the flour, baking powder, cocoa powder, and cinnamon. Set aside.

3. In the bowl of a stand mixer fitted with the paddle attachment, beat the butter and sugar on medium speed for about 3 minutes. Add the zest and eggs, one at a time, making sure each egg is fully incorporated before adding the next.

4. Add the coffee and mix until smooth.

5. Reduce the speed to low and add the flour mixture. Mix until all of the dry ingredients have been incorporated. Do not overmix.

6. Roll the dough into 1½-inch (4 cm) balls and place them 1 to 2 inches (2.5 to 5 cm) apart on an ungreased baking sheet. Bake for 10 minutes.

7. Transfer to a wire rack with aluminum foil underneath to cool.

8. **To make the icing:** In a small bowl, combine the confectioners' sugar, milk, and lemon extract, and mix until smooth. Drizzle the glaze over the cookies. Allow the icing to dry completely before serving.

NONNA CECILIA DEBELLIS'

SEVEN LAYER COOKIES

Dolci Tricolore

PREP TIME: 2 HOURS, 15 MINUTES • COOK TIME: 12 MINUTES • YIELD: SEVERAL DOZEN

I don't think I've ever met a person who didn't like seven layer cookies, otherwise called rainbow cookies. Nonna Cecilia learned to make this Italian-American classic cookie from her Commara Maria, who had come to America before her, and it quickly made its way into her repertoire.

4 large eggs, separated

1 cup (2 sticks, or 240 g) unsalted butter, at room temperature

1 cup (200 g) sugar

12 ounces (340 g) almond paste

2 cups (240 ml) all-purpose flour

Red and green food color

½ cup (160 g) apricot jam

4 ounces (113 g) semisweet chocolate

🥄 **Nonna Cecilia Says**
Some recipes say you should weigh the cookies down overnight to make sure they're pressed together. I used to put encyclopedias on them! But over time, I found that it wasn't really necessary and just giving them a good press with your hands is all you need.

1. Preheat the oven to 375°F (190°C).

2. In the bowl of a stand mixer fitted with the paddle attachment, beat the egg yolks and butter on medium speed until combined. Add the sugar and mix until incorporated. Break up the almond paste into small chunks. Add to the mixer and mix until smooth. Reduce the speed to low and add the flour.

3. In a small bowl, whisk the egg whites with a fork until foamy and add them to the mixer. Mix for a few minutes until a soft, uniform dough forms.

4. Divide the dough into 3 equal parts in 3 separate bowls. Leave one of the parts of dough the natural white color. Add the food color to the 2 remaining bowls to achieve your desired colors.

5. Spread the dough into 3 separate ungreased 12 × 8-inch (30 × 20 cm) baking pans. Bake for 10 to 12 minutes and let cool completely.

6. Line a clean work surface with parchment paper. Flip the green sheet out of the baking pan and lay it down first. Spread half the apricot jam over the green sheet. Place the white sheet on top of the green sheet and spread the remaining apricot jam. Place the red sheet over the white and press the sheets firmly together with your hands.

7. With a serrated knife, trim all 4 edges of the sheets to even them out.

8. Melt the chocolate in a double boiler or microwave, and then spread it over one side. Place in the refrigerator until the chocolate is dry, about 1 hour, or preferably overnight. Turn over to the other side so that the chocolate side is facing the parchment paper and spread the remaining side with chocolate. Refrigerate until the chocolate is set, about 1 hour.

9. Cut into 1½ × ½-inch (4 × 1.5 cm) cookies and serve.

CHOCOLATE-DIPPED ALMOND BISCOTTI

Biscotti alle Mandorle e Cioccolato

PREP TIME: 1 HOUR • COOK TIME: 40 MINUTES • YIELD: ABOUT 60 BISCOTTI

Sometimes you just crave the crunch of a good biscotto, and Nonna Rosetta's chocolate-dipped almond cookies deliver. You'll barely be able to wait for the chocolate to dry before taking a bite.

COOKIES

Butter, for greasing

3 cups (360 g) all-purpose flour, plus more for dusting and the pan

½ cup chopped unblanched almonds

3½ teaspoons baking powder

3 large eggs

1 cup (200 g) sugar

½ cup (120 ml) vegetable oil

1 teaspoon vanilla extract

2 tablespoons (30 ml) amaretto

CHOCOLATE DIP

1½ cups (260 g) chopped semisweet chocolate (about 9 ounces)

1 teaspoon vegetable oil

> **Nonna Rosetta Says**
> *Sometimes I add* Strega, *a traditional Neapolitan liqueur, to the batter for an extra kick.*

1. **To make the cookies:** Preheat the oven to 350°F (175°C). Butter and flour a baking sheet.

2. Spread the almonds out on an 11 × 7-inch (28 × 18 cm) baking pan and toast them for 5 to 7 minutes, until lightly golden. Transfer to a plate and set aside.

3. In a mixing bowl, whisk together the flour and baking powder. Set aside.

4. In the bowl of a stand mixer fitted with the paddle attachment, beat the eggs, sugar, vegetable oil, vanilla extract, and amaretto on medium speed until combined.

5. Reduce the speed to low and add the flour mixture. Mix until the flour is incorporated. Add the almonds and mix until they are fully incorporated.

6. Divide the dough into 4 equal parts and form each part into a loaf on the prepared baking sheet. Bake for 20 minutes.

7. Remove the loaves from the oven, let cool slightly, and then cut the loaves into 1-inch (2.5 cm) thick biscotti, placing them cut-side up on the baking sheet. Bake for an additional 20 minutes, turning over the biscotti halfway through. Transfer to a wire rack to cool completely.

8. **To make the chocolate dip:** Melt the chocolate and the vegetable oil in a double boiler or microwave. Dip the bottoms of the biscotti into the chocolate and place them on their sides to dry on a wire rack with foil underneath.

INDEX

ACKNOWLEDGMENTS

Thank you to my incredible dream team at Race Point Publishing for helping me bring my greatest dream to life. Thank you to Jeannine Dillon (and the wonderful Terry Spinelli) for trusting in me and reaching out to offer me the opportunity of a lifetime. You made me believe I could actually write this, and I am incredibly touched by how much passion and dedication you have put into the book. Many thanks to Merideth Harte and Erin Canning for working so closely with me and lending your time and talents. You have all made this experience feel like I was working with my closest girlfriends.

Special thanks to the wonderfully talented Evi Abeler, who captured the true essence of my Nonna in every one of her beautiful photographs. You have taught me so much, and this book would not be what it is without your time and patience. You are a true artist in every sense.

Thank you to John and Leona Seazholtz for always believing in me and my ideas with so much passion. Many thanks to Salvatore Asaro and the team at Botticelli Foods for taking a chance and trusting a sassy chick from Brooklyn to represent your products. It is my pleasure to work with an authentic Italian family business, and your faith in me means a great deal.

To all the fans and followers of *Cooking with Nonna*: Every day you all make it possible for me to do what I love and share my heritage with the world. Thank you all for caring about the recipes and these incredible women who have taught me so many lessons in the kitchen.

Thank you to all the *nonne* who have contributed their recipes and life stories throughout this book. You are all amazing women and incredible chefs, and every last one of you deserves a book all your own. Thank you for trusting me to be your voice. I am truly lucky to have been able to live this experience with all of you and make more memories while we wrote, laughed, and tested recipes. You have all made me feel like I was a part of your own families.

I would like to thank my family from the bottom of my heart. Leonardo, you are the greatest brother I could ever ask for. Thank you for being the first pair of eyes to read this manuscript and help me become a better writer. To my parents, Angela and Vito, thank you for fully supporting every crazy idea I have ever had. I could not have written this book without your unconditional love and guidance. I am who I am because you both never once told me to be realistic. A special thanks to my dad-ager, Vito: You are my strength when I am weak and you are the beating heart of *Cooking with Nonna*. I will never be able to repay you for all that you do.

Finally, to my Nonna: You are the strongest woman I have ever known. You selflessly give to those around you every day and never ask for anything back. Thank you for teaching me everything you know about food and embarking on this amazing journey with me. You are truly my best friend. *Ti voglio un mondo di bene.*

ABOUT THE AUTHOR

Rossella Rago is the host of the popular web TV series *Cooking with Nonna* (www.cookingwithnonna.com). For each episode of the show, Rossella invites an Italian-American *nonna* to cook with her and share traditional Italian recipes and fond memories of her childhood in Italy. Rossella has traveled the country and performed cooking demonstrations in numerous cities across the United States with local *nonne* as her partners.

Rossella spent her childhood in the kitchen with her maternal Nonna Romana, learning the long legacy of recipes from Puglia passed down through generations. Launching *Cooking with Nonna* TV has allowed Rossella to expand her culinary expertise to other regions of Italy, too. Rossella, together with her mother and her Nonna Romana, won the "Italiano Battle" episode of the Food Network's *24 Hour Restaurant Battle* in 2010. She lives in Brooklyn, New York.

MOLA DI BARI
CHIESA DI
S.M. LORETO

Guest Chec

K-DUPL / KC1

Sciddurlo Nino